MW01105337

Mentoring Away the Glass Ceiling in Academia

Mentoring Away the Glass Ceiling in Academia

A Cultured Critique

Edited by Brenda L. H. Marina

LEXINGTON BOOKS
Lanham • Boulder • New York • London

Published by Lexington Books
An imprint of The Rowman & Littlefield Publishing Group, Inc.
4501 Forbes Boulevard, Suite 200, Lanham, Maryland 20706
www.rowman.com

Unit A, Whitacre Mews, 26-34 Stannary Street, London SE11 4AB

British Library Cataloguing in Publication Information Available

Library of Congress Cataloging-in-Publication Data

Mentoring away the glass ceiling in academia : a cultured critique / edited by Brenda Marina.
pages cm
Includes bibliographical references and index.
ISBN 978-1-4985-1530-6 (cloth : alk. paper) -- ISBN 978-1-4985-1531-3 (electronic)
1. Women in higher education--United States. 2. Women college teachers--United States. 3. Women
college administrators--United States. 4. Mentoring in education--United States. 5. Discrimination in
higher education. I. Marina, Brenda Louise Hammett
LC1568.M46 2015
378.0082--dc23
2015010650

Printed in the United States of America

Contents

III: Steps toward Successful Mentoring

Foreword

I am honored to compose a foreword for *Mentoring Away the Glass Ceiling in Academia: A Cultured Critique*. This book explores, interprets, and illuminates the contemporary realities of gender equity in the labor market in general and in higher education in particular. The editor, Dr. Brenda Marina, is a scholar with considerable experience in higher education administration. Among her outstanding academic credentials are associate professor, assistant dean, program director, and student advisor. What is remarkable is that all these pursuits were accomplished concurrently while actively serving in professional leadership positions. The authors who participated in this collective work provide critical, insightful, and revealing details into what it is like to be a woman in various academic settings at varying stages in their careers. Their stories describe the sometimes overt and sometimes obscure obstacle—glass-ceiling realities—for women and how it has impinged on the lives of women in the academy. Furthermore, their personal stories speak to how mentoring has been a chisel for tapping on the glass ceiling as they have advanced in higher education. Dr. Marina's analyses of each chapter create a lively illumination adding a targeted dimension that proves to be useful in describing the intersections and interconnectedness of women, mentoring, and the glass ceiling in academia. This book will not disappoint professionals nor will it disappoint women as readers seeking to understand the importance of mentoring to their career advancement in higher education.

Since the publication of my article *Challenges, Choices, and Decisions of Women in the Academy: A Discourse on the Future of Hispanic, Black, and Asian Members of the Professoriate*, women continue to be critically underrepresented in the upper echelons of academia, both in the faculty ranks and among executive administration positions. *Mentoring Away the Glass Ceiling in Academia: A Cultured Critique* is simultaneously a fascinating, yet sobering, analysis of and extension of my work. Likewise, it is a lucid and masterful extension of the work of many who are dedicated to serving as mentors and improving the academic lives and paths for women educators. The critical conversations presented in this book align well with my research and the work of Jackson and Leon, and Kochan, Kent, and Green, just to name a few. The stories are absorbing and highly readable and help us better understand the places and spaces where and how the glass ceiling still exists.

The narratives and counternarratives in this book challenges traditional ways of knowing and doing by considering mentoring as a contemporary determinant of the glass ceiling in higher education. As you turn the pages of this book and read, you will witness situational experiences from graduate school to faculty positioning, with or without mentoring experiences and glimpses of the glass ceiling effect in place for women. There are many valuable lessons learned, and throughout the text you will also find the voice of hope and daily endeavors to shatter the glass ceiling in multiple spaces. I applaud the efforts of Dr. Marina for undertaking the editing of this important book and for bringing to light the thoughtful, astute, and moving voices of these women. I also wish to recognize the transparency of the contributors who opened their minds, hearts, and spirits to fill the pages of this edited volume.

This scholarship has implications for best practices at all levels in postsecondary settings to prepare and support women for careers in the global economy through mentoring and shifts in institutional climate. I am truly honored to have played this small role in writing the foreword for such a remarkable book.

Ramona Ortega, D.P.A.
Associate Professor and Faculty Fellow for Engagement;
Office of the Sr. VP and Provost
The University of Akron, Department of Public Administration & Urban Studies

REFERENCES

Jackson, J., and R. Leon. 2010. "Enlarging our Understanding of Glass Ceiling Effects with Social Closure Theory in Higher Education." In John C. Smart (ed.), *Higher Education: Handbook of Theory and Research*. New York: Springer.

Kochan, F., A. Kent, and A. Green. 2014. *Uncovering the Hidden Cultural Dynamics in Mentoring Programs and Relationships: Enhancing Practice and Research, Volume 4: Perspectives in Mentoring Series*. Charlotte: Information Age Publishing (IAP).

Ortega, Ramona, Brenda L. H. Marina, Lena Boustani Darwich, Eunju Rho, Isa Rodriquez-Soto, and Rajade Berry-James. 2013. "The Voices and Choices of Women in the Academy." *Journal of the International Association for the Study of the Global Achievement Gap*. Book 9. http://digitalcommons.georgiasouthern.edu/jiasgag/9.

Acknowledgments

First, foremost, and always, I thank God. I am blessed to be a leader, answering the call to serve. Second, I thank my publisher, Lexington Books, and Alissa, Carissa, and Nicolette for taking an interest in this topic and endeavor for composing this manuscript.

Third, I am indebted to those who accepted my invitation to share their research, programs, practices, and advice. Each personal experience and narrative has derived greater meaning to my purpose of mentoring women for leadership.

Lastly, and most important, I am thankful and grateful for my husband of thirty-six years, Frank. Without his constant encouragement and patience over the duration of this work, this book may not have come to fruition.

Introduction

This Is Where I Begin . . .

Brenda L. H. Marina

Over the past thirty-five years, a range of social, cultural, and structural-institutional ideologies have been identified as intervention strategies for breaking the glass ceiling in academia. Institutional practices and discourses are exemplars of how little attention has been paid to the relationship of mentoring and the social, cultural, and political dis/advantages for women's career paths in academia. There is a devastating consequence for women who lack mentorship at every juncture of their educational career. Additionally, the lack of educational scholarship on how women are (or are not) mentored factored into the cultural dynamics and conditions of academia is an issue. Scholarship has been produced with the goal of reducing structural barriers to the diversification of organizations. Such work has offered strategies such as mentoring for reducing the achievement gap for women and the glass ceiling effect for women of diverse backgrounds.

Findings from my qualitative research on women of color in higher education and leadership positions and my most recent literature analyses on the glass ceiling merited a re-examination of key findings and manifestations. My previous research question was: What are the important contemporary determinants in breaking the glass ceiling in higher education that have received minimal attention? The terms "mentoring," "religion," and "spirituality" were overwhelmingly distinguished as coping strategies. After a critical analysis, I had evidence (or the lack of evidence) regarding the determinants for breaking the glass ceiling that have received little attention and give rise to this conversation.

At one time the term "glass ceiling" was used mostly to refer to mainstream, upwardly mobile white women entering male-dominated professions. Today, the term is more broadly used to include all women from various professional points of view. From my womanist point of view, the glass ceiling is referred to the highest level that a professional woman can attain in a given professional field before running into an impasse in terms of achieving higher goals (Marina and Fonteneau 2012). The glass ceiling has often been virtually impermeable to many qualified women who wish to assume leadership roles in academia. As such, this amalgamation of the glass ceiling effect and mentoring women in academia adds a different dimension to the discussion. As new and different voices are added to the traditional notions of academic discourse, glass-shattering transformation can occur (2012).

Narratives by and about the experiences of women of diverse backgrounds in the United States and beyond the borders of this nation will shed needed light on the ways in which mentoring influences identity formation and internal coping mechanisms in environments often characterized by marginalization (Vargas 2002; Stanley 2006). Through these narratives, women of diverse backgrounds attempt to serve as "quasi mentors" and create spaces for other women to survive and thrive within the educational arena.

This text honors and extends previous work on the experiences of women academics from diverse backgrounds. Through this book, I call for new ways of understanding the vital role that narratives of women play in speaking truth to the power of mentoring. Utilizing a narrative approach, this text brings insights from women academics to exposé the extent to which politics, equity agendas, and mechanisms of quality assurances for mentoring have supported or failed these women. As such, I have asked the authors to bridge some of the knowledge gaps among women differently situated but engaged in academic workspaces.

This book provides examples of mentoring relationships, programs, and experiences interpreted from varied cultures and contexts. Culture implies a set of beliefs, assumption, norms, and traditions that are incorporated into the lives of those in a group. Culture exists in countries, racial and ethnic groups, in organizations and institutions, and within each of these there may be subcultures that have their own set of beliefs and values (Kochan and Pascarelli 2003). Context, similar to culture, is a framework, situation, circumstance, or environment. The chapter authors offer their cultured and gendered perspectives on mentoring from varied racial and ethnic backgrounds: African American, African American with a German parent, Asian (United Kingdom), black, Caucasian, Caucasian with Scandinavian and Native American (Chippewa) parents, Caucasian with one German parent and one Norwegian/French parent, English (United Kingdom), Jamaican, Korean, and Turkish. Furthermore, these perspectives on mentoring are from varied education levels, disciplines, and workspaces: business, education, mathematics, social work, STEM, undergraduate, graduate, early career, tenure-track faculty, tenured faculty, and administrators. The cultured and gendered dynamics of mentoring is not simple and straightforward (Kochan, Kent, and Green 2014; Marina 2014).

OVERVIEW

The first section of this book, "On the Road to Academe," is titled as such to help us consider the uneven terrain and journey that occurs from the onset of graduate education for women of diverse backgrounds (disciplines, cultures, age variance, and so on). In chapter 1, Jennifer M. Johnson and Jeanette C. Snider discuss the experiences of African American women in graduate school as compared to their white peers. This chapter explores how these two African American female graduate students, a master's student (graduated in 2011) and a doctoral student (graduated in 2013) engaged in positive mentorship relationships to achieve academic, professional, and personal success. Using personal narratives, they each share their formal and informal experiences with mentorship through interactions with their advisor, a tenured African American female faculty member, with their supervisors and professional colleagues, and with one another. Moreover, this chapter explores the question: How can the concepts of social and cultural capital be used to understand the importance of "social networks" and having a sense of the "culture of the academy" for minority students as they navigate academe?

In the following chapter, Krystal A. Foxx and Virginia C. Tickles explain that for many years, women who navigated through the STEM environment had to find their own way, oftentimes causing them to leak through the pipeline. They note that women who are less satisfied in the academic workplace are less likely to stay in STEM careers if they *feel* that they are less likely to advance within their career. Additionally, ethnic-racial groups and women continue to be underrepresented at higher education institutions, and women continue to be outnumbered in upper-level positions in the STEM workforce (Hill, Corbett, and St. Rose 2010).

This chapter provides the mentor's and mentee's reflections of their experiences while navigating the STEM culture both in academia and industry. Accounts of mentoring experiences supported by relevant literature help frame the importance of mentoring for women in general and for women of color in specific, because historically, this field was not an option for them. Personal experiences/stories and recommendations are shared with the hope that those who are interested in the retention of women of color in STEM and increasing diversity in the workforce can develop strategies to move forward the agenda of diversity and the need to increase the number of women in STEM and their opportunities for mentorship.

In chapter 3, Jean Ostrom-Blonigen and Cindy Larson-Casselton note that research consistently indicates that men are better positioned to secure organizational mentoring relationships than women (Ely, Ibarra, and Kolb 2011; Sandberg 2013) and that women are often disadvantaged in traditional formalized mentoring structures (Searby and Collins 2010; Zachary 2009). In 2013, success came in the form of doctoral degrees for these two women who began their graduate programs as strangers. Both older-than-average students, these women became friends and peer-mentors when each offered the other social support after life circumstances undermined the complete formation of normal, more formalized mentoring relationships. Further discussion focuses on social support, communication theory, and on how higher education institutions can be more proactive in mentoring older-than-average female graduate students during such times when they must also navigate life challenges.

In section II, "Tapping on the Glass Ceiling in Academe," career issues and concerns are described, highlighting the role of mentoring. This section calls attention to the positive and negative aspects of mentoring for women. Allison E. McWilliams explores the burdens associated with mentoring and women in the academy in the first chapter of this section. She contends that mentoring is often ascribed with positive attributes while ignoring the inherent power differentials that exist within those relationships. Because mentoring is often aligned with so-called "soft" skills and given to gendered positioning, women are asked to perform this role. As such, women potentially subject themselves to a "lesser" role than their male colleagues who adopt the roles of researcher and scholar. These power dynamics encourage women to be less inclined to serve as mentors, not more so; additionally, when women are effectively cut off from more senior mentors it perpetuates a system that exists on a "sink or swim" mentality.

Using both her own personal narrative as staff member, public service faculty, and administrator, as well as narratives of female assistant and associate professors from her doctoral research, this chapter explores how these power dynamics play out within the academy. What are these burdens of the insider-outsider that both allow us and prevent us from enacting the role of "mentor"? What burdens both allow us and prevent us from reaching the "power center"? What place of privilege do I occupy now that allows me to ask these questions? This chapter examines these questions and identifies some key takeaways for both women and the academy.

In chapter 5, Dian D. McCallum explains how workplace mentoring is highly regarded as one of the best means of inducting new members into an organization, providing a number of benefits for the mentor and mentee as well as the organization as a whole. She portends that some higher education institutions are not typically known for embracing workplace practices such as formal mentoring, as it might be commonly assumed. In other words, formal mentoring as an aspect of workplace socialization is not embedded in the organizational culture and is therefore not an explicit means of acclimating new faculty members into most of these institutions.

Noting that formal mentoring for faculty in higher education is a prominent feature or becoming more common in countries such as England, the United States, and Australia, in small island states such as Jamaica, formal mentoring for new academics is not yet ingrained in the institutional practices at one of the chief institutions of higher education. This chapter describes the "induction" experiences of two female academics in their beginning years of teaching at a higher education institution in Jamaica. McCallum highlights the role of informal mentoring as the main institutional mechanism that these female academics experienced as a part of their ongoing socialization into the university, specifically at the departmental level.

Following, Lillie Ben describes the mentor-protégé relationships from a Pan-Asian perspective. She contends that the outcomes of mentoring practices in the academic and business world of today are not well aligned with the concepts of mentoring principles. Furthermore, she discusses negative consequences, pointing to ambiguous philosophical issues around gender and ethnicity.

The purpose of Ben's chapter is four-fold: 1) First, to discuss best practices on mentorship principles; 2) second, to make transparent major issues and plausible solutions of mentorship differences around gender and ethnic philosophies as viewed from the academic and business world; 3) third, to highlight mentoring issues and plausible solutions from the viewpoint of Asian American women (that is, primarily Pan-Asian American females) in academe and business; and 4) fourth, to share her personal experiences as an Asian American woman mentor of six Asian American professional women protégés.

In chapter seven, Julie Haddock-Millar and Chandana Sanyal discuss preparing qualified women for upper-level and leadership positions in the United Kingdom (UK). They note that the Higher Education Institutional (HEI) environment is characterized by a distinct absence of sponsorship and developmental mentoring, resulting in very few female professors in many UK HEIs. The authors' experiences of both being mentored and mentoring others reflects many of the issues women face (although not exclusively), when making the transition from practice to academia. Haddock-Millar's story focuses on the impact of her decision to undertake a professional doctorate and her career journey to date in the world of academia. Sanyal's story explores her early impressions and encounters with "educational leaders" and how that has shaped her thinking and views of "academics." Additionally, Sanyal's story examines whether her non-western educational background and ethnicity, her values, beliefs, and culture immobilize her career progression. Additionally, she considers to what extent mentoring has supported her continued career development.

In section III, "Steps toward Successful Mentoring," the authors describe collaborative efforts that enhanced their professional development. For example, Tamara Bertrand Jones, JeffriAnne Wilder, and La'Tara Osborne-Lampkin describe Sisters of the Academy (SOTA). This institute was created to help facilitate the success of black women in academia by providing a support network. As scholars with similar research interests of mentoring, advising, and faculty development, they benefited from the collective "brain trust" that comes from a group with similar goals and interests. In this chapter, they discuss the role of peer mentoring in facilitating the development of social capital, which is necessary for success in the academy. They describe how participation in SOTA has influenced their scholarly productivity and contributed to their overall professional and personal development. Bertrand Jones, Wilder, and Osborne-Lampkin maintain that the stories of black women academics provide a deeper comprehension of the complexity of issues at the intersection of race and gender, and these complexities contribute to the often mysterious world of academia. . . . *Our experiences are valid and can be used to facilitate understanding of other black women's experiences, as well as generate future areas of inquiry.*

In chapter 9, Isaac A. Blankson, Venessa A. Brown, and Ayşe Y. Evrensel describe the support activities provided by a university for its faculty with an emphasis on female faculty. They discuss a grassroots support program that is provided by faculty for faculty. This chapter also discusses the different types of consulting and mentoring activities available for the faculty and where the gender-related differences appear. For example, GIFT (Group Instructional Feedback Technique) allows a consultant/mentor to ask a faculty member's students questions and share students' answers with the faculty member. The authors found that in all the diverse interactions between faculty members and consultants/mentors, the female mentees appeared to have a clear understanding of their challenge and could readily express these challenges. This chapter concludes with a summarization of their findings with areas of challenges and opportunities for female faculty.

In the last chapter of this section, Emma Previato, a professor of mathematics, focuses on the science, technology, engineering, and mathematics (STEM) disciplines because of the traditional underrepresentation of women. This chapter's scope includes discussion on professional associations that were created for women who select disciplines which are historically underrepresented by women and persons of color. The role of mentoring is demonstrated through the different types of mentoring structures.

In the concluding section of the text, I examine the stories through the lens of the theory of intersectionality, and offer a discussion on cultural patterns, variations, and similarities in mentoring utilizing Yosso's (2005) theory of cultural capital. The theory of intersectionality (Crenshaw 1991) began as an exploration of the oppression of black women in society. This theory suggests that various culturally and socially constructed categories, such as race, gender, and class, interact on multiple and often simultaneous levels, contributing to systematic social inequality. Intersectionality is an ambiguous and open-ended concept. Because of its vagueness and inherent open-endedness, it "initiates a process of discovery which not only is potentially interminable but promises to yield new and more comprehensive and reflexively critical insights" (Davis 2008, 78). Through this intersectional lens, I attempt to show how our mentoring experiences as women across cultures and around the globe are interconnected.

REFERENCES

Crenshaw, K. 1991. "Mapping the Margins: Intersectionality, Identity Politics, and Violence against Women of Color." *Stanford Law Review* 43(6): 1241–99.

Davis, K. 2008. "Intersectionality as Buzzword: A Sociology of Science Perspective on What Makes a Feminist Theory Successful." *Feminist Theory* 9(67–87): 733-768. Thousand Oaks, CA: Sage.

Ely, R. J., H. Ibarra, and D. M. Kolb. 2011. "Taking Gender into Account: Theory and Design for Women's Leadership Development Programs." *Academy of Management, Learning & Education* 10(3): 474–493.

Hill, C., C. Corbett, and A. St. Rose. 2010. *Why So Few? Women in Science, Technology, Engineering, and Mathematics*. Washington, DC: American Association of University Women.

Holmes, S. L., L. D. Land, and V. D. Hinton-Huston. 2007. "Race Still Matters: Considerations for Mentoring Black Women in Academe." *The Negro Educational Review* 58(1/2): 105–129.

Kochan, F., and J. Pascarelli. 2003. *Global Perspectives on Mentoring: Transforming Contexts, Communities, and Cultures*. Greenwich: Information Age Publishing, Inc.

Kochan, F., A. Kent, and A. Green. 2014. *Uncovering the Hidden Cultural Dynamics in Mentoring Programs and Relationships: Enhancing Practice and Research, Volume 4: Perspectives in Mentoring Series*. Charlotte: Information Age Publishing (IAP).

Marina, B. L. H. 2014. "A Cultural Connection to Identity Development for Graduate Female Students of Color." In F. Kochan, A. Kent, and A. Green (eds.), *Uncovering the Hidden Cultural Dynamics in Mentoring Programs and Relationships: Enhancing Practice and Research, Volume 4: Perspectives in Mentoring Series*. Charlotte: Information Age Publishing (IAP), 63–77.

Marina, B. L. H., and D. Y. Fonteneau. 2012. "Servant Leaders Who Picked up the Broken Glass." *Journal of Pan African Studies* 5(2): 67–83.

Sandberg, S. 2013. *Lean In: Women, Work, and the Will to Lead*. New York: Alfred A. Knopf.

Searby, L., and L. Collins. 2010. "Mentor and Mother Hen: Just What I Needed as a First Year Professor." *Advancing Women in Leadership Journal* 30(20): 1-16.

Stanley, C. A. 2006. "An Overview of the Literature." In Christine A. Stanley (ed.), *Faculty of Color: Teaching in Predominantly White Colleges and Universities*, 1–29. Bolton, MA: Anker Publishing Company, Inc.

Vargas, L. 2002. *Women Faculty of Color in the White Classroom: Narratives on the Pedagogical Implications of Teacher Diversity*. New York: Peter Lang Publishing.

Yosso, T. J. 2005. "Whose Culture Has Capital? A Critical Race Theory Discussion of Community Cultural Wealth." *Race, Ethnicity and Education* 8(1): 69–91.

Zachary, L. J. 2009. "Filling in the Blanks." *T+D* (May): 63–66.

I

On the Road to Academe

ONE

PhorwarD Progress

Moving Ahead through Mentorship in the Academy

Jennifer M. Johnson and Jeanette C. Snider

The majority of students attending college in the United States are women. Since the 1990s, women have outpaced men in both college enrollment and degree attainment rates (Lopez and Gonzalez-Barrera 2014). African American or black[1] women lead all racial/ethnic groups in college enrollment, with over 50 percent of individuals ages eighteen to twenty-four pursuing postsecondary education (Aud, Hussar, Johnson, Kena, Roth, Manning, Wang, and Zhang 2012). These enrollment trends are reflected in degree attainment rates as well. During the 2009–2010 academic year, 68 percent of the associate's degrees, 66 percent of the bachelor's degrees, 71 percent of the master's degrees, and 65 percent of the doctoral degrees conferred to African Americans went to women (Aud, Hussar, Johnson, Kena, Roth, Manning, Wang, and Zhang 2012). Despite these positive trends, black women continue to be underrepresented across various leadership roles in higher education (Croom 2011; Trower and Chait 2002). Black women represent merely 3 percent of full-time faculty, 1.39 percent of full professors, and the ranks of senior academic leaders and college presidents continue to be dominated by males across all U.S. institutions of postsecondary education (Kena, Aud, Johnson, Wang, Zhang, Rathbun, Wilkinson-Flicker, and Kristapovich 2014).

To encourage more black women to consider careers in academe, senior institutional leaders, both faculty and administrators, are called to serve as "mentors" for students beginning early in their undergraduate career. Going beyond a traditional student-advisor dynamic, mentors serve as visible role models, often with the willingness and capacity to provide the academic and professional guidance important for career advancement as well as the personal and emotional support needed to overcome potential barriers to success (Baker and Griffin 2010; Bova 2000; Grant 2012). Positive interactions with senior leaders across various disciplines in higher education can be critical in building strong networks with scholars and practitioners (Griffin and Reddick 2011), promoting positive perceptions of faculty-life (Fries-Britt and Turner 2005), and cultivating a sustained interest in leadership opportunities in the field (Davis 2010).

There are several approaches to cultivating mentorship relationships between students and institutional leaders. Successful relationships can be between mentors and students that take into consideration students' race, gender, academic, or professional interests, or all of the above (Grant 2012; Griffin and Reddick 2011; Johnson-Bailey, Valentine, Cervero, and Bowles 2008; Makobela and Green 2001). Additionally, peer mentorship is a critical source of support for black scholars. As Fries-Britt and Turner (2005) assert, the success of black Americans in higher education can be attributed in part to the opportunities they created for themselves with one another.

In an effort to understand the conditions that encourage and promote a sustained interest in pursuing faculty and senior administrative careers amongst black women, we share in this chapter how we each engaged in positive mentorship relationships throughout our collegiate and professional careers to achieve academic, professional, and personal success. Born and raised in the United States to American-born parents, we each identify as African American women (Jennifer Johnson's parents are each of African descent while Jeanette Snider's mother is of African descent and her father is of German descent). We share our early experiences with mentorship as well as the critical encounters through graduate school that contributed to our decisions to continue in academe. Utilizing scholarly personal narrative as our methodology (Nash 2004), we offer our experiences as a lens for understanding how black women can be encouraged to pursue careers in the academy through mentorship.

METHODOLOGY

We use scholarly personal narrative as the tool to share our individual experiences navigating the academy. A narrative begins with the "experiences as expressed in lived and told stories of individuals" (Creswell 2007, 54). Scholarly personal narrative, or autoethnography, focuses on the experiences of the author from their point of view, allowing for a restorying of the events, interactions, or circumstances that contributed to some outcome in relation to available academic research (Nash 2004).

Restorying is defined as "the process of reorganizing stories into some general framework . . . a causal link among ideas . . . that are not necessarily in chronological order" (Nash 2004, 56). In this case, this method is appropriate as it allows for us to use our own narratives about mentorship to examine the patterns and experiences of mentorship that sustain and promote progression through the academy at different points in our academy journey.

Our relationship began in 2009, as we began our graduate programs in a higher education program at a large research-intensive university. At the time, we were at different points in our careers. Jennifer was transitioning from a full-time position working for a college access program and beginning a PhD program, while Jeanette had just completed her bachelor's degree and was beginning a master's program. Our similar research interests, namely exploring the educational experiences of students of color, facilitated the pairing with the same faculty advisor, a tenured African American woman in the department. Following, we share our formal and informal experiences with mentorship beginning as undergraduates with institutional leaders, advisors, and peers, and continuing as graduate students and student affairs professionals with our colleagues, peer groups, and with one another.

PERSONAL NARRATIVES ON MENTORING

Contemplating the Academy

Jeanette Snider

Mentoring has always been a significant aspect of my educational experience. In my formative years, my parents served as my first mentors, always encouraging me academically. Although I had strong familial supports, I struggled early on academically and realized in middle and high school that my approach to school would look different than my peers. I developed a strong work ethic that propelled me into advanced courses and later into a selective university. This achievement did not come without the mentors that guided me throughout the educational system and helped me overcome my low self-efficacy and low self-esteem.

Entering into a selective predominately white institution (PWI), feelings of doubt resurfaced. I struggled to connect to my university and at times felt as though I did not deserve to attend such a prestigious institution. Instead of transferring, I began to spend more time with three black administrators around campus, which quickly manifested into strong mentoring relationships. Navigating through a selective PWI can be isolating, but my mentors gave me a place to feel comfortable to share my fears, worries, and struggles all while affirming me to achieve and persist in spite of those challenges. These relationships helped me plant roots on campus. Through these mentoring relationships I developed a passion for educational advocacy. As role models, my mentors exposed me to higher education as a "profession" and helped me become aware of the critical role administrators and faculty of color play in the matriculation of students of color (Chandler 1996). These authentic relationships would later influence my graduate studies and career goals (Padilla, Treviño, Gonzalez, and Treviño 1997).

Although I garnered tremendous support in my undergraduate years, graduate school was an entirely new obstacle. I immediately entered the program with extreme doubt and anxiety. I felt like an imposter and ill equipped to excel in the program (Johnson-Bailey 2004). Admittedly, I selected the master's program based on the relationships I observed between my advisor and her students during our admitted student welcome weekend. From one encounter, I sensed a mutual respect, trust, and support from my advisor toward her budding master's- and PhD-level students. I wanted to be part of that type of environment. It was in a course she taught in the most unlikely of circumstances that our mentoring partnership emerged.

In the program, not only did her presence and support motivate me to excel, but I found comfort and encouragement through her scholarly publications. I read one of her articles that she wrote with one of her mentees over ten years ago. Through their personal narratives, I realized the power of vulnerability and transparency in the academy. Her scholarly narrative highlighted the challenges both she and her mentee faced as an assistant professor and PhD student at a PWI. In my eyes, I was alone and incapable of completing my degree. The article selflessly allowed me to understand the struggles that are common in the academy and how to develop strategies to succeed. Although difficult to fathom, my mentor, a woman I hold in such high regard, felt tensions in the academy and with her abilities. Her vulnerability and courage to share what is often kept private in the academy gave me the agency I needed to persist and earn my master's degree.

One of the benefits of my graduate program was the ability to take courses with doctoral students. I was given the opportunity to work side-by-side with aspiring PhDs from diverse racial and ethnic backgrounds (Patton 2009). Originally, I never contemplated earning a PhD and at times I thought I would not finish my master's degree, but my classmates mentored me through the process. Whether they set up writing sessions at cafes or eateries, edited my papers, provided words of encouragement, or discussed research interests, I realized quickly how important peer mentors were in the graduate-level process (Packer-Williams and Evans 2011). As I completed my master's degree program and continued working on campus, I witnessed many doctoral students graduate; their ac-

complishments have inspired me to begin my pursuit of a doctoral degree. I look forward to continuing to pay forward all the aid I have
received throughout my educational and professional life.

PhD and Beyond

Jennifer Johnson

I would not be the woman I am today without the academic, professional, and personal mentorship I received over the years. Women from
diverse racial, socioeconomic, and educational backgrounds have played
a prominent role in my experiences. While I haven't always fully recognized it, these women, often teachers and counselors, truly motivated
and encouraged me to embrace my thirst for knowledge and would never let me shy away from being the "smart black girl" in the class (Fordham 2008). They maintained high expectations for me, and so of course, I
began to believe in myself even in the face of difficult times. My mentors
helped cultivate the confidence and conviction I needed to pursue a career in the academy.

In a lot of ways, I found college to be a different world. As an African
American woman from a low-income community, I struggled to find my
place in a space that was predominantly white and affluent (Ostrove and
Long 2007). The burgeoning confidence I had from my previous academic success was all but shattered, and I found it difficult to find faculty and
staff members that I could share my concerns with. From their perspective, my grade point average was solid, so by all accounts, I was doing
just fine and not in need of any additional support services (Freeman
1999). Having no one to turn to and not wanting to allow my vulnerabil-
ities to show, I put up a strong front; I became highly engaged socially
through student organizations and clubs and took on leadership roles
across campus. To my surprise, my involvement on campus allowed me
to cultivate mentorship relationships with people I did not expect: my
peers. Informal interactions with juniors and seniors, many of whom
were black men and women from Caribbean and African backgrounds,
really helped me realize that I was not the only person wrestling with
issues of belonging; I slowly I began to learn strategies to not only succeed but thrive in college (Padilla et al. 1997). As I moved through my
undergraduate experience, I saw it as my responsibility to "pay it forward" to the new students, sharing with them the keys to successfully
navigating the campus. I really tried to be a good mentor and role model
to others, but deep down I felt that I was still personally in need of
guidance from those more seasoned in their lives and careers.

From my experiences of mentoring students through their educational
journey, I finally found my calling—student affairs. Prior to starting a
graduate program in higher education, I was a middle school teacher, the

most important and challenging role I have ever had in my life. The experience helped me channel a sense of strength and resiliency that I did not realize I had. In comparison, graduate school was a breeze; no longer concerned with proving myself, I moved through the academic requirements of my master's program with ease. I also was able to finally connect with individuals who would become long-time mentors, two Caucasian faculty members in my program. My graduate school advisor, a newly minted PhD, embodied many of the qualities I wanted to cultivate as an academic. In her class, I started to really see myself not just as a practitioner but as a scholar and potential faculty person. Moreover, she was willing to get to know me and my story and how those experiences connected with my interest in student affairs. It was the first time I felt that someone in an academic role was willing to get to know me outside of the classroom context. Another female faculty member served as an important mentor through my master's degree program. A mid-career tenure-track faculty member, she followed a more traditional approach to mentoring, focusing on honing my writing skills and emphasizing the importance of academic knowledge. At the same time, she was a role model for work/life balance, stressing the importance of making time for her young family. Between these similar, yet diverse mentors and role models, I felt I had a good balance of both personal and intellectual support as I began to reflect on the type of career I wanted to pursue and why. Ultimately, they each played a role in my decision to apply to PhD programs. Thanks to their acknowledgment of and positive feedback on my writing, scholarly interests, and passion for education, I saw the academy as the place for me.

Having recognized the significance of maintaining positive relationships through graduate school in my experiences, I knew that this would be important in a doctoral program. I specifically looked for programs where there was a sense of community and limited competition for time with faculty. I applied to several programs, and my decision was strongly influenced by the opportunity to work with a renowned scholar with a reputation for mentorship. Knowing there were only a handful of tenured African American faculty women in my field, how could I pass up the opportunity to work with one? She immediately took me under her wing as a research assistant, and over the next four years I was able to gain hands on experience with research, academic writing, and presenting at conferences. Within my academic community, I found myself mentoring master's students, organizing study groups, serving as a sounding board and peer reviewer for my colleagues, and really stepping into the habits and practices of a faculty member-in-training. Moreover, as I continued working in student affairs, I was informally mentored by senior administrators and faculty members who encouraged (and at times pushed) me to take on various leadership roles both on campus and in the academic community. Through each of these experiences and opportunities, I saw academia as the space for me to thrive and make a lasting impact on the communities I hold dear. As I now begin my career as a faculty member, I continue to reflect on how all of the formal and informal mentorship experiences throughout my lifetime have cultivated and nurtured my self-confidence, academic interests, professionalism, and leadership skills. The academy can be a challenging space to navigate, but I really feel that I have the supports and networks needed to be successful along this journey.

DISCUSSION

As highlighted from our narratives, there were several commonalities in our educational experiences navigating academe that can be helpful when trying to encourage more black women to enter faculty and senior leadership roles. Across our experiences, mentorship came in a variety of forms. Before we identified "mentors," we found role models who embodied the confidence and poise we wanted to see in ourselves. Role modeling is the example an individual sets forth, both intentionally and unintentionally, by her everyday actions. Although the individual connections and experiences that spring from a strong mentoring relationship were crucial to our retention and matriculation process, at times it was the mere presence of successful students, faculty, and staff in the academy that made all the difference. Our role models embodied success; their strength and perseverance laid the footprints for younger students and junior faculty, such as us, to follow.

The literature is full of narratives regarding the challenges and pitfalls in the academy for women and students of color at all levels in their educational journey. Stereotypes, isolation, tokenism, and overt and covert forms of racism have plagued the experiences of students for generations (Ellis 2001; Gildersleeve, Croom, and Vasquez 2011; Tillman 2011). Our personal narratives, however, illustrate the ways mentorship interceded at each level to push us to new limits academically. Mentorship was particularly critical during our undergraduate years. Although praised as "high achievers" as high school students, college was a new space where we were forced to (re)discover and (re)assert our academic and social identities. During that phase of our experiences, mentorship came primarily from student affairs administrators and our peers. Relationships forged with these individuals were used to combat feelings of isolation, inequity, unfair treatment, and marginality, particularly as students of color attending predominantly white institutions (Bova 2000; Grant 2012; Johnson-Bailey 2004). Once these needs were met, we began to involve ourselves on campus, take on leadership roles, and see ourselves again as confident and capable scholars.

As graduate students, mentorship from faculty members was acutely significant, as close relationships with veteran scholars contributed to gains in academic knowledge, research skills and abilities, and independent scholarship. Grant (2012) postulates that black female graduate students' "intellectual capabilities are oftentimes doubted, and their research interest are often questioned or neglected" (104). Contrary to the prevailing literature, we had the opportunity to work with a handful of different faculty members who were supportive of our burgeoning interests. This was likely due to the fact that we were intentional in selecting graduate programs with faculty members who shared our research interests and perspectives in higher education. Taken together, across our undergraduate and graduate experiences, three categories of mentorship relationships emerged; mentorship with black women; mentorship across race and across gender; and mentorship with our peers, summarized below.

Black Women: Retaining One Another

Oftentimes students of color and women seek mentorship from members of their same race and gender (Patton 2009; Patton and Harper 2003; Tillman 2011). Daloz (1999) suggests that the very existence of these mentors from similar backgrounds "provides proof that the journey can be made" (207). Consistent with this theme, we each were intentional about seeking out mentorship from other black women. Given our shared identities, these same race and gender mentors were perceived as people who could relate to our educational challenges and social experiences in higher education (Fries-Britt and Turner 2005; Grant 2012; Packer-Williams and Evans 2011; Patton and Harper 2003). Fortunately, these expectations were met, most recently through our experiences with our advisor, a tenured African American woman, as well as with one another as peers in the graduate program. Working with an advisor who was both attentive to our needs and professionally connected in the field afforded us opportunities to teach, conduct research, present at conferences, and move successfully through academic milestones in our program. Moreover, she has continued to serve as a reference for us as we look to take advantage of career opportunities in higher education. Additionally, through our academic community, we had various opportunities to connect with one another, as well other black women who graduated from the program and were leading successful careers in higher education. These ongoing relationships continue to flourish and inspire us to grow professionally. According to Johnson-Bailey (2004), same-race mentors were one of the top factors in the retention of black female graduate students at a PWI. We believe that having the opportunity to work so closely with various individuals (both faculty and peers) who mirrored our social backgrounds and professional interests was instrumental in our timely graduation and interest to apply to PhD programs and tenure-track faculty careers. These positive experiences are the prerequisites to ensuring that more black women take on senior leadership experiences later in their career.

Finding Common Ground: Mentorship across Race and Gender

The underrepresentation of black female faculty and senior administrators make it virtually impossible for all black female graduate students to gain same race and gender mentors from their own department, if at all (Bova 2000; Burgess 1997; Grant and Simmons 2008). Although students have described fruitful cross-race and cross-gender mentor relationships, there are certain commonalities shared when describing successful relationships. First and foremost, trust has to be established between mentors and mentees. In some cases, black students feel as though they cannot be vulnerable with faculty members or advisors from different racial/cultural backgrounds due to the fear of being perceived as weak or incompetent (Patton and Harper 2003). From our experiences, we can each identify at least one non-black faculty member or senior administrator that we would consider to be mentors. These individuals embodied an ethic of care for our personal and professional growth that qualified them to be deemed as a mentor in our eyes. White female mentors, for example, provided support in terms of helping us gain a better understanding of the gendered roles/responsibilities and changing expectations for women in the field.

Also, research suggests that the approach to mentorship varies across gender. For example, male faculty members tend to provide more academic and career support for black women rather than emotional, personal, and/or cultural support (Patton 2009; Tillman 2011). In our experiences, black and Latino male mentors were particularly helpful in areas of academic and career support; serving as "Big Brother Academics" in our eyes. These individuals have also facilitated meetings with other professionals in the field (both men and women), leading to a variety of opportunities including internships, conferences, and speaking engagement. While potentially challenging, cross-race and cross-gender mentor relationships are common and can provide students with the information and support they need to persist and thrive in various educational and professional settings (Bova 2000; Packer-Williams and Evans 2011; Patton and Harper 2003).

Figuring It out Together: Peer Mentoring

Peer mentoring has emerged as a critical source of support, especially in the absence of opportunities to cultivate mentoring relationships with institutional leaders (Packer-Williams and Evans 2011). Research suggests harsh environments at PWIs leave a need for more emotional support structures, the understanding from peers and colleagues, or "sistering." Grant and Simmons (2008) define sistering as "relationships with other caring and nurturing women of color for social, professional, and spiritual support with networking opportunities" (509). In this sense, peers can help one another cope with subtle race-based injustices or microaggressions, increase positive self-identity and self-efficacy, and recognize and combat stereotypes (Packer-Williams and Evans 2011). Students can support each other informally through study groups or social gatherings, or more formally through "sister circles" or community of scholars programs (Patton 2009).

Peer mentorship also has advantages for individuals once they become faculty members and administrators. Packer-Williams and Evans's (2011) study exploring the experiences of new African American female faculty found peer mentoring as a means to "assist each other in scholarly efforts through collaborative research publications and presentations, to provide opportunities for members to voice their concerns and have them validated by other African American women in the academy, and to combat the isolation in the academy by participating in social events together held inside and outside of the university setting" (13). Many participated in these activities out of a desire to uplift younger doctoral students and aid in their academic process; illustrating the important cyclical consequences of positive mentoring (Grant 2012; Patton and Harper 2003). Taken together, as "sisters" in the academy, we took it upon ourselves to not just seek out mentorship from senior faculty and administrators but to look to one another for encouragement and motivation during times of challenge and to share the knowledge and practices needed to successfully navigate the academy. In our view, no single approach to mentorship would have propelled us to where we are today.

FUTURE DIRECTIONS IN MENTORSHIP

Based on the literature and our personal experiences, we make institutional recommendations to engage black women in mentoring practices that will cultivate future leaders in higher education. We assert that mentoring relationships may vary across different individuals. Some mentoring relationships can be strictly career orientated or academic in nature, while others are more about building social and personal connections. Consequently, the criteria used for matching mentors to mentees should be consistent with the nature and purpose of these pairings. Ultimately, the most important attribute of a mentoring relationship is the genuine interest on the part of both mentor and mentee to develop a mutually beneficial "partnership"—whether the relationship is for just a year, or if it will continue for several decades.

Most of our mentoring relationships developed informally through interactions with others during advisement meetings and research team sessions. Opportunities to meet and connect with one another in an academic setting laid the foundation for opportunities to expand outside of this single place and time. To increase the likelihood that these connections can be established, formalized mentoring programs at the university level must be created and supported to bring together students and junior faculty to mentors willing to advise them through their various stages in the academy. This can also help ensure that no single individual carries the burden of mentoring for all students. Formalized programs spread the responsibility and send a message from the top-down that the university values mentoring and acknowledges the tremendous benefits mentoring provides.

Efforts must be made at all levels of the academic spectrum to encourage burgeoning leaders to consider careers in postsecondary education. Oftentimes, mentoring programs target graduate students, and a more recent trend in mentoring has focused on black males. As we move forward as mid-level administrators and junior faculty members, formal and informal mentoring programs should continue to be encouraged and cultivated. Navigating the tenure process, for example, is an enormous undertaking, which often requires guidance and encouragement from senior leaders. Strategies must be put in place to ensure the success of underrepresented faculty. The cyclical effect of supporting quality faculty to mentor younger faculty and graduate students will perpetuate a sustainable pipeline of mentors for years to come.

CONCLUSION

Research suggests that the scarcity of black women in tenured faculty and senior administrative roles at four-year colleges and universities can be attributed to limited opportunities to cultivate meaningful relationships with knowledgeable others in the academy (Weidman and Stein 2003). To increase the representation of black women in tenured faculty and senior leadership positions across colleges and universities, it is important to understand the experiences, issues, and obstacles faced by these individuals as they attempt to navigate academe. One way to gain this information is through scholarly reflection on one's own experiences. Black women are complex, and consequently, the experiences of black women in the academy are challenging given the complex intersections of race and gender, as well as other identities such as ethnicity, religion, or sexuality (Baker and Griffin 2010; Patton and Harper 2003). As women of color in the academy, we found ourselves trying to understand how our multiple social identities influence our experiences and opportunities in higher education. Oftentimes we were confronted with challenges and barriers that may have prevented a seemingly smooth and forward progression through higher education. Mentorship, in various forms, was critical to our ongoing engagement in the academy and establishing the belief that we deserved to have a place at the table. Opportunities to hear the firsthand experiences of women who are successfully moving through academe can be helpful in this regard, and more research in this area should be encouraged.

The literature is latent with examples about the positive outcomes associated with mentoring relationships. Scholarship exploring the experiences of black women in the academy highlights the significance of positive mentor relationships on the retention, graduation, and career advancement of these women. Given our experiences with mentorship shared above, it is clear that mentorship early on can help students build the confidence and skills necessary to even contemplate applying to graduate programs. Contrary to previous findings outlining negative experiences of mentorship amongst women of color (Bova 2000; Gildersleeve, Croom, and Vasquez 2011; Tillman 2011) our experiences were overwhelmingly positive, suggesting that shifts in the academic landscape have begun to influence opportunities to cultivate a diverse pipeline to leadership roles in higher education. Through mentorship, graduate students and junior faculty of color such as ourselves can forge important networks and professional connections, learn how to successfully maneuver in the academy, and ultimately experience quicker professional success and more satisfying careers (Davis 2010; Grant 2012; Tillman 2011). Validation, affirmation, and nurturing from others provides a space where black women can both cultivate their talents and gain an appreciation of the value added by their presence in leadership roles across postsecondary education. Efforts made early will, without a doubt, help future generations of black women leaders as those who were mentored are more likely to mentor others. An essential benefits of mentoring is the development of academic talent within diverse communities, which ultimately will create a needed pipeline for black women to not only become faculty, deans, provosts, presidents, or chancellors, but to help transform the higher education landscape in ways that will positively impact the world.

NOTE

1. The term *African American* is used as the racial/ethnic descriptor for individuals of African descent born and raised in the United States. The term *black* is used as the racial/ethnic descriptor for individuals of African descent who have ancestors across the African Diaspora. When citing specific studies/articles, the terms *African American* or *black* is used as consistent with the original author.

REFERENCES

Aud, S., W. Hussar, F. Johnson, G. Kena, E. Roth, E. Manning, X. Wang, and J. Zhang. 2012. *The Condition of Education 2012* (NCES 2012–045). Washington, DC: U.S. Department of Education, National Center for Education Statistics. Retrieved from http://nces.ed.gov/pubsearch.

Baker, V. L., and K. A. Griffin. 2010. "Beyond Mentoring and Advising: Toward Understanding the Role of Faculty 'Developers' in Student Success." *About Campus*: 1–8.

Bova, B. 2000. "Mentoring Revisited: The Black Woman's Experience." *Mentoring & Tutoring* 8(1): 5–16.

Burgess, R. G., ed. 1997. *Beyond the First Degree: Graduate Education, Lifelong Learning, and Careers*. Bristol, PA: Open University Press.

Chandler, C. 1996. "Mentoring and Women in Academia: Reevaluating the Traditional Model." *NWSA Journal* 8(3): 79.

Creswell, J. W. 2007. *Qualitative Inquiry & Research Design: Choosing among Five Approaches*, 2nd edition. Thousand Oaks, CA: Sage.

Croom, N. 2011. "Finding Rainbows in the Clouds: Learning about the Full Professorship from the Stories of Black Female Full Professors." Graduate Theses and Dissertations. Paper 12168. Iowa State University.

Daloz, L. A. 1999. *Mentor: Guiding the Journey of Adult Learners*. San Francisco, CA: Jossey-Bass.

Davis, D. J. 2010. "The Academic Influence of Mentoring upon African American Undergraduate Aspirants to the Professoriate." *Urban Review* 42: 143–158.

Ellis, E. M. 2001. "The Impact of Race and Gender on Graduate School Socialization, Satisfaction with Doctoral Study and Commitment to Degree Completion." *The Western Journal of Black Studies* 25(1): 30–45.

Fordham, S. 2008. "Beyond Capital High: On Dual Citizenship and the Strange Career of 'Acting White.'" *Anthropology & Education Quarterly* 39(3): 227–246.

Freeman, K. 1999. "No Services Needed?: The Case for Mentoring High-Achieving African American Students." *Peabody Journal of Education* 74(2): 15–26.

Fries-Britt, S., and B. Turner. 2005. "Retaining Each Other: Narratives of Two African American Women in the Academy." *The Urban Review* 37(3): 221–242.

Gildersleeve, R. E., N. N. Croom, and P. L. Vasquez. 2011. "'Am I going Crazy?!': A Critical Race Analysis of Doctoral Education." *Equity & Excellence in Education* 44(1): 93–114.

Grant, C. M. 2012. "Advancing our Legacy: A Black Feminist Perspective on the Significance of Mentoring for African-American Women in Educational Leadership." *International Journal of Qualitative Studies in Education* 25(1): 101–117.

Grant, C. M., and J. C. Simmons. 2008. "Narratives on Experiences of African-American Women in the Academy: Conceptualizing Effective Mentoring Relationships of Doctoral Students and Faculty." *Internal Journal of Qualitative Studies in Education* 21(5): 501-517.

Griffin, K. A., and R. J. Reddick. 2011. "Surveillance and Sacrifice: Gender Differences in the Mentoring Patterns of Black Professors at Predominantly White Research Universities." *American Educational Research Journal* 48(5): 1032-1057.

Johnson-Bailey, J. 2004. "Hitting and Climbing the Proverbial Wall: Participation and Retention Issues for Black Graduate Women." *Race Ethnicity and Education* 7(4): 331-349.

Johnson-Bailey, J., T. S. Valentine, R. M. Cervero, and T. A. Bowles. 2008. "Lean on Me: The Support Experiences of Black Graduate Students." *The Journal of Negro Education* 77(4): 365-381.

Kena, G., S. Aud, F. Johnson, X. Wang, J. Zhang, A. Rathbun, S. Wilkinson-Flicker, and P. Kristapovich. 2014. *The Condition of Education 2014* (NCES 2014–083). Washington, DC: U.S. Department of Education, National Center for Education Statistics. Retrieved from http://nces.ed.gov/pubsearch.

Lopez, M. H., and A. Gonzalez-Barrera. 2014, March 6. "Women's College Enrollment Gains Leave Men Behind." *Pew Research Center*. Retrieved from http://www.pewresearch.org.

Makobela, R. O., and A. L. Green, eds. 2001. *Sisters of the Academy: Emergent Black Women Scholars in Higher Education*. Sterling, VA: Stylus.

Nash, R. J. 2004. *Liberating Scholarly Writing: The Power of Personal Narrative*. New York: Teachers College Press.

Ostrove, J. M., and S. M. Long. 2007. "Social Class and Belonging: Implications for College Adjustment." *The Review of Higher Education* 30(4): 363-389.

Packer-Williams, C. L., and K. M. Evans. 2011. "Retaining and Reclaiming Ourselves: Reflections on a Peer Mentoring Group Experience for New African American Women Professors." *Perspectives in Peer Programs* 23(1): 9-23.

Padilla, R. V., J. Treviño, K. Gonzales, and J. Treviño. 1997. "Developing Local Models of Minority Student Success in College." *Journal of College Student Development* 38(2): 125-135.

Patton, L. D. 2009. "My Sister's Keeper: A Qualitative Examination of Mentoring Experiences among African American Women in Graduate and Professional Schools." *The Journal of Higher Education* 80(5): 510-537.

Patton, L. D., and S. R. Harper. 2003. "Mentoring Relationships among African American Women in Graduate and Professional Schools." *New Directions for Student Services* (104): 67-78.

Tillman, L. C. 2011. "Sometimes I've Felt Like a Motherless Child: Being Black and Female in the Academy." In S. Jackson and R. G. Johnson (eds.), *The Black Professoriate: Negotiating a Habitable Space in the Academy*, 91-107. New York: Peter Lang.

Trower, C., and R. Chait. 2002. "Faculty Diversity: Too Little for Too Long." *Harvard Magazine* 104(4): 33-37, 98.

Weidman, J. C., and E. L. Stein. 2003. "Socialization of Doctoral Students to Academic Norms." *Research in Higher Education* 44(6): 641-656.

TWO

I Am My Sister's Keeper

A Dual Mentoring Perspective of Women of Color in STEM

Krystal A. Foxx and Virginia C. Tickles

WHAT IS MENTORING?

Mentoring is defined as a series of meaningful interactions that occur between an experienced individual and a person in need of personal and professional support (often referred to as a protégé). The mentoring process requires, at the least, a mentor (a wise person) providing advice or counsel to a protégé or junior (Kram 1985; Mezias and Scandura 2005; Paglis, Green, and Bauer 2006). According to Chesler and Chesler (2002), a mentor is someone who bears the role and responsibility of assisting, supporting, and developing protégés through exposure to information and resources that might be unknown to them. Mentors appear in many forms such as a role model, leader in community, friend, professor/administrator, and advisor/counselor (Amelink 2009; Anderson and Shannon 1988; Fagenson 1989) and in the higher education arena might assist protégés in navigating through college in both undergraduate and graduate programs and career paths (Blake-Beard, Bayne, and Crosby 2011; Crisp and Cruz 2009). Some mentors may be very selective in choosing new mentees (protégés) to mentor (Johnson 2007); however, both, protégés and mentors, grow during the mentoring process (Ragins and Kram 2007) especially those that exhibit mutual respect, trust, understanding and empathy for each other (National Academy of Sciences, National Academy of Engineering, and Institute of Medicine 1997). Mentoring relationships are not just limited to a single mentor and protégé, but can be conceptualized as a relationship between a network of mentors and a protégé over the entire career span of a protégé or can be seen as a team mentoring approach, which is a group of mentors and protégés (Higgins and Kram 2001; Lankau and Scandura 2002; Mezias and Scandura 2005).

Mentoring relationships can be seen as both formal and informal (Amelink 2009; Cobb et al. 2006) with formal relationships being initiated by an organization or program with prescribed times and requirements, while informal relationships occur as a result of two people who desire to meet because of perceived mutual interest and interpersonal comfort and connection (Allen, Poteet, and Burroughs 1997; Amelink 2009; Douglas 1997; Gaskill 1993; Kram 1983, 1985). There are several types of mentoring relationships that can form; some that are common to the cultured and global context of the academic and professional setting described in this chapter are hierarchical (relationship between mentor and protégé in which mentors have the information and more power), apprentice (mentor aids protégé in becoming valued member of profession), co-mentoring (both mentor and protégé share responsibility and power), and peer mentoring (peers provide personal and professional support to one another) (Amelink 2009; Buell 2004; McGuire and Reger 2003; Touchton 2003). Notwithstanding the types of mentoring that exist, research shows that mentoring is very beneficial to all parties involved including the mentor, protégé, and organization (if hosting a formal mentoring program) (Allen 2003; Amelink 2009; Aryee, Chay, and Chew 1996; Fagenson 1989).

GLOBAL IMPORTANCE OF MENTORING WOMEN OF COLOR IN STEM

Globally, diversity continues to be pivotal in science, technology, engineering, and mathematics (STEM) higher education and the workforce. This is primarily because the creation of new and innovative ideas and products from people of diverse backgrounds and experiences allow countries to be competitive with each other (Slaughter and McPhail 2007). STEM fields remain responsible for over half of the U.S.' economic growth in areas such as research, educational endeavors, and workforce (Malcolm, Chubin, and Jesse 2004) yet people in the sciences in Singapore, Chinese Taipei, Japan, Korea, England, Hungary, Czech Republic, Slovenia, Hong Kong, and the Russian Federation have higher scores in sciences than the United States (Gonzales, Williams, Jocelyn, Roey, Kastberg, and Brenwald 2009). Additionally, Machi and Heritage (2009) explains that the United States is not directing as much attention on STEM fields in comparison to other countries around the world. Hughes (2009) found that in 2008 the United States produced far fewer engineers than other countries such as China and India. Furthermore, Turkey, Greece, and France produce two to three times as many physics graduates than the United States (De Welde, Laursen, and Thiry 2007).

Although we see an increase in ethnic-racial diversity in the United States with the expected population to be majority persons of color by 2043 (United States Census Bureau 2012), ethnic-racial groups and women continue to be underrepresented at higher education institutions and women continue to be outnumbered in upper-level positions in the STEM workforce (Hill, Corbett, and St. Rose 2010). Statistics indicate that in 2011 women made up only 26 percent of those in STEM careers, and underrepresented ethnic-racial groups made up roughly 17 percent with even less of a percentage being women of color (Landivar 2013). In other countries, women in STEM face similar challenges Specifically, DeWandre (2002) found that women researchers in Italy advanced far less than their male counterparts in national labs and that 50 percent of biology graduates in the United Kingdom are women even though only 9 percent of women hold professor positions. Internationally, underrepresentation of women is based on cultural aspects due to both policies and differences that have an impact on diversity in the workforce and in education (De Welde, Laursen, and Thiry 2007; Linn 2007). Therefore, the urgency to increase diversity in STEM higher education and the STEM workforce with underrepresented groups such as women and persons of color should remain a global priority for all STEM companies and academic institutions.

According to Hill, Corbett, and St. Rose (2010), one way that college and university administrators can recruit and retain more women in STEM fields is by increasing mentoring opportunities. Mentoring is said to be a necessary component for the advancement of women, especially women of color, in STEM fields because for many years women who navigated through the STEM environment had to find their own way, oftentimes causing them to leak through the pipeline. In general, research reveals that women that are less satisfied in the academic workplace are less likely to stay in STEM careers if they feel that they are less likely to advance within their career (Amelink 2009). Additionally, women of color experience feelings of loneliness, isolation, and/or disillusionment in STEM fields. However, mentoring has been known to decrease these feelings in women of color and student participation in formal mentoring programs has been shown to improve the retention of undergraduate women majoring in the STEM fields (Amelink 2009; Kahveci, Southerland, and Gilmer 2006). Overall, mentoring women of color in STEM has been known to be an effective strategy for aiding in the personal and academic success of women who navigate through academia and in STEM disciplines (Amelink 2009).

This chapter describes the personal stories of two black women who both have experiences navigating through STEM disciplines in higher education. It also provides reflections of their mentoring experiences prior to enrolling into higher education and their need for mentoring opportunities while navigating the STEM culture. Narrative in the form of stories has the power to change and direct the lives of others (Noddings 1991; Rushton 2004). Therefore, the narrative of personal accounts of mentoring and the lack thereof, supported by relevant literature, will help frame the importance of mentoring for all—but specifically women of color in a field historically dominated by white males (Amelink 2009). The information provided in this chapter is intended to reach higher education via STEM program administrators, STEM faculty members, STEM employers, and/or other relevant persons in the STEM workforce who are invested in increasing diversity in the workforce and understanding mentoring and its effects on the retention of women of color in STEM. Throughout this chapter, personal experiences/stories will be shared not just to highlight the challenges that women of color face in a STEM environment but to encourage the intended audience through various recommendations to continue developing strategies to move forward the agenda of diversity and the mentoring support needed to increase the number of women of color in STEM.

MY SISTER: THE MENTEE'S EXPERIENCE

Over several decades, mentoring has been an effective approach in aiding black students in the adaptation of their higher education environments and academic success (Strayhorn and Terrell 2007). Mentees (also known as protégés) can have several mentors at one time (Higgins and Kram 2001; Lankau and Scandura 2002; Mezias and Scandura 2005), which is apparent as this woman of color tells her story of being mentored by various family, family friends, and community leaders during her years of secondary education. This part of the narrative story reflects on the mentee's (woman of color one) first encounters of mentoring prior to attending a higher education institution. It also highlights how mentoring shaped both the personal and professional development of this woman of color prior to engaging in STEM in higher education.

First Accounts of Mentoring: A Reflection of My Mentors

As I reflect on my journey of mentoring, my first interactions with mentors were a result of informal occurrences. Growing up in a small rural town, where everyone knows one another, mentoring was a community affair for me. The proverb "it takes a village to raise a child" never reigned more accurate to describe my mentoring experiences. At an early age, mentoring became important to me, and it provided a stronger connection to my family and friends as well as my community.

As a child, I grew up with parents who were active in the community, which made others feel responsible for nurturing and creating a leader in me, both in school and the community. Several of my first encounters of mentoring took place in my hometown, resulting in me gaining a network of mentors, who, to this day, continue to guide and influence both my personal and professional decisions.

In particular, my family and family friends (parents, grandmother, aunts, and church community) were mentors. As a result of my interactions with them, I gained an understanding of the role that mentors should play and developed my own identity as a mentor. One lesson that I learned from mentorship from my parents was that one great quality of a mentor is to be able to envision or offer more to an individual than what they currently see or have. While I understand that not all mentors are visionaries or invest this type of effort into their protégés, my parents understood the importance of this factor. At the time, my mother had attended a community college and my dad had dropped out of school to take care of his family, yet they collectively pushed me to excel in everything including academic and personal matters. Because I was a potential first-generation college student, there was a push to see greater in me so my parents motivated me to go to college and get involved to ensure that I would be connected to the right people and resources. The motivation they provided was more than enough, but having them steer me in a positive direction connecting me to the right resources and people made my journey to pursue higher education much easier.

Alongside my parents, mentoring moments with my grandmother and aunts were important during my middle and high school years. I come from generations of strong women in my family including my grandmother who was very active in the community and served both locally in roles such as pastor, teacher, and volunteer/community mentor, and a role internationally as a mission worker in Africa and Bahamas. My grandmother was the epitome of a servant leader and mentor. She always assured me that my life mattered and that my purpose was significant. She, along with my aunts, made me realize that mentoring was necessary, and they would often encourage me and connect me to others who helped me to productively carry out my personal and professional goals while also helping others. My grandmother's mentorship and wisdom, as well as shadowing and witnessing some of her experiences as a leader in the community, were vital to my development in becoming a mentor to others. I remember some of the challenges my grandmother faced in leading and working with diverse people. Despite those challenges, she did not let people change her character. She would always say "Treat people the way you would want to be treated no matter what" and would give to others, which inspired me to be a hands-on leader and mentor.

There were also three other women who provided mentorship during my high school years. One was my assistant principal, a family relative and active community leader who was responsible for preparing me for various aspects of college since I did not attend any pre-college preparation programs nor had a financial plan for college. I remember the process of preparing for college, and there would be times when I would literally sit in her office during breaks, fill out college applications and scholarships, and seek her advice about college and campus life. I was a first-generation college-bound student with minimal knowledge of the college process. The literature shows that first-generation students face challenges such as adapting to the college/university environment, preparing academically, integrating socially with peers, and interacting with faculty (Chen 2005; Ishitani 2003; Kim and Sax 2009; Martínez, Sher, Krull, and Wood 2009). This mentor would answer all of my questions and guide me as I prepared, which taught me that a mentor is someone with multiple experiences that are necessary to the growth of a person. She was significant in developing my leadership and academic rigor and suggested that I take particular courses at the local community college to be a well-advanced student; become more involved in leadership positions such as officers and active members of student clubs/organizations; and get more active in my community. She also encouraged me to stay out of trouble by avoiding the wrong crowd and peers who were not of a positive influence.

Two other women, who were both teachers while I was in high school, had a major influence on me. I would often find myself talking with these two ladies during lunch breaks and after school just to hear of historical events that had taken place in my community or to talk about new resources that were available at my high school. These particular women would also encourage me to push myself more in the classroom or to get more involved socially because they personally knew my parents would want me to be successful in all of my educational endeavors. These were not just teachers but mentors who were vested in developing me to become a well-rounded student and leader while in high school.

Overall, I don't know what I would have done without all the mentors that have shaped my abilities over the years. My family and community played a major role in my decision to attend and persist in college. All mentors that I've gained took time to get to know me not only as a student and future leader, but also as an individual. They assisted in developing my skills and knowledge and motivated me to learn and prepare for my personal and professional goals.

REFLECTIONS OF JOURNEY INTO STEM HIGHER EDUCATION

The first part of the narrative tells the story of how mentoring evolved for a first-generation woman of color who was the protégé and how mentoring shaped her personal and professional experiences prior to attending a university to engage in STEM. This particular section also introduces the other woman of color who was a first-generation female STEM student with excellent skills in mathematics obtained during her high school years. Together, their combined stories of experiencing STEM at a predominantly white institution (PWI) and a historically black college and university (HBCU) are told to understand the challenges that women of color often face in STEM disciplines such as engineering, mathematics, computer science, and many other related disciplines. It is the goal of this part of the narrative to highlight commonalities in both stories to understand how underrepresented groups in STEM (particularly black, Latino, Native American, or women in STEM) often feel isolated and culturally alienated; have minimal interactions with faculty and even peers, and lack the support and positive interactions and mentoring needed to successfully navigate through STEM while pursuing higher education (Amelink 2009; Foor, Walden, and Trytten 2007; Landivar 2013). The first reflection is the mentee's experience of pursuing STEM at a university followed by the reflective thoughts of the mentor who pursued and obtained a degree in engineering.

A Search for Mentorship

Woman of Color (One)

While in middle and high school, I grew to love mathematics and be highly skilled in advanced mathematics courses. Additionally, I competed in high school student clubs where I developed more knowledge of the medical sciences. Other than taking advanced and college-preparatory mathematics and science courses and participating in science-related student organizations, I didn't have too many connections to STEM prior to attending a university. I knew that I wanted to go into a STEM discipline when I pursued my undergraduate education but wasn't sure of the exact major. My experiences as a member of the student club focused on the medical sciences, along with my love for mathematics led me to initially pursue biomedical engineering during my first year as an undergraduate student.

I remember attending a pre-orientation program for students of color at my undergraduate institution and connecting with other biomedical engineering students of color. Although I started out eager about the major and was excited to have found a few new college friends, I stayed in the biomedical engineering major only briefly. My reason for switching the major was partly due to the tough science courses, but also due to the challenge of adjusting to the college environment because of the pressure to balance getting involved in student organizations and maintaining excellent grades. At times, it was all very overwhelming, which led to my transition from being enrolled as a biomedical engineering student to testing out other STEM disciplines such as computer science and mathematics. When I committed to being a mathematics major, I began working part-time as both a grading assistant and tutor for the mathematics center. I had a few friends in the major that I would study with as well as access to professors and other resources in the department, but didn't have the necessary mentoring support from professors or peers in the discipline. The rigorous coursework, need for mentorship, and lack of desire to further engage in mathematics led to a change in academic major.

Throughout the changing of majors from one STEM discipline to the next, I noticed a pattern. I noticed that I would often feel distant when it came to studying with peers or interacting with faculty (especially in computer science and engineering) and would find preparing for class or a test challenging at times. Research shows that less interaction with peers and faculty, issues with isolation and school/classroom climate play a major role in the reason of why students of color do not stay in STEM (Anderson and Kim 2006; Ancar 2008; Hurtado et al. 2011). Consistent with the research literature, I experienced a cold environment while in certain STEM disciplines and would see only a few women of color in my classes. The school/classroom climate and fewer interactions with others such as peers and faculty in those STEM disciplines created a disconnect from learning; however, I persisted and still graduated in a STEM discipline.

Immediately following my undergraduate career, I began working in the field of education. In addition to STEM, I had a strong passion for education and would often work with middle and high school students in various educational roles such as academic tutor and mentor/volunteer with educational organizations during my undergraduate years. I also wanted to help address some of the challenges youth, particularly youth of color and potential first-generation college students, are facing such as high dropout rates, low academic performance while in high school, and challenges navigating higher education institutions. After my experiences navigating a higher education institution, I wanted to make sure that other first-generation college students had the right resources and opportunities that they needed to better prepare them for college. Therefore, I worked in educational nonprofit organizations and pursued graduate education.

One role, in particular, allowed me to assist students with college and career opportunities by providing them with mentors from their own community. This particular experience taught me a lot about how mentoring worked from both the perspective of the mentee and mentor; and what resources should be received by mentoring pairs while in a mentoring relationship. Being in this role, I knew that I had found the right career path and was able to mentor students and aid in areas such as formal programming for college preparation and access to internships related to math, science, and medical professions. This role also led to a new mentor in my life who had received her doctorate and worked in education for over thirty years. This person served as a career mentor and pushed me to become a better leader and would often provide opportunities for me to enhance leadership skills such as managing others and public speaking. I learned from this mentor that being passionate about what you are doing is necessary to lead others and that delegating responsibilities and utilizing all team members' skills are important for carrying out the mission of the organization. I also admired this mentor's charismatic leadership presence, and it provided the example I needed as I developed my leadership skills. Her mentorship guided me in my pursuit of my doctorate.

Through my doctoral education, I was given opportunities to work in research assistantships with professors in my department and serve in leadership roles such as a mentor for first-year doctoral students for my department's graduate student organization. My research assistantships allowed me to not only enhance my research skills but interact with professors and administrators in my department as well as the college. Additionally, I was re-introduced to STEM through a research opportunity with a professor and began to study the theories and scientific reasoning as to why persons of color including women face several challenges in the STEM environment. While conducting doctoral research, I am able to talk with students in STEM, particularly students of color in engineering, and understand students' experiences to help future women and students of color who pursue STEM. Additionally, I serve as a member on a STEM committee for an organization geared toward women of color in academia and receive many opportunities to collaborate and get mentored by women of color scholars while in the academy. Although mentoring was not readily available during my undergraduate experience, mentorship has been found through my graduate education and allowed me to mentor and be a resource to other students and peers. I've learned that seeking the right resources and being resourceful is important for being an effective mentor and for being mentored.

Woman of Color (Two)

The climate for women pursuing engineering degrees was ripe when I graduated high school, and with all the money floating around for high achievers, companies were eager to offer scholarships to females, even more so, African American females. Many PWIs had just started their

dual degree programs with some of the HBCUs, and women were entering these programs in hopes of obtaining degrees in engineering. I did
not know what an engineer was or did at that time; however, I followed
the suggestion of my high school counselor who thought that with my
math skills I could easily become an engineer and earn a lucrative salary.
Coming from a family of nine children, the idea of earning a salary that
exceeded what the adults in my family had earned indicated success to
me. After researching what engineers do, the thought of possibly design-
ing cars, engines, computers, appliances, airliners, or jets seemed unique-
ly different and interesting. When I told the males in my life of my desire
to be an engineer, many of them laughed and quickly dismissed my
boasting as just another one of my ploys to compete with the boys. They
doubted my ability to achieve simply because I was a female. I just assumed that they were sick of the girls in the neighborhood constantly
challenging and oftentimes beating them in every sport imaginable from
kickball to baseball, at least until we all started reaching an age of maturity. My inner drive to be all that I could be, regardless of race or gender,
made me the right person to take on such a task and I did. While I didn't
have many issues concerning race while in school at that time, I had seen
the hardships of race displayed from moving into an all-white neighborhood as a child. The white families started slowly moving out of the
neighborhood and would not allow their kids to play with most of us
(kids of color). I had, however, dealt with issues internal to my own race
where the lighter skinned achievers/students of color were often times
chosen to be the top student or class representative above the darker
skinned achievers/students of color, even though sometimes the darker
skinned students were clearly the top student.

I was totally oblivious to all the sacrifice and hard work that it would
take to achieve the goal of becoming an engineer. I had always been a
high achiever; however, the luxury of never having to really work hard
for anything in the educational arena quickly became a thing of the past
as soon as I began the college experience. Though it wasn't necessarily
difficult, it was time consuming and required me to focus more and use
more critical thinking and time management skills to excel. Looking back
at my college experiences, I realized my immaturity and that I failed to
utilize all of the resources available to me while embarking on such a
journey. I simply did not know what to expect or how to move around in
this new environment. I vaguely knew at the onset that this would be a
male-dominated field, but I assumed it would be dominated with more
males in my classes than females and that wasn't always the case. There
appeared to be an almost equal number of males and females in the
classroom. Still, that wasn't a problem for me. I had brothers, as well as
male classmates and friends who I matriculated with previously, and I
always managed to rise to the top and still master the subject matter. The

males in the class were not the issue. The issue was the faculty and their perception of females in STEM.

As I reflect back, I'm reminded of an incident with a male professor that hit me at my inner core. Not only did he have an issue with my femaleness, but he also had an issue with my skin complexion and the fact that I was the top scorer in his classroom. For him, and he stated it as such, I just didn't look or dress the part of someone who should be setting the bar for the grades on his chemistry exam. My female friends and classmates, who heard the comments, defended my honor, but I did not. His comments left me confused, tormented and lost. I did not quite understand the depth of the comments he made so I internalized them and acted as if his comments did not matter. I knew it was an insult, but I couldn't understand it coming from him for he was black like me. We were at a HBCU and we were on the same team, so I thought. The only other option available to me at that time was for me to verbally retaliate, but I was smart enough to know that this wasn't the environment to do so and didn't even know what to say about something that even I didn't understand.

As I look back on the incident, a mentor, maybe even a female just like me, could have made all the difference in the world in understanding how I felt and at the same time could have redirected my energy for more positive productive results. Instead, I became quiet in class, participated less and stopped applying myself in this professor's class. Why should I stay engaged? I felt defeated. If those who are trained to teach me didn't think I was worthy of the type of education I was pursuing, then who? I had always achieved, received the support from those around me, but this was new and different to me. Not only was the comment directed toward me being a female, but I was also "too ethnic" for his preference of a student. He had a problem with my shade of blackness, my hair, me. He was color struck. I did not fully understand that my journey in STEM was more than just a new journey for me; it was new for them too. The instructors I encountered in high school demanded and applauded effort, these here in college, not so much. It was clear that I was a female in a male's world, and how dare I outshine them. And, if I was to be included, I needed to look more mainstream including having a lighter shade and softer presence. Carini, Kuh, and Klein (2006) suggest that students of color's interactions with faculty that are of positive quality relationships are highly linked with students' academic performance. Cole (2008) reveals that negative feedback and student's distance from faculty led to lower grades or GPA and indicates challenges with self-efficacy and confidence.

I soon left that institution, and thought a college close to home where the love and support of my parents near would be more suitable. The home environment was one of familiarity, and even if issues occurred here, I could deal with it because it was home. Throughout my life I have always had a strong support network in my family. My parents, grand-parents, aunts, and uncles all demanded our absolute best. Our name in the community was equated to high standards of excellence, extreme intelligence, and to achieve less required great effort. I never really looked at my family as mentors. In my mind, that was just what families did. They supported one another. It wasn't until my early years in college that I discovered that not all students had the support of parents, friends, teachers, community leaders, and neighbors. I understood then that I was fortunate because I had come from a family of intellectuals and high achievers who supported me. The path for higher education had already been paved for me and there was no reason for me to struggle.

I thought being close to home was supposed to make my educational experience in STEM better since the newly entered institution, a PWI, came highly recommended. So, I expected a more positive and fruitful experience. Not only did I not have support from the professors, but also there were very few black students in the major. I was studying petrole-um engineering and very few of the students in my field were black or female like me, and to top it off, none were eager to include me in their study groups or share advice they had received from past students in this discipline. At the PWI, I worked and experienced in solitude while at least at the HBCU, I had my classmates, who looked and related to me and would study with me. At this PWI, I had no one and realized that I had transferred into an even worse situation. At the first college, I at least had the support of my peers and was leading academically in the class-room even though struggling to be socially accepted by others including a black male professor. I wasn't struggling with the lessons or the learn-ing process but with coping with all other social issues and politics sur-rounding degree attainment. I left the first institution simply because I didn't feel like I was getting any guidance. In reality it was a better situation than the second institution. I soon left the second institution, the PWI, because it was not a good academic fit either. I was starting to doubt my ability to persist, but I was passionate about my education and was determined to find my way.

It didn't take long to find another route in my journey of obtaining an engineering degree. One of my classmates at the first institution knew the challenges I was having and suggested yet another transfer where she had found refuge. And for me, I simply had nothing to lose. I was already lost and was willing to try something new to get my educational goals back on track, so I found my way to another HBCU. But, this time there were more females in my classes. The professors of which were mostly male, didn't seem to care if you were female or not, and the campus was appealing to me. This change could have been the result of an increase in my maturity based on my prior two educational experiences, but as I look back and reflect, there simply were no mentors in sight to help me navigate through this process. The professors merely taught the courses and some would help with other areas if they were asked, but for the most part, we were on our own. Because of the sudden influx of women, especially women of color in STEM, I don't believe that professors fully understood their role in retaining and aiding in the academic and personal success of the women of color. How do you provide mentorship to students if you don't recognize their needs? When I reflect back on my many experiences, and the experiences I've since had, I clearly see the value a mentor would have had in helping to shape the careers for me and my former classmates. I lost valuable time finding my own way and encountered many detours, roadblocks, and brick walls. Navigating as a black female in an environment that was traditionally for white males was clearly a challenge since it was undergoing construction (and still is undergoing construction to include more racially and ethnically diverse students).

MY SISTER'S KEEPER: THE MENTOR'S EXPERIENCE

Mentoring can take form in various ways such as peer mentoring, hierarchical mentoring, apprentice mentoring, and co-mentoring (Amelink 2009; Buell 2004; McGuire and Reger 2003; Touchton 2003); which can shift the power position for the mentor. Mentors can share the responsibility of power and knowledge with protégés or take on the role as the more knowledgeable and skilled person who the protégés look to for advice and hands-on guidance. This part of the narrative explains the mentor's decision to be a resource and guide for others who desired to be an engineer, especially young women of color. The narrative also explores the differences of mentoring in various settings such as higher education/academia, the community of the mentor, and a STEM industry.

It Takes a Village: The Decision to Mentor Others

Becoming a mentor was not an intentional decision for me because I never realized that other women were struggling to excel in this field. Those who matriculated in college with me and had put in the time and hard work succeeded in their studies and obtained meaningful jobs. The work environment was a new experience for me, and I assumed that the challenges I was having were typical of any work environment. It wasn't until later in my career that I realized "we" (women of color) were still missing from the field. I chalked up all of my experiences in the STEM workplace as simply being a difficult place to navigate indifferent to race or gender. The educational curriculum and work environment, I assumed were just tough spaces because I saw many people struggle (for example, male, female, all races). I never really noticed "our" presence or absence in the workforce until I had been there for a while and saw that the numbers of women of color weren't getting any better. I guess I expected there to be few women of color in the workforce, but I also expected gradual change. I noticed that there were very few blacks and very few women, and in many encountered spaces I was the only one. I had always been a high achiever, and simply thought that becoming an engineer was only afforded to those who could excel. I saw students struggle with math and sciences in high school and in college and believed that some people simply didn't appear to have what it took, but I did because I had survived. It became clear to me that the reality of having always excelled limited my ability to see the STEM work environment for what it really was until I started struggling for my very own survival in the workplace. At that moment, I looked around and saw that not only was I struggling with the environment but I had no one to talk to or listen to understand the issues I was facing . . . there was no one.

Talking to my parents and grandmother always proved fruitful, as they kept me grounded in knowing that my negative feelings, lack of excelling in the environment, limited promotions, and being isolated from important meetings and high invisible projects had nothing to do with me. They kept me believing in me, but it didn't correct the loneliness, frustrations, and the feeling that I didn't belong. Research shows that these feelings are often common of women of color like me in STEM disciplines (Amelink 2009; Herzig 2004; VanLeuvan 2004). My parents didn't understand, because for most women in this field, black women for sure, the STEM field was unchartered territory and I was breaking new ground. My parents, grandparents, aunts, uncles, cousins, and friends had not been in this place. Some had finished college, some were teachers and one a professor, but no female in my family before me had enrolled and worked in a STEM profession. They couldn't possibly know how to help me and suddenly I felt more alone.

I rationalized my first job experience to being a Southern girl out of place in the Midwest, so I found another position "Down South," where the Southern hospitality was bound to show itself in the making of my career. Though the environment was better, I quickly realized that it wasn't the geographic location and that the environment wasn't going to improve to an appropriate level of professionalism unless I demanded equity and asserted myself in spite all the roadblocks. Even still, there was no real mentoring being done, not for me. I had to blindly move in the direction of my intuition, doing what felt right to maintain in the job I was hired to do even though I had no clear path of direction.

It wasn't until I ran into individuals in the community, at church, in the ballpark, in my hometown, and at my class reunions that I was excitingly and surprisingly seen as a black female engineer. These individuals wanted me to talk to their nieces, daughters, and cousins that were going into the field. It was at that moment that I saw the value of being a mentor and how it would have made a difference in my very own navigation as a previous STEM student and now STEM professional. It wasn't until those phone calls, questions, conversations, concerns, and spoken fears from others that I realized that "it takes a village" to help us navigate the STEM terrain, and I was in a position to make a difference. Many of the young girls I encountered and their parents asked for my input before they entered a STEM field, and many of them continue to ask for advice/direction during their matriculation in STEM. Some I believe will engage my expertise until that day when I am no longer able to give it. To think, where was my village then and what would my successes look like if I had that resource available to me? My own shortcomings and lack of support was reason enough for me to mentor and guide others who came behind me so that they can achieve their dreams and avoid leaking out of the STEM pipeline like I almost did.

Mentoring Women in STEM

Industry

Mentoring in the workplace provided me with the unique opportunity to give back. I had the opportunity to select my mentees each summer for approximately three months while serving in a minority-mentoring program at work. I always chose a black female or inner-city female who came from a large family because I knew the challenges from that type of family structure. The goal for me was to try to choose someone just like me to allow myself the opportunity to be the best mentor possible to someone who I felt could relate on many levels. Additionally, I also knew that mentors like me were rare and wanted to seize every opportunity I could to make a difference in someone else's life. I wanted to give them accurate accounts of what it takes to navigate the STEM profession and to prepare them for the journey ahead. I wanted them to understand that no matter how intelligent, creative, well-spoken, and confident they were, they would always be in a position of proving themselves to others in the field. Furthermore, I chose the opportunity to mentor to expose them to all aspects of the environment to avoid the culture shock that I had experienced. The best part of mentoring is helping others to understand that they are the owners and navigators of their careers and that they shouldn't relinquish that power to anyone. The other important advice to be shared with protégés on being successful is that being at the right place at the right time in a conducive and supportive environment conducive is vital for the success of women of color. I currently still mentor my protégés, and what I've learned is that mentors will support, promote, and advocate for you consistently.

Academia

Mentoring in academia proved to be productive and fruitful. The students I mentored in industry all came from STEM programs at HBCUs, and I began to notice a pattern and consistency in the commonalities of attitudes and behaviors that needed the attention of a mentor. I enrolled in a program that allowed me to leave the industry and serve as a visiting professor at the university level for a few years. There I taught courses, advised students, supported design projects and student organizations, wrote grants, and managed summer pre-college programs among a plethora of other duties. In essence, I was involved at every level of the students' educational experience in the places where I could provide the most impact. In that experience, I learned that all students need mentoring. Some recognize it while others don't. Those who recognized it and truly understood the value I was able to bring in terms of mentoring, engaged me every opportunity possible. Those who didn't recognize it, navigated on their own. Some, especially those I saw struggling, I reached out to and offered to help them along the way. Some received mentoring well while others rejected it and continued to strive or struggle, depending on where they were in the educational process. I also observed that very few professors mentored the students. Those who were mentors recognized the need for mentoring and availed themselves. Others mentored because they understood it to be necessary for the campus climate and not because they were passionate about it, which taught me that mentoring comes from a genuine desire to see students succeed and to know that you've done your best to promote their success. Mentoring is less about self and more about building and nurturing others, advancing society, enhancing professional growth, and giving back to a greater good.

Community

Mentoring in the broader community also exists outside of the STEM environment. Community programs, pre-college programs, and church affiliated programs all provide avenues for mentoring students in STEM. During my stint in teaching, I was fortunate enough to direct and manage a pre-college STEM program for students in grades three to eleven for a summer and entire school year (approximately every other Saturday during the school year). The most enlightening part of this experience was to see the gleam and glare in the eyes of the students who were amazed that I looked like them, talked their language, and had achieved what I have thus far in life. Being able to draw that kind of connection on a personal level meant a lot to them, and it revealed itself in the questions they asked about my experiences as well as the questions they asked during the sessions. This time was also the perfect opportunity for me to use college-age students who I had mentored, to serve as mentors for these younger students. I was not only mentoring but also teaching others how to mentor and give back as well as understand the importance of mentoring. At the end of the program, the parents thanked me for being a beacon in their child's eyes. Through this experience, I found that there are a lot of brilliant and critical thinking future scientists and engineers of color like me that exist, who just need a lifeline, guide, or someone who has achieved similar feats to reach back and support them along the way.

I also served as a mentor in a "blind mentoring" project in a STEM field of high-achieving high school students through a community college. This project was instrumental in allowing an exchange of trust and expertise without any knowledge of the students' or mentors' race, ethnicity, gender, name, class, or experience. The mentee simply trusted the mentor's input in support of the requirements needed to complete the project and implemented it without reservation. The mentor willfully supported the student, blind to who s/he was, which made the relationship pure and free of biases. In the end, mentors and mentees were revealed. My mentee turned out to be a woman of color who thrived and won the overall competition. This experience began to make me think about many of the aspects we encounter while mentoring and working in the STEM environment.

INSIGHTS FOR HIGHER EDUCATION INSTITUTIONS FROM BOTH PERSPECTIVES

The stories of these two black women who navigated the STEM environment highlight some of the traditional issues that the literature suggests exist as to why women of color face difficulties in STEM disciplines and even choose not to stay in them. Those issues include lack of academic preparation in STEM prior to enrolling into college; disengagement while in the discipline; feelings of isolation due to a hostile climate, negative relationships with faculty, and lack of advising and support (Amelink 2009; Foor, Walden, and Trytten 2007; Herzig 2004; VanLeuvan 2004). Specifically, both the mentee and mentor experienced social isolation from peers and became disengaged due to the lack of mentoring and instructional/coaching support from professors and other administrators/ professionals who had the ability to mentor someone in a STEM major.

Additionally, their stories also highlight that the roles of race and gender must be more critically considered in understanding the impact it has in the STEM educational environment and workplace. The mentor's story of navigating through three higher education institutions and being judged based on the color of her skin and femininity also illustrate stereotype threat, in which the threat of being a woman and a person of color can be viewed through the lens of a negative stereotype or the fear of doing something that would confirm that stereotype suppresses academic performance for the student associated with the group being stereotyped (Bell, Spencer, Iserman, and Logel 2003; McGee and Martin 2011). This atmosphere created by stereotype threat was experienced in the mentor's story in the particular instance of interacting with a male professor in which he had an issue with her being a black woman and excelling in his classroom because she did not "look the part or dress the part for someone who should be setting the curve in Chemistry." Furthermore, race played a role in the mentor's story of attending a PWI and being excluded from the social constructs surrounding the educational process. It was unclear whether the intersection of race and gender issues was present, but research shows that black women are victims of "the double bind" (Ong, Wright, Espinosa and Orfield 2011).

Both stories can inform mentoring practices for women of color who will pursue a STEM education and/or career. Mentoring is not the only solution to addressing the issues of representation of women of color in STEM, since women report they receive less mentoring than men at all levels of postsecondary education and in post-doctoral experiences (Nolan, Buckner, Marzabadi, and Kuck 2008). Therefore, we offer the following suggestions in maximizing the mentoring experiences of women of color who are planning to seek or are currently enrolled in STEM educational institutions and careers.

Suggestions for the Protégés and Mentors

a. First, mentees or protégés should not be afraid to seek support from individuals who have seniority in the STEM educational and professional environment. There are individuals who are more than willing to assist and were once in need of support as well. Besides, mentoring can improve protégés self-confidence and communication.

b. Second, mentees and mentors should understand the mentoring relationship and craft that relationship to complement the goals and expectations of the mentee with the skills and abilities of the mentor. Mentoring relationships take on many forms. They work best when the relationship is mutually beneficial to both parties. Protégés usually expect this relationship to follow a more hierarchical structure, but oftentimes the form may change during the actual process (Amelink 2009).

c. Third, mentors do not know everything. This is where having several mentors with varying strengths can be of benefit to the mentee. The goal is to build a team of people (who may not know one another), to aid in helping with navigating through the STEM terrain. Mentors should encourage the protégé to network and seek out mentors for all areas of their life. This can be through involve-

ment in formal mentoring programs as they are beneficial to protégés as well. Having more sources of support provides a well-
rounded mentoring relationship and does not put more bearing or
weight on one specific mentor.

d. Fourth, mentees must assert themselves by using the information
provided by the mentors to make the best decision. Mentees must
own their decisions, regardless of the input provided by mentors,
as the context and the methods of the organization through which
they are maneuvering will vary. Mentors are only providing their
protégés with information based on their experiences to help them
understand some of the pitfalls and unwritten rules that the mentees may not be aware of while building their own experiences.
Thus, mentees must understand that they are the person ultimately
responsible for their educational and career goals.

e. Fifth, some mentoring relationships happen naturally; others need
cultivating. There is nothing wrong with that. If a mentoring relationship is no longer serving either party, it is okay to seek mentorship elsewhere. As with anything else, cordiality and respect during this transition has its advantages.

f. Sixth, it is wise to have at least one mentor that can relate to the
personal (for example, gender-wise, social, cultural, racial, geographical) perspective of the mentee. A mentor who understands
the background, goals, and desires of a mentee can be beneficial in
mentoring the total person, not just the student, or the STEM employee, but the person and the wealth of culture and value that
they may possess (Yosso 2005). Specifically, for women in STEM,
research shows that once women in STEM careers enter the field,
they continue to face barriers including low publication rates and
lack of work-life policies that allow women to balance multiple
roles associated with career and family (Bystydzuenski 2004; Koehler 2008; Sullivan 2007). Therefore, a female mentor in the profession will be vital for being able to show how to balance career and
home factors.

g. Lastly, mentors should always provide input that is in the best
interest of the mentee first. Providing them with options and allowing them to decide their path will serve to build a better relationship. When opportunities arise that fit well with the goals of
the protégé, encourage their participation explaining both the benefits and pitfalls. Remember that protégés look at mentors as a
model of excellence and that honesty and trust are important tools
in building the rapport of the mentoring relationship.

When taking all these things into consideration, the mentoring experience can help to lessen those feeling of isolation, low confidence, disillusionment that black women in STEM often feel in the STEM environment

(Amelink 2009; Foor, Walden, and Trytten 2007; Herzig 2004; VanLeuvan 2004). In fact, mentoring women in engineering careers can increase their confidence, improve their communication skills, and provide a clearer picture of educational and performance expectations in both the academic and workplace environment (Brainard and Ailes-Sengers 1994; Brainard and Carlin 1998; Chesler, Boyle Single, and Mikic 2003; Frestedt 1995). Other literature also suggests that early exposure to mentoring in secondary education; specifically pairing female students with women scientists increase the female students' chances of pursuing a STEM career (McLaughlin 2005). These positive outcomes and the justification of a stronger presence for women in STEM supports the need for increased mentoring avenues for women, particularly women of color who choose to matriculate or work in a STEM field. The stories in this chapter are being shared to show the complexities that exist for women of color navigating STEM disciplines at higher education institutions and working in the STEM field. These stories provide accounts of both positive and negative experiences in STEM and aid in understanding how providing and receiving mentoring support to or from others can shape or hinder the process.

Implications for Mentoring Women of Color in STEM

The types of mentoring, for both formal and informal processes, have not changed much from the 1980s to 2000s nor has there been much of a shift in the increase of mentoring for women, particularly women of color in STEM. Therefore, one suggestion for future research is to conduct a more in-depth examination of the historical timeline of both formal and informal processes of mentoring for women of color in STEM both in higher education and the STEM profession over the past thirty years. This will allow practitioners and researchers to understand how mentoring needs to evolve to better suit the needs of women who are receiving education and/or working in a male-dominated field such as STEM.

Additionally, more research is needed on the role that both gender and race play in STEM mentoring relationships; particularly, further examination of whether cross-gender mentoring, same gender, or same race/ethnicity mentoring relationships promote more or less socialization, confidence, and productivity in STEM fields (Amelink 2009). Furthermore, more research studies should be conducted to determine what factors are vital to effective mentoring relationships for women of color in STEM for the purposes of providing a guide that can be used globally for formal mentoring in STEM educational programs and STEM careers.

REFERENCES

Allen, T. D. 2003. "Mentoring Others: A Dispositional and Motivational Approach." *Journal of Vocational Behavior* 62: 134–154.

Allen, T. D., M. L. Poteet, and S. M. Burroughs. 1997. "The Mentor's Perspective: A Qualitative Inquiry and Agenda for Future Research." *Journal of Vocational Behavior* 51: 70–89.

Amelink, C. 2009. "Overview: Mentoring and Women in Engineering." *SWE-AWE-CASEE.* Retrieved from http://www.engr.psu.edu/awe/misc/ARPs/ARP_Mentoring_overview120408.pdf.

Ancar, L. N. 2008. "Social and Academic Factors of Success and Retention for Students of Color at a Predominantly White Institution in Agricultural and Engineering Based Disciplines." ProQuest Dissertations and Theses. (230661399).

Anderson, M. E., and A. L. Shannon. 1988. "Toward a Conceptualization of Mentoring." *Journal of Teacher Education* 39: 38–42.

Anderson, E., and D. Kim. 2006. "Increasing the Success of Minority Students in Science and Technology." Washington, DC: American Council on Education.

Aryee, S., Y. W. Chay, and J. Chew. 1996. "The Motivation to Mentor among Managerial Employees." *Group and Organization Management* 21: 261–277.

Bell, A. E., S. J. Spencer, E. Iserman, and C. R. Logel. 2003. "Stereotype Threat and Women's Performance in Engineering." *Journal of Engineering Education* 92(4): 307–312.

Blake-Beard, S., M. L. Bayne, and F. J. Crosby. 2011. "Matching by Race and Gender in Mentoring Relationships: Keeping our Eyes on the Prize." *Journal of Social Issues* 67(3): 622–643.

Brainard, S. G., and L. Ailes-Sengers. 1994. "Mentoring Female Engineering Students: A Model Program at the University of Washington." *Journal of Women and Minorities in Science and Engineering* 1(2): 123–135.

Brainard, S., and L. Carlin. 1998. "A Six-Year Longitudinal Study of Undergraduate Women in Engineering and Science." *Journal of Engineering Education* 87(4): 369–375.

Buell, C. 2004. "Models of Mentoring in Communication." *Communication Education* 53(1): 56–73.

Bystydzuenski, J. M. 2004. "(Re)gendering Science Fields: Transforming Academic Science and Engineering." *NWSA Journal* 16(1): viii–xii.

Carini, R., G. Kuh, and S. Klein. 2006. "Student Engagement and Student Learning: Testing the Linkages." *Research in Higher Education* 47(1): 1–32.

Chen, X. 2005. *First Generation Students in Postsecondary Education: A Look at their College Transcripts* (NCES 2005-171). U.S. Department of Education, National Center for Education Statistics. Washington, DC: U.S. Government Printing Office.

Chesler, N. C., P. Boyle Single, and B. Mikic. 2003. "On Belay: Peer Mentoring and Adventure Education for Women Faculty in Engineering." *Journal of Engineering Education* 92(3): 257–262.

Chesler, N. C, and M. A. Chesler. 2002. "Gender Informed Mentoring Strategies for Women Engineering Scholars: On Establishing a Caring Community." *Journal of Engineering Education* 91(1): 49–55.

Cobb, M., D. L. Fox, J. E. Many, M. W. Matthews, E. McGrail, G. T. Sachs, D. L. Taylor, F. H. Wallace, and Y. Wang. 2006. "Mentoring in Literacy Education: A Commentary from Graduate Students, Untenured Professors, and Tenured Professors." *Mentoring and Tutoring* 14(4): 371–387.

Cole, D. 2008. "Constructive Criticism: The Role of Student-Faculty Interactions on African American and Hispanic Students' Educational Gains." *Journal of College Student Development* 49(6): 587–605.

Crisp, G., and I. Cruz. 2009. "Mentoring College Students: A Critical Review of the Literature between 1990 and 2007." *Research in Higher Education* 50: 525–545.

DeWandre, N. 2002. "Women in Science: European Strategies for Promoting Women in Science." *Science* 295: 278–279.

De Welde, K., S. Laursen, and H. Thiry. 2007. "Women in Science, Technology, Engineering and Math (STEM)." *ADVANCE Library Collection*, Paper 567.

Douglas, C. A. 1997. *Formal Mentoring Programs in Organizations: An Annotated Bibliography*. Greensboro, NC: Center for Creative Leadership.

Fagenson, E. A. 1989. "The Mentor Advantage: Perceived Career/Job Experiences of Protégés versus Non-Protégés." *Journal of Organizational Behavior* 10(4): 309–320.

Foor, C. E., S. E. Walden, and D. A. Trytten. 2007. "'I Wish that I Belonged More in this Whole Engineering Group': Achieving Individual Diversity." *Journal of Engineering Education* 96(2): 103–116.

Frestedt, J. L. 1995. "Mentoring Women Graduate Students: Experience of the Coalition of Women Graduate Students at the University of Minnesota, 1993–1995." *Journal of Women and Minorities in Science and Engineering* 2(3): 151–170.

Gaskill, L. R. 1993. "A Conceptual Framework for the Development, Implementation, and Evaluation of Formal Mentoring Programs." *Journal of Career Development* 20: 147–160.

Gonzales, P., T. Williams, L. Jocelyn, S. Roey, D. Kastberg, and S. Brenwald. 2009. "Highlights from TIMSS 2007: Mathematics and Science Achievement of U.S. Fourth- and Eighth-Grade Students in an International Context." Washington, DC: National Center for Education Statistics.

Heckel, R. W. 2008. *A Global Study of Engineering Undergraduate and Doctoral Degrees Awarded in Ninety-One Countries*. Retrieved from http://www.engtrends.com/IEE/Global_Web.pdf.

Herzig, A. 2004. "Slaughtering this Beautiful Math: Graduate Women Choosing and Leaving Mathematics." *Gender and Education* 16(3): 379.

Higgins, M. C., and K. E. Kram. 2001. "Reconceptualizing Mentoring at Work: A Developmental Network Perspective." *Academy of Management Review* 26: 264–288.

Hill, C., C. Corbett, and A. St. Rose. 2010. *Why so Few? Women in Science, Technology, Engineering, and Mathematics*. Washington, DC: American Association of University Women.

Hughes, B. 2009. "How to Start a STEM Team." *Technology Teacher* 69(2): 27–29.

Hurtado, S., et al. 2011. "'We Do Science Here': Underrepresented Students' Interactions with Faculty in Different College Contexts." *Journal of Social Issues* 67(3): 553–579.

Ishitani, T. T. 2003. "A Longitudinal Approach to Assessing Attrition Behavior among First-Generation Students: Time-Varying Effects of Pre-College Characteristics." *Research in Higher Education* 44: 433–449.

Johnson, W. B. 2007. *On Being a Mentor: A Guide for Higher Education Faculty*. Mahwah, NJ: Lawrence Erlbaum Associates.

Kahveci, A., S. A. Southerland, and P. J. Gilmer. 2006. "Retaining Undergraduate Women in Science, Mathematics, and Engineering." *Journal of College Science Teaching* 36(November—December): 34.

Kim, Y. K., and L. J. Sax. 2009. "Student-Faculty Interaction in Research Universities: Differences by Student Gender, Race, Social Class, and First-Generation Status." *Research in Higher Education* 50: 437–459.

Koehler, E. 2008. "Women in STEM Fields Still Need Support." *Laser Focus World*, January.

Kram, K. E. 1983. "Phases of the Mentoring Relationship." *Academy of Management Journal* 26: 608–625.

Kram, K. E. 1985. *Mentoring At Work*. Glenview, IL: Scott Foresman.

Landivar, L. C. 2013. "Disparities in STEM Employment by Sex, Race, and Hispanic Origin." *American Community Survey Reports*, ACS-24. Washington, DC: U.S. Census Bureau.

Lankau, M., and T. A. Scandura. 2002. "An Investigation of Personal Learning in Mentoring Relationships: Content, Antecedents, and Consequences." *Academy of Management Journal* 45: 779–791.

Linn, M. 2007. "Women in Science: Can Evidence Inform the Debate?" *Science* 317: 199–200.

Machi, E., and F. Heritage. 2009. "Improving U.S. Competitiveness with K-12 STEM Education and Training. Heritage Special Report. SR-57. A Report on the STEM Education and National Security Conference, October 21–23, 2008." *Heritage Foundation*. Retrieved from ERIC database.

Malcolm, S. M., D. E. Chubin, and J. K. Jesse. 2004. *Standing our Ground: A Guidebook for STEM Educators in the Post-Michigan Era*. Washington, DC: AAAS Publication Services.

Martínez, J. A., K. J. Sher, J. L. Krull, and P. J. Wood. 2009. "Blue-Collar Scholars?: Mediators and Moderators of University Attrition in First-Generation College Students." *Journal of College Student Development* 50(1): 87–103.

McGee, E. O., and D. B. Martin. 2011. "'You Would Not Believe What I Have to Go through to Prove my Intellectual Value!' Stereotype Management among Academically Successful Black Mathematics and Engineering Students." *American Education Research Journal* 48: 347–1389.

McGuire, G. M., and J. Reger. 2003. "Feminist Co-Mentoring: A Model for Academic Professional Development." *National Women's Studies Association Journal* 15: 54–72.

McLaughlin, R. 2005. "Girls in Science." *Science Scope* 28(7): 14.

Mezias, J. M., and T. A. Scandura. 2005. "A Needs-Driven Approach to Expatriate Adjustment and Career Development: A Multiple Mentoring Perspective." *Journal of International Business Studies* 36(5): 519–38.

National Academy of Sciences, National Academy of Engineering, and Institute of Medicine. 1997. *Adviser, Teacher, Role Model, Friend, on Being a Mentor to Students in Science and Engineering*. Washington, DC: National Academy Press.

Noddings, N. 1991. "Stories in Dialogue: Caring and Interpersonal Reasoning." In C. Witherell and N. Noddings (eds.), *Stories Lives Tell: Narrative and Dialogue in Education*, 157–170. New York: Teachers College Press.

Nolan, S. A., J. P. Buckner, C. H. Marzabadi, and V. J. Kuck. 2008. "Training and Mentoring of Chemists: A Study of Gender Disparity." *Sex Roles* 58(3/4): 235–250.

Ong, M., C. Wright, L. L. Espinosa, and G. Orfield. 2011. "Inside the Double Bind: A Synthesis of Empirical Research on Undergraduated and Graduate Women of color in Science, Technology, Engineering and Mathematics." *Harvard Education Review* 81(2): 172–208.

Paglis, L. L., S. G. Green, and T. N. Bauer. 2006. "Does Adviser Mentoring Add Value? A Longitudinal Study of Mentoring and Doctoral Student Outcomes." *Research in Higher Education* 47(4): 451.

Ragins, B. R., and K. E. Kram. 2007. *The Handbook of Mentoring at Work: Theory, Research, and Practice*. Thousand Oaks, CA: Sage Publishing.

Rushton, S. P. 2004. "Using Narrative Inquiry to Understand a Student-Teacher's Practical Knowledge while Teaching in an Inner-City School." *The Urban Review* 36(1): 61–79.

Scandura, T. A., and M. A. Von Glinow. 1997. "Development of the International Manager: The Role of Mentoring." *Business and the Contemporary World* 9: 95–115.

Slaughter, J., and I. McPhail. 2007. "New Demands in Engineering, Science and Technology." *The Black Collegian*. Retrieved from http://www.Blackcollegian.com/index.php?option=com_content&view=article&id=255:john-brooks-slaughter&cat-id=37:industry-reports&Itemid=116.

Strayhorn, T. L., and M. C. Terrell. 2007. "Mentoring and Satisfaction with College for Black Students." *The Negro Educational Review* 58(1–2): 69–83.

Sullivan, B. 2007. "Closing the Engineering Gender Gap: Viewers Like You." *New England Journal of Higher Education*, 26–28.

Touchton, J. G. 2003. "Women's Ways of Mentoring." *NASPA NetResults*.

United States Census Bureau Report. 2012. *U.S. Census Bureau Projections Show a Slower Growing, Older, More Diverse Nation a Half Century from Now (Press Release)*. National

Population Projections: 2012 to 2060. Retrieved from http://www.census.gov/newsroom/releases/archives/population/cb12-243.html.

VanLeuvan, P. 2004. "Young Women's Science/Mathematics Career Goals from Seventh Grade to High School Graduation." *Journal of Educational Research* 97(5): 248–267.

Yosso, T. J. 2005. "Whose Culture Has Capital? A Critical Race Theory Discussion of Community Cultural Wealth." *Race Ethnicity and Education* 8(1): 69–91.

THREE

Navigating the Turbulent Boundaries of a PhD Program

A Supportive Peer-Mentoring Relationship

Jean Ostrom-Blonigen and Cindy Larson-Casselton

Formalized mentoring relationships are typically developed by an organization for the purpose of advancing the mentee's standing within an organization via this typically short-term, structured process (Inzer and Crawford 2005; Zachary 2009). Conversely, informal mentoring relationships are typically based in friendship, longer term, and initiated by either the mentor or the mentee for the purpose of benefitting the mentee in some manner (Inzer and Crawford 2005). Yet, both types of mentoring relationships tend to favor males over females (Cole 1981; Etzkowitz, Kemelgor, and Uzzi 2000; Moore and Sagaria 1991; O'Brien 2014).

Graduate study degree completion is problematic (Bowen and Rudenstein 1992; Mansson and Myers 2012) and mentoring is crucial for graduate student success (Mansson and Myers 2012). A recent EBSCO (academic search premier) database search for scholarly journals for the six-year period from 2008 to 2014 using the search terms "higher education" and "graduate student mentoring" yielded only 169 articles. This chapter describes our journey as two older-than-average doctoral students who inadvertently formed an informal mentoring relationship that ended in friendship once we obtained our degrees. We believe that our relationship, which provided us with the support necessary to complete our respective degrees, was worthy of study to determine whether it, or other relationships like it, can be used in informal and formal mentoring.

OUR PHD JOURNEYS

This is our story: two women's journeys in the pursuit of their PhD degrees. Although different, our stories, outlined in a chart (see table 3.1, end of chapter) as the stories of "Jean" and "Cindy," resonate along a parallel chord that may be applied to future mentoring research.

Jean

Jean was born in the Midwest of the United States in 1962 and is the oldest of three girls. Jean's father is Scandinavian and Native American (Chippewa). Jean's mother is German. In college, Jean majored in accounting and management information systems and is a certified public accountant (1983 bachelor's degree). Jean married in 1987 and had two children, who were born in 1991 and 1992. In 2002, at the age of thirty-nine, Jean made the decision to obtain a doctorate degree in communication. Eleven years later, Jean graduated with a doctor of philosophy degree in 2013. While pursuing her degree, Jean experienced many life-events common to a middle-aged married woman with children, such as the high school graduation of both of her children. In addition, during the pursuit of her PhD degree, Jean had a hysterectomy (which put her into immediate menopause), was diagnosed with sleep apnea, and changed jobs five times. Additionally, Jean's family battled cancer many times: her mom, who had cancer in 1999, was again diagnosed in 2001, 2003, and 2012; her dad was diagnosed in 2004; and her sister in 2004, 2006 (during which time Jean donated stem cells to her sister), and 2007. In 2006, Jean's son was a passenger in a car accident in which his friend was killed, and in 2009, that same son began his daily journey to beat drug addiction. In 2011, Jean welcomed a grandchild. In 2012, Jean's husband was diagnosed with cancer. In 2013, Jean and her husband separated and were subsequently divorced in 2014.

Cindy

Cindy was also born in the Midwest of the United States in 1957. Cindy is the middle child of three, with an older sister and a younger brother. Cindy's father is Norwegian. Cindy's mother is French and Norwegian. In college, Cindy majored in communication studies (1980 bachelor's degree); she also has a master's degree in communication studies (1982 master's degree). Cindy married in 1983 and has two children, who were born in 1991 and 1993. In 2001, at the age of forty-three, Cindy made the decision to obtain a doctorate degree in communication. Twelve years later, Cindy graduated with a doctor of philosophy degree in 2013. In addition to pursuing her degree as an older-than-average student, Cindy also went through menopause and had both children graduate from high school. Cindy's dad was diagnosed with prostate cancer (2005), kidney cancer (2008), and had heart valve replacement (2010). In 2007, Cindy lost her husband following a short battle with cancer.

REVIEW OF LITERATURE

Oftentimes, graduate students indicate that the most important role that mentors serve are functions of guidance and support (Cronan-Hillix, Gensheimer, Cronan-Hillix, and Davidson 1986). This chapter examines how social support, coupled with the theory of communication privacy management (CPM) was employed in our relationship as two older-than-average female students in pursuit of our PhD degrees. Social support is the perception and actuality that one is cared for (Ma, Quan, and Liu 2014). As described in their 2012 Annual Mentoring Institute conference paper (Larson-Casselton, Ostrom-Blonigen, Bornsen, and Erickson 2012), social support has been conventionally used in health communication and consists of four primary types of support: 1) emotional, a sharing of life experiences; 2) instrumental, tangible aid; 3) informational, advice/ suggestions; and 4) appraisal, information for self-appraisal (House 1981)—whereas CPM, although native to the interpersonal communication-studies discipline, has not yet been readily used in mentoring research. CPM (Petronio 2000, 2002), most frequently linked to family studies, has been used in "predicting and explaining boundaries and the regulation of revealing and concealing private information in dyadic, family, group, or organizational systems" (Baxter and Braithwaite 2008, 282). CPM consists of six principles: 1) ownership, 2) control, 3) rules, 4) coownership, 5) negotiated rules, and 6) boundary turbulence. Following, we further discuss these two concepts.

Social Support

Theoretically, mentoring appears to be very complementary to social support. However, despite the apparent resemblance of the two concepts, and despite previous calls for integration (McManus and Russell 1997), Giblin and Lakey (2010) state "the two literatures have developed mostly in isolation" (772). There are many definitions of social support found in the literature. Although different terminology is used in many of them, the definitions possess common characteristics. All of the definitions imply some type of positive interaction or helpful behavior provided to a person in need of support (Rook and Dooley 1985). A communication theory approach to social support, this concept is traditionally considered to be the exchange of verbal and nonverbal messages conveying emotion, information, or referral, to help reduce someone's uncertainty or stress, and "whether directly or indirectly, communicate to an individual that she or he is valued and cared for by others" (Barnes and Duck 1994, 176).

The primary components of social support focus on the actions that people undertake that function to help others manage problems and stresses. House (1981) defined social support as "an interpersonal transaction involving one or more of the following: (1) emotional concern (liking, love, empathy), (2) instrumental aid (goods and services), (3) informational (about the environment), or (4) appraisal (information relevant to self-evaluation" (39). One of the key elements of social support focuses on the steps necessary to help others manage their problems and stress (Larson-Casselton, Ostrom-Blonigen, Bornsen, and Ericksen 2012, 2013). As noted from our previous studies mentoring fulfills the emotional, instrumental, informational, and appraisal components in direct, indirect and verbal and nonverbal capacities (Larson-Casselton, Ostrom-Blonigen, Bornsen, and Ericksen 2012, 2013). We have also come to believe that informal mentoring is more readily adaptive when emotional components are involved.

Social Support in Interpersonal and Organizational Communication

Social support has been used across a wide array of disciplines (Burnett and Buerkle 2004; Geist-Martin, Ray, and Sharf 2003; Hubbell and Hubbell 2002) including psychology, medicine, and sociology. Support groups help individuals to see that they are not alone and that others share their frustrations and feelings. Supportive interactions can lessen distress and enhance recovery from traumatic experience and may include messages that offer expressions or behaviors of caring and concern (Larson-Casselton 2007). Social support has also been used in the workplace to indicate job satisfaction (Harris, Winskowski, and Engdahl 2007) and leader effectiveness (McDonald and Westphal 2011).

Harris, Winskowski, and Engdahl (2007) state "The source of support may be a supervisor, mentor, or colleague and the content of the support may include information, appraisal, assistance with tasks, or emotional support" (150). In face-to-face support, the exchange usually begins by establishing relationships based on other commonalties (Larson-Casselton 2007). Additionally, there is little question that face-to-face social support in healthcare has both a direct and indirect effect on the physical and mental health of caregivers (Geist-Martin, Ray, and Sharf 2003). "[Informal] mentoring fulfills the emotional, instrumental, informational, and appraisal component[s of social support] in ways that are both direct and indirect and in ways that are both verbal and non-verbal" (Larson-Casselton, Ostrom-Blonigen, Bornsen, and Ericksen 2012, 2).

THE THEORY OF COMMUNICATION PRIVACY
MANAGEMENT (CPM)

Communication privacy management (CPM) theory, developed by Petronio (1991), is defined as a "method of understanding the ways people manage the dialectical tensions of disclosing and protecting privacy" (Petronio and Jones 2007, 202). Originally dubbed communication boundary management (Petronio 2000, 2002), CPM's foundation is in social psychology (Baxter and Braithwaite 2008), particularly Altman's privacy regulation work (Allman 1998; Margulis 2003; Morr Serewicz and Petronio 2007; Petronio 2004). A rules-based privacy management system, CPM, unlike self-disclosure, is comprised of levels of metaphoric boundary structures of varied permeability (Afifi 2003; Caughlin and Petronio 2004; Petronio 1991, 2000, 2002, 2004, 2009; Petronio and Durham 2008).

CPM has six principles of private information management that represent the organizing boundary structures that interlink individuals: 1) ownership, 2) control, 3) rules, 4) co-ownership, 5) negotiated rules, and 6) turbulences or regulation of privacy breakdowns (Petronio 2002, 2010). Communication boundary structures have different levels (Petronio 2000) that accommodate alliances (Golish and Caughlin 2002) or hierarchies; such as a mentoring alliance. Inevitably, because there is an inherent risk in sharing private information, individuals seek to manage that risk by controlling what information they share with others (Afifi 2003; Allman 1998; Duggan and Petronio 2009; Morr Serewicz and Petronio 2007). The dialectical tension between revealing and concealing is very real (Afifi 2003; Petronio 2000, 2002). Tension (Ostrom-Blonigen 2013) or relief (Larson-Casselton 2013) may occur between being public with private information or remaining private.

The first principle, ownership, acknowledges both the sharing of private information and the boundaries that surround that information (Petronio 2002). Communication boundaries are either permeable, allowing information to move internally and externally, or impermeable, intentionally impeding information flow (Morr Serewicz and Petronio 2007; Petronio 2010). Thus, ownership describes how, and perhaps why, people both conceal and reveal their private information to others.

The second principle, control, is revealed in the constructing of boundary signals (Afifi 2003; Duggan and Petronio 2009; Petronio 2007). Communication privacy boundaries afford the information owner a sense of control (Allman 1998; Duggan and Petronio 2009) and are often developed to be compatible with the owner's existing relationship levels (Afifi 2003). Boundary controls can be permeable, allowing information sharing, or rigid, restricting information sharing (Caughlin and Afifi 2004; Golish and Caughlin 2002). Private information does not become owned by another until the one who owns the information reveals it to another person or persons.

The third principle, rules, typically mirror an individual's values. Privacy rules, stated or unstated, govern the exchange of information (Afifi 2003; Golish and Caughlin 2002; Helft and Petronio 2007; Petronio 2000, 2002) in family (Afifi 2003), marital relationships (Petronio 1991), and organizational settings (Ostrom-Blonigen 2013). Complex relationships produce complex rule systems (Golish and Caughlin 2002; Helft and Petronio 2007; Morr Serewicz and Petronio 2007; Petronio 2010). In an effort to ease dyadic tensions, rules are established in many communication relationships to enforce boundaries surrounding/guarding private information. As rules are developed, communication boundaries usually become less permeable. Rules also depict how open or closed the privacy boundary will be to protect the privacy of the information (Larson-Casselton 2013) and are usually developed based upon the criteria of: (a) culture, (b) gender, (c) motivation, (d) context, and (e) risk-benefit ratio (Petronio 2000, 2002, 2004; Petronio and Durham 2008).

The fourth principle of CPM is shared boundaries or co-ownership (Petronio 2000, 2002, 2004; Petronio and Caughlin 2006; Petronio and Durham 2008). Co-ownership of information indicates that the confidant is in a position to decide whether to reveal the information to someone else or to keep the information private. Petronio and Reierson (2009) contend that this principle forms the basis for a fundamental understanding of how privacy management and confidentiality are linked together. Information disclosures can place the recipient in a position of power (Petronio 2009, 2010), especially if the disclosure catalyst is emotion (Petronio 2010). Similarly, disclosure can make the discloser vulnerable (Serewicz and Petronio 2007).

The fifth principle of CPM, negotiated rules, governs the collective communication boundaries between individuals and give those individuals within the collectively held boundary the ability or the right to share information with those outside the boundary (Petronio and Caughlin 2006). Individuals and groups use rules to manage their communication decisions (Caughlin and Afifi 2004; Petronio 2000, 2002). At times, information owners are unwilling (Morr Serewicz and Petronio 2007) to share their information, and at other times, co-owners have knowledge but are prohibited from sharing what they know (Golish 2003; Petronio 2010). When information is revealed by others, ownership of the information is relinquished, thus allowing other people to share control over the privacy boundary that protects the private information.

The sixth and final principle of CPM is boundary turbulence. A change or an event, unexpected, intentional, or simply perceived, in predictable conversation patterns or in communication rules can cause communication boundary turbulence (Afifi 2003; Petronio 2000, 2002). Additionally, when relationships are altered as a result of a new or situational grouping of individuals (Golish and Caughlin 2002), a significant change (for example, funding shortfall or technology innovation), or life event

(Afifi 2003; Petronio 2000), privacy boundary rules may change. In their work with family members, Petronio and Caughlin (2006) found: "Boundary coordination may be compromised when rule expectations are fuzzy to one of the shareholders, when the context of the situation is defined differently by one or more . . . members, or when assumptions about informational ownership are dissimilar" (46). Privacy breaches may occur or be triggered by boundary turbulence (Duggan and Petronio 2009), or when attempts to control or coordinate the communication of private information fail (Morr Serewicz and Petronio 2007). Turbulence occurs when expectations are violated about how privacy boundaries surrounding private information should be handled: "It is through analyzing the turbulence and how families [or other relationships] respond to it, that researchers can better understand how to manage it" (Afifi 2003, 735).

CPM in Interpersonal and Organizational Communication

CPM has also been used in a wide variety of disciplines. In health communication, CPM has been used to explain the physician-patient dyadic when physicians neglect their disclosure obligations (Helft and Petronio 2007). In family health situations, CPM helps to describe privacy-boundary relationships that develop when family and friends serve as healthcare advocates (Petronio, Sargent, Andea, Reganis, and Cichocki 2004). Additionally, CPM has been used to describe the privacy-boundary relationships that occur when a young child (Duggan and Petronio 2009) or an adult (Ostrom-Blonigen 2007; Petronio and Ostrom-Blonigen 2008a; Petronio and Ostrom-Blonigen 2008b) becomes seriously ill. CPM work also has been used in research involving physicians and their families as they seek to navigate work boundaries (Petronio 2006). Health communication researchers have also used CPM to gain a better understanding of boundary management rules (Petronio, Reeder, Hecht, and Mon't Ros Mendoza 1996), to assess the appropriateness of health-diagnosis disclosures (Greene and Serovich 1996), and to investigate the privacy concerns of nursing-home residents (Petronio and Kovach 1997).

CPM has also been employed in family systems. Specific efforts in this area include triangulation, loyalty conflicts, and the formation of various alliances (Afifi 2003; Golish and Caughlin 2002; Thompson, Petronio, and Braithwaite 2012). In her work with stepfamilies, Afifi (2003) found that meta-communication, described as communication about communication (Bateson 1951), or "directly confront[ing] the person with whom there is a problem" (Afifi 2003, 744) appears to be the most successful method in minimizing boundary conflicts. Finally, within group systems, CPM has also provided a better understanding about the communication boundaries of other cultures (Faulkner and Mansfield 2002). For example, CPM has been used to measure the privacy rules employed by college student bloggers (Child, Pearson, and Petronio 2009). In organizational settings, CPM has been used to describe the communication boundaries within a research university regarding the provisioning of technology (Ostrom-Blonigen 2013).

OUR PREVIOUS WRITINGS

In a 2011 study, working with two additional colleagues (Larson-Casselton, Ostrom-Blonigen, Bornsen, and Ericksen), we used ethnographic self-interviews to examine the informal mentoring relationship(s) of four older-than-average female doctoral students and concluded that all four forms of social support (informational, appraisal, instrumental, and emotional) were present within the interactions of these women. In a 2012 online pilot survey of three older-than-average male doctoral students, together with two additional colleagues (Larson-Casselton, Ostrom-Blonigen, Bornsen, and Ericksen 2012), we found that each of the men chose to describe a formal mentoring relationship with either their advisor or one of their doctoral committee members. Of further interest was that none of the men's responses included an emotional support component; yet, examples of informational, instrumental, and appraisal support were all found in the men's responses. Although the response rates to our 2013 online survey, following the pilot study, were lower than hoped for (n = 6), we and another colleague (Larson-Casselton, Ostrom-Blonigen, Bornsen, and Ericksen 2012) found those identifying as "male" (n = 3) once again chose to describe a formal mentoring relationship with either their advisor or one of their doctoral committee members, which did not include emotional support. Whereas the female respondent (n = 1) once again described an informal mentoring model, highlighting the importance of emotional support. The remaining two respondents chose not to identify their sex.

Finally, Ostrom-Blonigen conducted a 2013 focus group of five females; three had completed their PhD degree as older-than-average students, one had completed her PhD degree as a traditional-aged student, and one had completed her master's degree as a traditional-aged student. Four of the women, with the exception of the traditional-aged PhD student, chose to describe informal mentoring relationships that included all four types of social support. Interestingly, the traditional-aged PhD student described a formal mentoring relationship with her advisor; yet also claimed all four types of social support were evident in their mentoring relationship. When further questioned about her formal mentor, the traditional-aged PhD student indicated that her mentor was female and younger than most PhD advisors in her department.

Social Support in Mentoring

The application of social support to a higher education mentoring relationship is appropriate. During the past several years, the social support of mentoring in higher education has been recognized as important to the person/organizational fit among nursing faculty administrators and nursing faculty (Gutierrez, Candela, and Carver 2012), first-generation students (Luckett and Luckett 2009), the first-year experience (Hall and Jaugietis 2011), and the self-report competence of student nurses and midwives (Lauder et al. 2008). Additionally, correlations have been found in the integrated research of perceived support and psychosocial mentoring and perceived support and career mentoring among medical resident physicians (Giblin and Lakey 2010).

CPM in Mentoring

The application of communication privacy management (CPM) to a higher education mentoring relationship is appropriate. CPM and mentoring relationships have yet to be linked in the literature. However, understanding the communication privacy boundaries could be an important aid to mentoring relationships within higher education. For example, in their 2009 work with students and faculty, Hosek and Thompson used CPM to explore the communication rules and boundaries that frame private disclosures of instructors when communicating with their students; repeating their study from a student-perspective might provide faculty/mentors and student/mentees with valuable insight about common communication privacy boundaries for these groups. Whereas, in their 2012 work with academic advisors and college student athletes, Thompson, Petronio, and Braithwaite used CPM to examine the privacy rules that academic advisors employ related to the private information disclosed to them by student/athletes. Such insights may assist with training academic advisors (Thompson, Petronio, and Braithwaite) who mentor student-athletes. CPM studies such as these may also be important in developing training curriculum for academic advisors/mentors in other disciplines.

METHOD

"The autoethnographer is someone who helps to form and reform the constructs that she or he studies" (Anderson 2006, 382). Autoethnography has been defended by interactionists as serving an important place in the innovation of qualitative methods (Anderson 2006). Using autoethnography, the researchers' biased experience in their own culture creates a rich narrative framework (Chang 2008; Muncey 2010; Siddique 2011) for analysis. According to Anderson, there are two types of autoethnography: evocative and analytic. For purposes of this study, analytic auto-ethnography was employed. The five key elements of an analytic auto-ethnography (Anderson) include: 1) complete member researcher status, either as an opportunist or a convert, 2) analytic reflexivity, 3) narrative visibility of researcher's self, 4) dialogue with informants beyond self, and 5) commitment to theoretical analysis.

For this particular study, analytic autoethnography is especially applicable because of our unique experiences of mentoring each other over a seven-year period. Additionally, all five key elements of an analytic auto-ethnography were present: 1) we were opportunistic (by occupation) members of a PhD degree program, 2) throughout our doctoral journey, we discussed our seemingly unique relationship, 3) our experiences were clearly evident as outlined in this chapter, 4) additional voices were added to ours as evidenced through the inclusion of our previous studies on this topic, and 5) our application of social support and communication privacy management theory demonstrates our commitment to theoretical analysis.

Case Studies

Tellis (1997) believes, done correctly, a single site study will "satisfy the three tenets of the qualitative method: describing, understanding, and explaining" (14). Yin (1994, 2004, 2009) has argued that single site studies, properly executed, have merit. To be effective, a single case study must establish parameters that can be applied to later research (Tellis 1997). Case study literature provides many examples of the merit of single site studies (Tellis 1997; Voss, Tsikriktsis, and Frohlich 2002; Yin 2009). We believe that our relationship is representative of an average (Yin 2009) informal mentoring relationship between older than average female students. Additionally, as was one of the goals of this project, single site studies can provide more in-depth examples and richer details.

OUR FINDINGS AND LIFE APPLICATIONS TO THEORY

Two objectives characterize the rationale for our study. The first objective was to examine the role that social support plays in the informal mentoring relationship. The second objective was to discover how the principles of communication privacy management theory might impact an individual's choice to adjust or regulate the revealing or concealing of their private information in an informal mentoring relationship.

Social Support

For us, graduate coursework provided a basis for commonality that resulted in the establishment of our relationship. Once established, our face-to-face supportive interactions evolved into an informal mentoring relationship that helped each of us become successful in our quest toward a PhD. Our supportive interactions were both verbal and non-verbal.

Direct emotional support was evidenced when Jean attended the funeral services for Cindy's husband, despite having never met him. An example of indirect emotional support has been our adoption of the phrase "we just need to be done with this now." Verbal emotional support has been in evidence in our expressions of concern for the other, particularly during times of sorrow and strife. Examples of non-verbal emotional support have been in evidence in our ability to help make the other feel supported even while sitting in silence for several hours while working on our individual projects. Additionally, humor has played a significant role in our non-verbal mentoring relationship support; for example, one morning a week for many years, we would meet at a table under a picture of Paul Bunyan and Babe, the Blue Ox, at a local coffee shop. (Paul Bunyan is a hero of giant-like physical stature in American folklore, dating back to pre-1910, who symbolizes the spirit and vitality of the American frontier, along with his ever-present companion, Babe, a gentle giant ox of a blue color [http://americanfolklore.net/folklore/paul-bunyan/].) The camaraderie was such that just the mention of Paul Bunyan still brings smiles.

Direct instrumental support was in evidence when Jean and another colleague wrote a re-entry into graduate school email for Cindy following a year-long academic absence after the death of her husband. An example of indirect and non-verbal instrumental support was Jean's act of taking a parking ticket off Cindy's windshield and paying it without her knowledge. Verbal instrumental support was repeatedly exhibited in our willingness to meet at 6:30 a.m. most Saturday mornings throughout our academic careers.

Direct and verbal informational support was in evidence when a colleague, having already completed her PhD described details and offered support to us. An example of indirect informational support was Jean's advice that Cindy consult the campus information technology help desk for assistance with her computer. Non-verbal informational support was offered many times when we would email articles to one another that pertained to the other's study.

Direct appraisal support was in evidence in the reading of each other's work and in the offering of constructive criticism. An example of indirect appraisal support was Cindy and Jean reminding each other to "get started" because "the hardest part is getting started." Non-verbal appraisal support was offered when we called upon each other as data coders.

CPM

The use of CPM to examine the informal mentoring relationship serves as an initial step to advance the importance of this type of mentoring in the academic world. Mansson and Myers (2012) state, "for more than four decades, scholars have argued rightfully that the quality of this relationship is important to advisees' academic success, yet they have neglected to examine how this relationship is maintained" (323). This study contributes to the academic mentoring research by introducing CPM as a lens through which the informal mentoring relationship can be further studied as a means to increase mentee success in academic programs.

Prior to 2007, we maintained self-ownership over our private information. We maintained control of our private information by keeping fairly impermeable communication boundaries. In this "safe" relationship, rules were minimized. In 2007, with the turbulence created by the death of Cindy's spouse, Jean sought to establish co-ownership with Cindy by negotiating a set of rules that redefined their relationship.

With one exception, the traditional-aged female PhD student, more communication boundary permeability was evident in informal mentoring relationships and emotional support was an important component of those informal relationships. Traditional formal mentoring structures use strict relationship rules that may prohibit an emotional component, which could contribute to the increase permeability of privacy rules found in informal mentoring relationships.

CONCLUSION AND FUTURE DIRECTION

For the past four decades there has been a growing body of advisor/ advisee mentoring research; however, the majority of these studies have focused almost entirely on the positive outcomes while ignoring how these relationships are sustained over time (Mansson and Myers 2012). With this autoethnographic case study we provide a means to extend the sustainability of these relationships by showing how informal peer mentoring might be used to foster success in academia. As a result, we agree that autoethnography "stimulate[s] more discussion of working the spaces between subjectivity and objectivity, passion and intellect, and autobiography and culture" (Ellis and Bochner 2000, 761).

From our work thus far, we believe that a social support gap exists in traditional formalized academic mentoring structures that typically emphasize the instrumental, informational, and appraisal components of mentoring support. These formalized structures either ignore or, in some cases, purposefully avoid the emotional component of social support. As older-than-average female students, our autoethnographic case study shows how informal peer mentoring was used to bridge that emotional support gap for older-than-average female students who struggle with other life challenges in ways that are direct and indirect and in ways that are verbal and non-verbal.

Due to institutional restrictions surrounding the emotional support academic advisors are able to provide their advisees, non-permeable communication boundaries around topics such as the life challenges an older-than-average female student faces, which may impact her academic success, are typically not discussed in the advisor/advisee relationship. CPM theory provides a mechanism to describe how communication privacy boundaries can be successfully navigated in a formalized academic mentoring program when communication rules are put into place early in the mentoring relationship that protect co-owned information, particularly that of an emotional nature, held by both the mentor/advisor and the mentee/advisee. In addition, CPM theory provides a valuable framework from which to examine the management of formal academic mentoring communication boundaries in ways that allow for another level of permeability through the establishment of informal peer mentoring programs that partner students, particularly older-than-average female students.

The limitations that surrounded this study are participant related in terms of diversity in gender, ethnicity, and age. We both are from the Midwest of the United States, are female, identify as Caucasian, and were in our early forties when we began our PhD programs. An additional limitation includes the limited sample size in most of our studies. Considering the limitations of our study, we are continuing this work with a larger and more diverse participant population. Our current study, which is already underway, includes a transcultural application that seeks to address the limitations we noted. If you have a mentoring story that you would like to tell, please email one of us (jean.ostrom-blonigen@ndsu.edu or clarson@cord.edu), and we will direct you to our current study materials. If you have not had the opportunity to experience a mentoring relationship or if you have had a negative experience with a mentoring relationship in the past, it is our hope that our chapter provides you with insights that give you the power to change the outcomes of your future mentoring relationships. For us, informal peer mentoring was the key to our success and we both look forward to a lifetime of future collaborations.

Table 3.1.

The Charted Stories of Jean and Cindy

Background Data	Jean	Cindy
Year of Birth	1962	1957
Ethnicity	German Scandinavian Native American (Chippewa)	Norwegian French
Age at PhD Decision	39 (in 2002)	41 (in 2000)
Personal Health during PhD Journey	Good overall Hysterectomy—2007	Good overall Migraines
Marital Status during PhD Journey and the Writing of This Chapter	1987—Married 2013—Separated 2014—Divorced	1983—Married 2007—Widowed
Education	1981—AS Business Administration 1983—BS Accounting 1999—BS Management Info. Systems 2013—PhD Communication	1980—BA Communication 1982—MA Comm. Studies 2013—PhD Communication
Employment during PhD journey	Full-time, but changed positions within the same organization five times	Full-time with the same organization
Children	2 boys—1991 and 1992	2 girls—1991 and 1992

REFERENCES

Afifi, T. D. 2003. "'Feeling Caught' in Stepfamilies: Managing Boundary Turbulence through Appropriate Communication Privacy Rules." *Journal of Social and Personal Relationships* 20: 729–755.

Allman, J. 1998. "Bearing the Burden or Baring the Soul: Physicians' Self-Disclosure and Boundary Management Regarding Medical Mistakes." *Health Communication* 10: 175–197.

Anderson, L. 2006. "Analytic Autoethnography." *Journal of Contemporary Ethnography* 35(4): 373–395. doi: 10.1177/0891241605280449.

Barnes, M. K., and S. Duck. 1994. "Everyday Communicative Contexts for Social Support." In B. Burleson, T. Albrecht, and I. G. Parson (eds.), *Communication of Social Support: Messages, Interactions, Relationships and Community*, 175–194. Thousand Oaks, CA: Sage.

Bateson, G. 1951. "Information and Codification: A Philosophical Approach." In J. Ruesch and G. Bateson (eds.), *Communication: The Social Matrix of Psychiatry*, 168–211. New York: Norton

Baxter, L. A., and D. O. Braithwaite. 2008. "Relationship-Centered Theories of Interpersonal Communication." In L. A. Baxter and D. O. Braithwaite (eds.), *Engaging Theories in Interpersonal Communication: Multiple Perspectives*, 281–283. Thousand Oaks, CA: Sage Publications, Inc.

Bowen, W. C., and N. L. Rudenstein. 1992. *In Pursuit of the PhD*. Princeton, NJ: Princeton University Press.

Burnett, G., and H. Buerkle. 2004. "Information Exchange in Virtual Communities: A Comparative Study." *Journal of Computer Mediated Communication* 9: 1–24.

Caughlin, J. P., and T. D. Afifi. 2004. "When Is Topic Avoidance Unsatisfying? Examining Moderators of the Association between Avoidance and Dissatisfaction." *Human Communication Research* 30: 479–513.

Caughlin, J. P., and S. Petronio. 2004. "Privacy in Families." In A. L. Vangelisti (ed.), *Handbook of Family Communication*, 379–412. Mahwah, NJ: Erlbaum.

Chang, H. 2008. *Autoethnography as Method*. Walnut Creek, CA: Left Coast Press.

Child, J., J. Pearson, and S. Petronio. 2009. "Blogging, Communication, and Privacy Management: Development of the Blogging Privacy Management Measure." *Journal of the American Society for Information Science and Technology* 60(10): 2079–2094.

Cole, J. R. 1981. "Views: Women in Science: Despite Many Recent Advances, Women Are Still Less Likely Than Men to be Promoted to High Academic Rank, and Few Have Full Citizenship in the Informal Scientific Community." *American Scientist* 69: 385–391. doi: 10.2307/27850530.

Cronan-Hillix, T. C., L. K. Gensheimer, W. A. Cronan-Hillix, and W. S. Davidson. 1986. "Student's Views of Mentors in Psychology Graduate Training." *Teaching of Psychology* 13(3): 123–127. doi: 10.1207/s15328023top1303_5.

Duggan, A., and S. Petronio. 2009. "When Your Child Is in Crisis: Navigating Medical Needs with Issues of Privacy Management." In T. Socha and G. Stamp (eds.), *Parents and Children Communicating with Society: Managing Relationships outside of Home*, 117–132. New York: Routledge.

Ellis, C., and A. P. Bochner. 2000. "Autoethnography, Personal Narrative, Reflexivity: Researcher as Subject." In N. K. Denzin and Y. S. Lincoln (eds.), *Handbook of Qualitative Research*, 2nd edition, 733–768. Thousand Oaks, CA: Sage.

Ely, R. J., H. Ibarra, and D. M. Kolb. 2011. "Taking Gender into Account: Theory and Design for Women's Leadership Development Programs." *Academy of Management, Learning & Education* 10(3): 474–493.

Etzkowitz, H., C. Kemelgor, and B. Uzzi. 2000. *Athena Unbound: The Advancement of Women in Science and Technology*. UK: Cambridge University Press.

Faulkner, S. L., and P. K. Mansfield. 2002. "Reconciling Messages: The Process of Sexual Talk for Latinas." *Qualitative Health Research* 12: 310–328.

Geist-Martin, P., E. B. Ray, and B. Sharf. 2003. *Communicating Health: Personal, Cultural, and Political Complexities*. Belmont, CA: Wadsworth.

Giblin, F., and B. Lakey. 2010. "Integrating Mentoring and Social Support Research within the Context of Stressful Medical Training." *Journal of Social and Clinical Psychology* 29(7): 771–796.

Gibson, S. 2006. "Mentoring of Women Faculty: The Role of Organizational Politics and Culture." *Innovative Higher Education* 31: 63–79.

Golish, T. D. 2003. "Stepfamily Communication Strengths: Understanding the Ties That Bind." *Human Communication Research* 29(1): 41–80.

Golish, T. D., and J. P. Caughlin. 2002. "'I'd Rather Not Talk about It': Adolescents' and Young Adults' Use of Topic in Stepfamilies." *Journal of Applied Communication Research* 30: 78–106.

Greene, K., and J. M. Serovich. 1996. "Appropriateness of Disclosure of HIV Testing Information: The Perspective of PLWAs." *Journal of Applied Communication Research* 24: 50–65.

Gutierrez, A. P., L. L. Candela, and L. Carver. 2012. "The Structural Relationships between Organizational Commitment, Global Job Satisfaction, Developmental Experiences, Work Values, Organizational Support, and Person-Organizational Fit among Nursing Faculty." *Journal of Advanced Nursing* 68(7): 1601–1614. doi: 10.1111/j.1365-2648.2012.05990.x.

Hall, R., and Z. Jaugietis. 2011. "Developing Peer Mentoring through Evaluation." *Innovation Higher Education* 36(1): 41–52. doi: 10.1007/s10755-010-9156-6.

Harris, J. I., A. M. Winskowski, and B. E. Engdahl. 2007. "Types of Workplace Social Support in the Prediction of Job Satisfaction." *The Career Development Quarterly* 56: 150–156.

Helft, P., and S. Petronio. 2007. "Communication Pitfalls with Cancer Patients: 'Hit and Run' Deliveries of Bad News." *Journal of American College of Surgeons* 205(6): 807–811.

Hosek, A. M., and J. Thompson. 2009. "Communication Privacy Management and College Instruction: Exploring the Rules and Boundaries that Frame Instructor Private Disclosures." *Communication Education* 58: 327–349. doi: 10.1080/03634520902777585.

House, J. S. 1981. *Work Stress and Social Support*. Reading, MA: Addison Wesley Publishing Company.

Hubbell, L., and K. Hubbell. 2002. "The Burnout Risk for Male Caregivers in Providing Care to Spouses Afflicted with Alzheimer's Disease." *Journal of Health and Human Services* 2: 115–132.

Humphreys, M. 2005. "Getting Personal: Reflexivity and Autoethnographic Vignettes." *Qualitative Inquire* 11(6): 840–860. doi: 10.1177/1047800404269425.

Ibarra, H., N. M. Carter, and C, Silva. September 2010. "Why Men Still Get More Promotions than Women: Your High-Potential Females Need More than just Well-Meaning Mentors." *Harvard Business Review*, 80–85.

Inzer, L. D., and C. B. Crawford. 2005. "A Review of Formal and Informal Mentoring: Processes, Problems, and Design." *Journal of Leadership Education* 4(1): 31–50.

Larson-Casselton, C. 2013. *Navigating the Turbulent Dual Role of Parent/Coach* (Unpublished doctoral dissertation). Fargo, ND: North Dakota State University.

Larson-Casselton, C., J. Ostrom-Blonigen, S. Bornsen, and S. Erickson. 2012. "Mentoring Made It Happen." In N. Dominguez (ed.), *Facilitating Developmental Relationships for Success*. Paper presented at 5th Annual Mentoring Conference, Albuquerque, NM (91–99). Albuquerque, NM: University of New Mexico.

Larson-Casselton, C., J. Ostrom-Blonigen, S. E. Bornsen, and S. L. Erickson. 2013. "Mentoring Made It Happen: Or Did It?" In N. Dominguez (ed.), *Impact and Effectiveness of Developmental Relationships*. Paper presented at 6th Annual Mentoring Conference, Albuquerque, NM. Albuquerque, NM: University of New Mexico.

Lauder, W., R. Watson, K. Topping, K. Holland, M. Johnson, M. Porter, . . . and A. Behr. 2008. "An Evaluation of Fitness for Practice Curricula: Self-Efficacy, Support and Self-Reported Competence in Preregistration Student Nurses and Midwives." *Journal of Clinical Nursing* 17(14): 1858–1867. doi: 10.1111/j.1365-2702.2007.02223.x.

Luckett, K., and T. Luckett. 2009. "The Development of Agency in First Generation Learners in Higher Education: A Social Realist Analysis." *Teaching in Higher Education* 14(5): 469–481. doi: 10.1080/13562510903186618.

Ma, Z., P. Quan, and T. Liu. 2014. "Mediating Effect of Social Support on the Relationship between Self-Evaluation and Depression." *Social Behavior and Personality* 42(2): 295–302. doi: 10.2224/sbp.2014.42.2.295.

Mansson, D. H., and S. A. Myers. 2012. "Using Mentoring Enactment Theory to Explore the Doctoral Student-Advisor Mentoring Relationship." *Communication Education* 61(4): 309–334.

Margulis, S. T. 2003. "On the Status and Contribution of Westin's and Altman's Theories of Privacy." *Journal of Social Issues* 59(2): 411–429.

McDonald, M. L., and J. D. Westphal. 2011. "My Brother's Keeper? CEO Identification with the Corporate Elite, Social Support among CEOs, and Leader Effectiveness." *Academy of Management Journal* 54(4): 661–693.

McManus, S. E., and J. E. A. Russell. 1997. "New Directions for Mentoring Research: An Examination of Related Constructs." *Journal of Vocational Behavior* 51: 145–161.

Morr Serewicz, M. C., and S. Petronio. 2007. "Communication Privacy Management Theory: Ethical Considerations." In B. B. Whaley and L. Turner (eds.), *Explaining Communication: Contemporary Theories and Exemplars*, 257–274. Mahwah, NJ: Lawrence Erlbaum Associates.

Moore, K. M., and M. D. Sagaria. 1991. "The Situation of Women in Research Universities in the United States: Within the Inner Circles of Academic Power." In G. P. Kelly and S. Slaughter (eds.), *Women's Higher Education in Comparative Perspective*, 359. New York: Springer.

Muncey, J. 2010. *Creating Authoethnographies*. London: Sage.

Murray, M. 2001. *Beyond the Myths and Magic of Mentoring: How to Facilitate an Effective Mentoring Process*, 2nd edition. San Francisco: Jossey-Bass.

O'Brien, K. R. 2014. "Access to 'Good' Mentoring for Underrepresented Group Members." *Learn, Share, and Grow*. Paper presented at 26th Annual International Conference, Gilbert, AZ: International Mentoring Association.

O'Brien, K. E., A. Biga, S. R. Kessler, and T. D. Allen. 2010. "A Meta-Analytic Investigation of Gender Differences in Mentoring." *Journal of Management* 36(2): 537–554. doi: 10.1177/0149206308318619.

Ostrom-Blonigen, J. 2014. *Learn, Share, and Grow*. Focus group conducted at 26th Annual International Conference, Gilbert, AZ: International Mentoring Association.

Ostrom-Blonigen, J. March 2007. *Emerging from the Cocoon: Reestablishing Privacy Boundaries Breached by Illness*. Unpublished paper presented at the Central States Communication Association Conference, Minneapolis, MN.

Ostrom-Blonigen, J. 2013. *Funding the Technology of a Research University*. Unpublished doctoral dissertation. Fargo, ND: North Dakota State University.

Petronio, S. 1991. "Communication Boundary Management: A Theoretical Model of Managing Disclosure of Private Information between Marital Couples." *Communication Theory* 1(4): 311–335.

Petronio, S. 2000. "The Boundaries of Privacy: Praxis of Everyday Life." In S. Petronio (ed.), *Balancing the Secrets of Private Disclosures*, 37–49. Mahwah, NJ: Lawrence Erlbaum Associates.

Petronio, S. 2002. *Boundaries of Privacy: Dialectics of Disclosure*. New York: State University of New York Press.

Petronio, S. 2004. "The Road to Developing Communication Privacy Management: Narrative in Progress, Please Stand By [Special Issue]." *Journal of Family Communication* 4: 193–208.

Petronio, S. 2006. "Impact of Medical Mistakes: Negotiating Work-Family Boundaries for Physicians and Their Families." Forum on Family and Work Boundaries. *Communication Monographs* 73(4): 462–467.

Petronio, S. 2007. "Translational Research Endeavors and the Practices of Communication Privacy Management." *Journal of Applied Communication Research* 3: 218–222.

Petronio, S. 2009. "Privacy." *Encyclopedia of Human Relationships*. Retrieved September 1, 2010, from http://www.sageereference.com/humanrelationships/Article_n419.html.

Petronio, S. 2010. "Communication Privacy Management Theory: What Do We Know about Family Privacy Regulation?" *Journal of Family Theory & Review* 2: 175–196.

Petronio, S., and W. Durham. 2008. "Understanding and Applying Communication Privacy Management Theory." In L. A. Baxter and D. O. Braithwaite (eds.), *Engaging Theories in Family Communication*, 309–322. Thousand Oaks, CA: Sage Publications, Inc.

Petronio, S., and S. M. Jones. 2007. "When 'Friendly Advice' Becomes a Privacy Dilemma for Pregnant Couples: Applying Communication Privacy Management Theory." In L. Turner and R. West (eds.), *Family Communication: A Reference for Theory and Research*, 201–218. Thousand Oaks, CA: Sage Publications, Inc.

Petronio, S., and S. Kovach. 1997. "Managing Privacy Boundaries: Health Providers' Perceptions of Resident Care in Scottish Nursing Homes." *Journal of Applied Communication Research* 25: 115–131.

Petronio, S., and J. Ostrom-Blonigen. July 2008a. *The Logic of Privacy and the Management of Disclosure—Implications and Applications of Communication Privacy Management: Emerging from the Cocoon: Reestablishing Privacy Boundaries Breached by Illness.* Participant panel at the International Association for Relationship Research Conference, Providence, RI.

Petronio, S., and J. Ostrom-Blonigen. November 2008b. *Family Factor—Learning to Face Health Predicaments: Family Stress of Managing Privacy during Cancer Care the Second Time Around.* Participant panel at the National Communication Association Conference, Panel Participant, San Diego, CA.

Petronio, S., and J. Reierson. 2009. "Regulating the Privacy of Confidentiality: Grasping the Complexities through Communication Privacy Management Theory." In T. Afifi and W. Afifi (eds.), *Uncertainty, Information Management, and Disclosure Decisions: Theories and Applications,* 365–383. New York: Routledge.

Petronio, S., H. M. Reeder, M. L. Hecht, and T. M. Mon't Ros-Mendoza. 1996. "Disclosure of Sexual Abuse by Children and Adolescents." *Journal of Applied Communication Research* 24: 181–199.

Petronio, S., J. Sargent, L. Andea, P. Reganis, and D. Cichocki. 2004. "Family and Friends as Healthcare Advocates: Dilemmas of Confidentiality and Privacy." *Journal of Social and Personal Relationships* 21: 33–52.

Powers, J. D., and D. C. Swick. 2012. "Straight Talk from Recent Grads: Tips for Successfully Surviving Your Doctoral Program." *Journal of Social Work Education* 48(2): 389–394.

Rook, K. S., and D. Dooley. 1985. "Applying Social Support Research: Theoretical Problems and Future Directions." *Journal of Social Issues* 41(1): 5–28.

Sandberg, S. 2013. *Lean In: Women, Work, and the Will to Lead.* New York: Alfred A. Knopf.

Searby, L., and L. Collins. 2010. "Mentor and Mother Hen: Just What I Needed as a First Year Professor." *Advancing Women in Leadership Journal* 30(20): 1–16.

Serewicz, M. C. M., and S. Petronio. 2007. "Communication Privacy Management Theory." In B. B. Whaley and W. Santer (eds.), *Explaining Communication: Contemporary Theories and Exemplars,* 257–274. Mahwah, NJ: Lawrence Erlbaum Associates.

Siddique, S. 2011. "Being In-Between: The Relevance of Ethnography and Auto-Ethnography for Psychotherapy Research." *Counseling and Psychotherapy Research* 11(4): 310–316.

Tellis, W. 1997. "Introduction to Case Study." *The Qualitative Report* 3(2). Retrieved April 3, 2012, from http://www.nova.edu/ssss/QR/QR3-2/tellis1.html.

Thompson, J., S. Petronio, and D. O. Braithwaite. 2012. "An Examination of Privacy Rules for Academic Advisors and College Student-Athletes: A Communication Privacy Management Perspective." *Communication Studies* 63(1): 54–76. doi: 10.1080/10510974.2011.616569.

Voss, C., N. Tsikriktsis, and M. Frohlich. 2002. "Case Research: Case Research in Operations Management." *International Journal of Operations & Production Management* 22(2): 195–219.

Yin, R. K. 1994. "Discovering the Future of the Case Study Method in Evaluation Research." *Evaluation Practice* 15(3): 283–290.

Yin, R. K. 2004. *The Case Study Anthology.* Thousand Oaks, CA: Sage Publications, Inc.

Yin, R. K. 2009. *Case Study Research: Design Methods,* 4th edition. Thousand Oaks, CA: Sage Publications, Inc.

Zachary, L. J. 2009. "Filling in the Blanks." *T+D* (May): 63–66.

II

Tapping on the Glass Ceiling in Academe

FOUR

Burdens of the Gifted

Moving inside the Margins

Allison E. McWilliams

Despite the gains that women have made within higher education—in today's four-year colleges and universities, female undergraduate students outnumber males, and women can be found at all ranks of university administration and faculty—female professors remain largely outnumbered by their male counterparts and increasingly so ascending the ranks. The most recent Integrated Postsecondary Education Data System statistics show that, for full-time faculty at degree-granting institutions, male assistant professors outnumber female 11.6 percent to 11.3 percent, male associate professors outnumber female 11.8 percent to 8.6 percent, and male professors outnumber female 16.9 percent to 7 percent.[1] This quantitative disparity has implications both for the culture of the institution and for the lived experiences of women within it, as fewer women in leadership positions means fewer female role models and mentors for female students and early-career academics, greater burdens on women to serve in these roles, and the perpetuation of male-centered interpretations of success.

The importance of examining these lived experiences is supported by other recent work investigating the challenges faced by today's women within higher education, challenges which include a pervasive bias toward women in their professional roles, difficulties balancing professional and personal demands, and an unequal burden of service. Each of these challenges contributes to women's marginalization within the academy, pressure to conform and to perform to standards which have been articulated for a "gender-neutral" employee, and hard choices between professional and personal lives (Hewlett et al. 2008; Monroe, Ozyurt, Wrigley, and Alexander 2008; Glazer-Raymo 2008).

This chapter explores the burdens specifically associated with mentoring and female academics. Mentoring is one way that new employees can learn how to be successful within organizations. Academic development traditionally has been left to a sort of apprenticeship process that starts in graduate school and is rooted in those informal advisory relationships that develop between faculty and students. These relationships define how a student learns to be a professor. In choosing an academic major, students are socialized into that disciplinary area of study through informal mentoring by their academic advisors; through observation and conversation students learn the norms and requirements for success in that particular field. Throughout this process, academic mentors provide "crucial insider information," as well as teaching "about the subtleties of local politics and organizational power. Good mentors teach protégés strategies for managing conflict and coach them on setting short- and long-term goals. Also, they teach protégés norms that set the acceptable range of behaviors" (Johnson and Ridley 2008, 16). These informal mentors are a fundamental part of students' socialization processes to the academy and the disciplines.

But not everyone is provided this hand up: "faculty members are more likely to mentor students whose professional interests are similar to their own and remind them of themselves" (Johnson and Ridley 2008, 161). This so-called "academic cloning" (Rice 1986, 18) persists into the profession:

> Faculty members are naturally attracted to junior colleagues who conjure images of themselves. Protégés are sought out who show interest in the senior members' career trajectories, who have similar interests, and who are most apt to become accomplished like-minded researchers, thereby furthering the senior faculty member's academic lineages. As a result, White men, who occupy the majority of positions of authority in business and academe, are more inclined to mentor other White men. Women and minorities in positions of authority are in short supply in the workforce and thus are unable to meet the demand for same-culture mentoring. (Zellers, Howard, and Barcic 2008, 559)

As well, just because one has been selected for mentoring does not mean that the relationship will be a positive or productive one.

Mentoring is often aligned with so-called "soft" skills and identified as "service" work that is given to gendered positioning: women, as "emotional caretakers," are assumed to be more capable of picking up this role; therefore, more women are asked to perform it. Because there are fewer women within the institution, those who are there are burdened with fulfilling this role disproportionately to their male colleagues. And, in performing the role of mentor, women subject themselves to a "lesser" position than their male colleagues, who are thus more able to adopt the roles of researcher and scholar, which are established measures of success within the academy. These power dynamics encourage women to be less inclined to serve as mentors, not more so. And when junior academics are effectively cut off from more senior mentors it perpetuates a system that exists on a "sink or swim" mentality.

Using both my own personal narrative as staff and faculty, as well as narratives of female assistant and associate professors conducted as part of my doctoral research, this chapter explores how these burdens play out within the academy. While not examining any specific institutional policy, in order to identify key takeaways for both women and the academy the chapter is guided by the goals of a feminist critical policy analysis, which employs five elements: 1. It poses gender as a fundamental category; 2. It is concerned with the analysis of differences, local context, and specificity; 3. The data is the lived experience of women, and the biases of the researcher are assumed to be a part of the research and subject to the same critical inquiry; 4. The goal is to change institutions (and not to just add women); and 5. It is an interventionist strategy, "openly political and change-oriented" (Bensimon and Marshall 1997). It is my hope that the stories shared here will illuminate a side of academia that is too often pushed to the margins and lead to positive change.

ORGANIZATIONAL SOCIALIZATION: LEARNING THE RULES

Organizational socialization is the process by which individuals are folded into and learn how to become successful members of an organization (Van Maanen 1977). At the beginning of one's career, she is a stranger to the organization, an outsider. Over time, she learns to distinguish normal from abnormal behavior and is thus better able to locate herself within that setting. For the organization, socialization plays an important reproduction role as well, as "new members must be taught to see the organizational world as do their more experienced colleagues if the traditions of the organization are to survive" (Van Maanen and Schein 1979, 211). The work of a faculty member, at least in part, is to create more faculty who are thus enabled to perpetuate the norms and beliefs of the institution of higher education.

Academia has always played a key role in preparing students for the professions, beginning with the clergy and eventually including medicine, business, and law (Becker 1961; Olsen and Whittaker 1977; Reid 1994; Schleef 2006). More recently, the institution of higher education has been studied for its socialization of future academics (Weidman, Twale, and Stein 2001; Austin 2002). Graduate education, Austin notes, provides multiple avenues of socialization for students: to graduate school, to the academic profession, and to the discipline. Further complicating this learning process, today's workplace is characterized by increasing student diversity, new technologies, changing approaches to learning, expanding workloads, and changing job markets. Using data from a four-year, qualitative, longitudinal study, Austin found not *better* preparation for these changing roles and expectations but a "lack of systematic professional development opportunities, minimal feedback and mentoring from faculty, and few opportunities for guided reflection. Although some students had faculty mentors who guided them carefully through the process, most did not" (2002, 104). Academic socialization, in other words, is neither a consistent nor an institutionalized process, and dependent upon the discipline, institution, or individual.

MENTORING

Mentoring is a specific, strategic intervention that is used to socialize individuals to an organization. As Kram (1985) first noted, mentors provide two distinct functions within organizations: *career functions*, which prepare mentees for their roles and advancement, and *psychosocial functions*, which enhance the mentee's personal growth, sense of identity, and self-efficacy. Limited research within the higher education setting has supported that these functions occur there as well (Cawyer, Simonds, and Davis 2002; Schrodt, Cawyer, and Sanders 2003; Paglis, Green, and Baert 2006).

Mentoring research often assumes positive impacts for these relationships, especially for mentees. While the potential benefits from serving as a mentor have been researched, including personal satisfaction, recognition, and rejuvenation, less emphasis has been placed on the potential costs, including loss of time, perceptions of nepotism, and poor performance reflecting negatively on the mentor (Ragins and Scandura 1999). Problems can arise when there is a lack of time and training devoted to the relationship, personal and professional incompatibility, lack of commitment and unrealistic expectations, and when it becomes a burden added to an already heavy workload (Ehrich, Hansford, and Tennant 2004). Additionally, much of the research touting positive outcomes simplifies the relationship into mentored versus non-mentored individuals without acknowledging the potential harm that so-called "marginal mentors" can do, individuals who "may disappoint their protégés or may not meet some or even most of their protégés' developmental needs" (Ragins, Cotton, and Miller 2000, 1178).

Particularly relevant to this chapter, Tolar (2012) examined the mentoring experiences of high-achieving women, who "identified mentoring as a critical factor in their development, both as a help and a hindrance" (174). Mentors provided opportunities and cleared roadblocks that helped to advance participants' careers. Mentors were identified as positive role models and as inspirations for the participants themselves to serve as role models for others. But the participants also described challenges associated with mentoring, including lack of access to mentors; dysfunctions in the mentoring relationships including inappropriate communication, conflicting messages, and learning how to respectfully disagree with one's mentor; and challenges associated with finding mentors, particularly female mentors. Cross and Armstrong (2008) also explored the experiences of senior women and their need to gain access to learning networks. The women often formed networks through "incidental learning" as a strategy to deal with the "old boys' network"; by observing this network in action and realizing they were being treated differently, the women then sought out male mentors who granted access to their previously closed networks. This strategy then was passed on through informal female networks. Other authors recently have argued for the development of mentoring networks rather than trying to find one mentor to address all developmental needs (Higgins and Kram 2001; de Janasz, Sullivan, Whiting, and Biech 2003; de Janasz and Sullivan 2004). These networks lessen the burden for any one mentor to be the "be-all, end-all" fount of knowledge and wisdom but also increase the burdens on mentees to find multiple individuals to play this role.

PERFORMING GENDER

Traditional examinations of women within higher education have been based on positivistic number-counting: the number of women within the academy, their ranks, salary inequities, and so on in comparison to men. While a useful starting place, such number-counting does not get us to the level of understanding structural foundations. More recent work has looked to the actual lived experiences of female academics in order to make sense out of organizational structures and systems. "Gendered institutions," Joan Acker (1992) informs us, means that gender is present "in the processes, practices, images and ideologies, and distributions of power in the various sectors of social life. . . . The law, politics, religion, the academy, the state, and the economy are institutions historically developed by men, currently dominated by men, and symbolically interpreted from the standpoint of men in leading positions, both in the present and historically" (567). But, as Ropers-Huilman points out, "women are grounded in communities and life experiences that affect how their identities as women are constructed. Women faculty construct their identities in ways that incorporate the complex and contradictory expectations of all their roles, oftentimes leading to a finely tuned, yet at least partially subconscious, dance of identities" (2008, 35). And this "dance of identities" does not fit so neatly into a gendered organizational structure.

The genderless institution assumes that all individuals have equal opportunity to be successful there as long as you follow the rules: It is possible to reach the center. Researchers have examined inside-outsider positioning in terms of what women need to do to gain the coveted insider status, to move from margin to center (see, for example: Forisha 1981; Aisenberg and Harrington 1988; Moore 1988; Aronson and Swanson 1991; Collins 1991; Luke and Gore 1992; hooks 2000; Christman 2003). According to the inside-outsider theory, women must allow themselves to be socialized in accordance with roles prescribed for them by the white patriarchy: either maintaining an inferior, "feminine" status or changing themselves in ways that make them more like men. There are a set of identifiable norms and standards for acceptable behavior, which can be taught to new members and which must be learned in order to be successful. Anyone who does not learn these norms and standards will not be allowed into the organization; anyone within the organization who does not behave accordingly will be forced out. The academy has been created by and for men, and is shaped to their values, beliefs, and behaviors. For a woman to succeed on the inside she must either adopt these values, beliefs, and behaviors, or risk being seen as a threat, "an anomaly and an exception, obviously a mistake, and hence is better tolerated cloaked in invisibility and lack of recognition" (Forisha 1981, 17). Witz and Savage (1992) label this the "paradox of women's organizational experiences": women must "behave like men but not *be* men and behave unlike women and yet be women" (53).

The "glass ceiling" and the "maternal wall" are two commonly cited reasons for women's difficulties with ascending the organizational ranks. In the first, women are prevented from moving up through limited roles and access to mentors; in the second, women are assumed unable to fulfill professional expectations due to their competing role as mother (Williams 2000). One cannot possibly be "good mother" and "competent professional" at the same time. Not only do these competing roles force women to choose between their personal and professional lives, it is also a choice they must make on the job. Performing the role of mentor, serving as the "emotional caretaker," is equated with that of "good mother" and therefore placed in opposition to "competent professional."

CONSTRUCTING IDENTITIES WITHIN HIGHER EDUCATION

As Harding (1987) informs us, "in the best of feminist research, the purposes of research and analysis are not separable from the origins of research problems" (8). The questions that guide this chapter have developed from my own troubled efforts to understand how *I* construct my identity within the academy and how that impacts my interactions with others. Therefore, first I share narratives from interviews with female assistant and associate professors at Southern Research University (SRU) conducted in 2007–2008 as part of my doctoral research (McWilliams 2008). Their stories describe how they interpret success, their experiences with mentoring, and how they try to role model behavior and mentor others.

Interpretations of Success

The women at SRU describe varying degrees of success with the transition to their faculty roles and find that their socialization has occurred mainly on the job, through trial and error, and with little formal training or formal mentoring past graduate school. The burden is squarely on the shoulders of the individual to learn the rules for success, even before she reaches her first professional position. Those who do not acquire this knowledge during graduate school are at a "severe disadvantage" as one assistant professor puts it, because there is not enough time once in the job to both learn the role and to publish enough to make tenure. One newly tenured associate professor calls this process "baptism by fire." And for the professors in the sciences there is an added challenge because there is a considerable disconnect between the training process that occurs in graduate school and what is expected in the job. As professors, those in the sciences describe needing skills in personnel management, financial management, grant writing, and other practices involved in running a successful small business, often with budgets of several million dollars. So while they have been trained at the bench, in science, Amanda, an associate professor says, "We should have had to take psychology, administration, finances, accounting, I mean, good Lord." She recalls what her graduate school mentor once told her, in describing this training process: "Nobody would ever run a company by only hiring people that didn't know what they were doing and fire them once they were trained."

While the burden may be on the individual to learn the role, expectations of acceptable behavior quickly are made clear: at SRU the emphasis is on research above all else. The teaching role at SRU is "not emphasized," according to one assistant professor of business. Indeed, she notes, "If anything, there's a major backlash if people sense that you're too into it. You know, you can really get yourself in trouble if people think you're like really too into teaching, or spending too much time on it or something." Carter, an associate professor in the sciences, puts it another way: "You can be the single worst teacher *in the world!* And still get tenure if you have papers and grants. . . . The University would rather have my seven million dollars of extramural funds than have me get really outstanding teaching evaluations from the students as opposed to just average ones. That distinction doesn't matter to the University" [emphasis hers]. Even the professors of English aren't immune to this institutional move, as one associate professor notes that at times she feels like a "cog in the corporation." One of her colleagues, an assistant professor, describes it as an ongoing struggle: "I'd like to think that we were here to sit around and think big thoughts and solve the problems of the world, but I'm constantly confronted with this idea that there are grades to be awarded, there is success and there is failure."

Experiences with Mentoring

The women of SRU also describe mixed experiences with mentors both in graduate school and in their professional roles. Since the socializing work of professors is to create more professors, there is not a lot of guidance provided for alternative careers outside of higher education, which several of the women express regret over. As one of the assistant professors of science notes, "You're not told that you could teach at a very small college and not do research. Or you could be an editor for a journal. Or, you know, you could do investment banking, where you give advice on start-up ventures. So there's a huge amount of things that people can do with a PhD in science but we're never actually told." This lack of information-sharing puts the burden on students to do that investigative work on their own, without guidance or mentoring from others. And, as these women describe it, by the time graduate students figure out that there are other options they are too far down the path toward academia to change professional directions.

Jane also describes lacking critical knowledge of career options for someone with a PhD in English. She recalls that her college advisors told her *not* to go to graduate school: "They said, graduate school is miserable, and you're going to be totally unhappy, and you're a nice person and we don't want to see that happen. And that's it! There was no real information about what field this was, the difficulty of getting jobs, exactly what made graduate school so tough and miserable, there was no discussion of that." Now that she is an assistant professor, Jane recounts the difficulties of being advised by a well-intentioned senior male colleague who was too advanced in his career to understand the realities and challenges faced by a young female assistant professor. She has experienced "people who were very aggressive, and wanted to be my mentor, and wanted to give me a lot of advice, and then you know would express disappointment at me if I didn't take their advice." The power dynamics in mentoring cannot be ignored.

Several of the participants describe "great" females and "amazing" mentors who have helped them to learn their roles. For some of the women, mentors in college and graduate school served as professional role models who helped them to create their identities as professors.

Christy, an assistant professor, believes she was accepted into one of the top programs in the country in her field thanks to one of these mentoring relationships: "So I just was really fortunate, I believe, to have, just been able to, you know, be mentored by this remarkable person who was so patient and so kind and gave me this amazing opportunity that I never felt that I deserved." One of her colleagues, Virginia, recalls a formative conversation with a professor in college: "I was like, so I could be a professor? And he's like, yeah, of course you could be a professor! It was like a real awakening for me that like, oh, these people are not like these bastions of brilliance rather than people in a profession, working hard." On the one hand we see the all-too-common notion that we, as women, don't deserve to be here, that we're best left on the margins. And on the other, the idea that, with hard work, we too can be successful here and get to the center.

Role Modeling: The Burdens of Gender

Now that they are in their professional academic roles, these women are acutely aware of their position as role models and the potential burdens it entails. Jane notes that female students "need to see women in positions of power to imagine that they too could be in that same position of power, that they too could be a faculty member or a scientist or a researcher or an activist." It is, she says, one of the important things that female academics contribute to the field, in addition to teaching and research: "Just by being. Just by being visible as a female academic, they could be inspiring or helping their female undergraduates to look at the world differently." Women carry a responsibility to move inside the margins and to help other women to create their identities.

Several of these women note the burden of doing "emotional caretaking." Because there is a perception that they will be "more empathetic" than their male counterparts due to their gender, more students seek out women versus men for advice and counsel. As Amanda notes, "Students walk in the door with unwanted pregnancies to bad marriages to I had one that was getting death threats. I mean, I do think if the students have a problem they're more likely to come and talk to a female professor than a male professor. Certainly for the female students that's the case. So I get a lot." This perception puts an extra burden on female faculty like Amanda, both for those women who are not so empathetic and have to therefore perform yet another role, and because there are fewer women to share that burden within the academy. It is a never-ending circle: women are perceived as emotional caretakers and thus are saddled with the extra burden of caring for students' emotional needs; and, because they are positioned in these encounters to care for their students' emotional needs, they are perceived as emotional caretakers. While a male colleague would be better able to refuse such positioning (indeed, would not be so positioned in the first place), a woman who similarly refused would be labeled as cold, unfeeling, or worse. Women are expected to play the role of "good mother" within the institution and in doing so will no longer be seen as "competent professional."

The burden of gender is enacted in other ways within the institution. When asked to serve on university-wide committees, one of the associate professors notes that very often she is the only woman in the room or one of only two. She refers to this burden of service as feeling responsible to be a "good girl." Because there are so few women in the institution, she feels she cannot refuse service assignments when they are offered; it is important to have women in the room. But, because there are so few women in the institution it means women are burdened with more of the service load, which takes time away from their ability to produce research, which therefore diminishes their role as serious academics within the eyes of the institution which has so burdened them. At the same time, being outside the white, male majority within the institutional structure can provide women with an extra layer of mentoring and networking that the men may not have: "I have an all-girls' network by now," this associate professor notes. "I'll walk into a room, very often, and there will be women from all over campus, and, you know, we kind of recognize each other."

Many of these professors, in their efforts to be seen as "competent professional" and move closer to the center, have privileged career over family and now wonder if that was the right choice. As one assistant professor says, "We can devote a lot more time to our careers. Now, is that a blessing or is that a burden? I don't know. Because at the same time I think that I missed my time. Because I feel like I've put so much into my career that I can't take that back." Due to their own experiences in the academy with these hard choices, many of these professors now work to make sure they are mentoring their students about the realities of the profession, the sacrifices involved, and the alternatives. And they advise these future faculty members to seek out a couple of senior mentors, to build their networks, and to find out about those informal unwritten norms that are key to success there.

MOVING CLOSER TO THE CENTER: BURDENS AND OPPORTUNITIES

Often as I was interviewing the women of SRU, I was struck by how their stories mirrored my own, even though we have followed very different paths. I too have often felt like my socialization to the academy has been "baptism by fire." As I have moved from the margins closer to that elusive center, I am increasingly struck by the lack of development and intentional mentoring within the academy, and how that hand up is granted to some, including myself, and not others. Why was it offered to me and not to others? What is my obligation, now that I am closer to that center, to be a role model and mentor? How does my position there both privilege and burden me? These are the questions that I struggle with, even as I work to create my identity within the norms of the very institution that causes that struggle.

Interpretations of Success

My first professional role in higher education following graduate school was a staff position supporting public service faculty who were teaching leadership and management development to public sector employees across the state. I spent several years in this role with increasing responsibility for developing curricula, planning conferences, managing budgets, and performing other clerical duties. It was meant to be a temporary position following my master's degree while I figured out where I was going, and I certainly didn't expect to be at the university very long. For reasons both personal and professional I ended up staying there for fifteen years.

When I started, I did not know anything about teaching leadership, being a public service faculty member, or how to be successful in my staff role. There was no formal training or orientation to my duties. My socialization came on the job, through trial and error, much like it did for many of the women at SRU. Unlike those women, I wasn't trying to meet expectations related to promotion and tenure; if anything I was performing a very traditional, female role as support staff to the male-oriented faculty role. My role models and mentors at that time were other women serving in equivalent supporting roles, many of whom lacked a college degree. This led to confusion on my part and my first professional identity crisis: in terms of experience these women knew more than me and certainly were more competent in their roles; in terms of academic credentials and expectations (my own, my family's, society's) I should have been at a more advanced position. I spent a lot of time wondering where I was supposed to be and what I was supposed to be doing and finding little personal or professional guidance to that end.

My first promotion was to a higher staff role, which moved me up the hierarchy to a position above my female co-workers. This led to a lot of anger on their part and further confusion for me. I was proud of my professional achievement and felt that I deserved it, yet also felt guilty for letting my co-workers down. I had done what I was "supposed" to do and moved up the organizational chart. It was a promotion that I had earned by demonstrating my professional competence. But professional competence doesn't make you the "good girl." A couple of years later I was promoted from staff to faculty, which allowed me to take on teaching and greater management responsibilities. I had moved closer to the center. But when a male colleague congratulated me on this achievement, I asked him not to talk about it, as I did not want to incur further animosity from my co-workers. At the same time, I was angry that I wasn't allowing myself to feel pride in my own professional accomplishment.

Learning to be a public service faculty member was once more a process of trial and error and learning on the job. Again, there was no formal orientation to or training for this role; if anything I was thrown into the deep end and advised to swim. I had not yet earned the PhD or benefited from that graduate school socialization. My now faculty colleagues had spent years working in the public sector prior to joining the university, which gave them authority and subject matter expertise which I lacked. I chose to observe many of them in their teaching roles and took note of what they did so that I might adopt their behaviors as my own. While effusively supportive and willing to share resources with me, there was no formal mentoring from these colleagues on effective teaching practices, student development, or how to successfully behave as a competent faculty member, nor did the institution expect or ask them to serve in this capacity. To do so would take them away from their expected roles that included more than a hundred days of teaching in locations around the state. I often felt like an imposter in front of the classroom teaching seasoned public sector employees how to be more effective leaders, when it felt like I had only read about what that meant. I quickly learned to adopt a "fake it 'til you make it" attitude and found that this went a long way toward being successful, whether teaching a class on leadership, facilitating a strategic planning process, leading policy analysis projects, or engaging with my faculty colleagues.

Experiences with Mentoring

Although I received little training or formal orientation to the various and specific job functions, I benefited from the guidance and support of many informal mentors who helped to shape my professional identity. On my first week in my first staff role, my supervisor approached me and said, "You seem like you have a lot of skills and talents beyond this job. What is it that you want to do, and how can we help you to get there?" Those are, I have discovered over the years, rare and powerful words to say to a young person. Over time, this same supervisor created many opportunities for me, including supporting my promotion from public service assistant to public service associate, which is the equivalent of moving from assistant to associate professor. As a woman who herself had moved successfully up the hierarchy to associate vice president, she served as a powerful role model for me of what a professional woman could look like. There were also several male mentors who provided ongoing "life lessons" regarding professional behavior and expectations. When faced with a significant workplace ethical situation, for instance, it was one of these male mentors whom I reached out to for advice. "You build your reputation, every single day, in every *little* thing you do," he said to me then, words that I have repeated to myself and others many times over the years.

I also developed deep, meaningful relationships with a group of diverse, accomplished women, both faculty and staff members. Both Caucasian and African American, one with a JD and others with PhDs, single and married, mothers of adult children, young children, and childless, these women helped to teach me how to do my job effectively and served as role models for personal and professional success. I watched them navigate the white male power structure both inside and outside the university, fight for issues and people whom they believed in, and weather organizational changes with grace and resilience. I also watched them abdicate their personal lives to that of the profession, giving everything they had to demonstrate that they were more "competent professional" than "good mother"; at the same time, it was these same women who were taking care of me and showing me the way. This was my personal learning network, and it is these same women whom I return to when faced with professional challenges and opportunities to this day.

Role Modeling: The Burdens of Gender

I am now in an administrative role at a different university, directing university-wide mentoring initiatives and programs. It is my role and goal to build a culture of mentoring on our campus, which gives me ample opportunity to think about how we can better prepare the next generation for their professional roles, both inside and outside the academy. Invariably, I also end up in the role of mentor as well, both to students and to colleagues, who seek me out to discuss their choices, decisions, and career paths. Like the women at SRU, I regularly have students and colleagues alike in my office in tears, in personal and professional distress. Do they seek me out because it's in my title? Is it because I'm a woman? Is it because I'm willing to give the time? Perhaps it is a combination of all three of these things. I find the opportunity to do this emotional caretaking both a great privilege and an enormous burden that drains my personal resources and ultimately hinders my abilities to be fully successful both inside and outside the institution.

Perhaps because of the role models and mentors who have guided me, I have devoted my whole self to being the "competent professional." I now find myself single and without children and likely without the opportunity to ever make that happen. I recall vividly how a male friend once told me that I was "intimidating" to men because of my professional and educational achievements. Though they respected me, they would much rather be with the "good girl" than with the "competent professional." I have had the benefit of many great mentors along the way, male and female, who advised me on my professional choices, and I credit them all on getting me to where I am now. But not one of them advised me on my personal choices. I find now that I wish that I had had *those* conversations along the way, too, and as a result, like the women of SRU, I now work to make sure that I am having those conversations with others.

I am also quite aware what my status as a single professional without children does for me and how it burdens me. Because I am able to work nights and weekends and fly off at a moment's notice, because I have demonstrated my willingness to privilege the "competent professional" over the "good mother," I am afforded opportunities that my married colleagues with children do not equally receive. And I must recognize that on most days I am OK with that choice, and that it is a *choice* that I have made. Successful lives come in many different forms, married and not, with kids and without. Those lives should be personal, individual choices, not professional consequences. At the same time, my choices mean I am often unfairly burdened with these opportunities. The institution often unconsciously gives a pass to those who have to make it to the soccer or baseball game or home by dinner. The burdens work both ways. And, every time that I uphold those standards as the only standards for success, I must recognize I potentially do harm to those who follow.

In my former faculty role I was asked to develop a new leadership program for faculty and staff at the university. I knew it would be challenging, and I was not certain I would be completely successful. Once more I would be facing the "sink or swim" dichotomy. It would expose me to senior leadership in ways I had not been, previously, and in ways I wasn't entirely sure that I wanted to be. In that moment another one of my male mentors came to me. "Here is what I've learned," he said. "You will never do worse being closer to the power center." Those words stick with me, to this day. Being closer to the center gives you access and the ability to make change in ways that you cannot from the margins, and my experience bears this out: on balance, I have not done worse for being closer to the center. But that move also limits your ability to see the changes that need to be made. Those who are closer to the center, I have found, often lack the mentorship that would make them most effective in those roles.

A friend and colleague once said to me, "You know, it's not *your* job to make those you work for better at *their* jobs." And, there is some truth to that. But I do feel that it is my responsibility to make the organization that I am a part of a better place for my having been in it. This same friend is the one who first introduced me to the phrase, "burden of the gifted." Those who are willing and able to take up the slack often do and thus more often are expected to do so. We burden those who are most gifted in both subtle and overt ways. So now I am the closest to the center that I have ever been. I am there due to the gifts and the talents that I bring and the hand up that has been offered to me so many times over the years. And in that role, and particularly as a female in that role, I have both the opportunity and the burden of being a role model to others. I have both the opportunity and the burden to make sure that doors are opened up to others, as they have been to me. Being closer to the center does not alleviate these burdens, it only enhances them. And if I choose not to pick up that mantle, most likely no one would notice. But what am I doing, then, for those who come after me? How am I making this place better for those who follow?

CONCLUSIONS AND KEY TAKEAWAYS

As the stories of the women of SRU and my own story shared here demonstrate, socialization to the academy is often left to chance, whether through adequate graduate school preparation, effective mentoring, or personal trial and error on the job. The disproportionate number of men versus women within the upper ranks of the academy unfairly burdens women to be effective role models and mentors for the women who follow. There is an assumption that women, as "emotional caretakers," are naturally equipped to serve as mentors, especially for other women. When men are forced to serve as mentors, they can lack the critical knowledge of the particular experience of women in the academy. When they aren't, women are potentially cut off from opportunities and knowledge critical to their success. While having more women in the higher ranks will alleviate some of this burden, it is not the quick fix that it appears to be. We must not continue to assume that women, just because they are women, are better suited to these roles. The institution should create structures and processes by which all faculty and staff can find and develop effective mentoring relationships and learning networks, both formal and informal. While I firmly believe in the benefits of those informal mentoring relationships on which so much of academic socialization is based, I also believe it is incumbent upon the institution to put into place structures and processes to support those relationships and to ensure equal access to them. We can and should train both mentors and mentees so that they can be successful in these roles and ensure that no one person or group of persons is unfairly burdened with this service.

So much of what I have learned about being successful in higher education has come through observation, listening, and paying attention. We hold onto norms and rules of behavior like some closely guarded secret that we will give you access to only once you finish your pledging process. I will always remember, in my former faculty position, observing the hiring process for two faculty members, one who was male, and one who was female. It was the exact same position, and yet we were offering the male considerably more money. When I questioned this, the answer was blunt and simple: "She didn't ask." I have learned more from moments like these about what it takes to be successful in higher education than I have from any formal education or development process. And while this perpetuates the sink-or-swim mentality, it should not diminish the value of doing that observation and listening work. The individual must take ownership for her own career and choices. As one of the SRU faculty put it, "I've seen people wipe out here too. Men wipe out. I think, are you not listening? Because I do see a lot of coaching along the way."

A lot of this chapter has discussed the various "roles" that individuals perform within the institution, an essentializing practice at best. Any performance is an opportunity to consider alternative performances, new and as yet unthought of performances. A move inside the organization, closer to the center, provides women the opportunity to disrupt the norms and expectations for success. As more women move up the organizational ranks, there are greater opportunities to change these performances. What might an institution look like that equally privileged "good mother" *and* "competent professional"? What might one look like that privileged mentor over scholar? At the same time, a move closer to the center increases the burdens to conform to the institutional norms. I must recognize that where I sit now affords me the opportunity to ask these questions in ways that others cannot. And it burdens me, too, to be a role model for success that all too often conforms to these norms.

If there is anything that an institution of higher learning should know how to do well, it is how to grow and develop its people. Theories and practices of effective organizational socialization have shown that new members must be taught the rules and norms of behavior so that they can be most effective there. But in higher education we seem to operate under the assumption that new employees will just figure it out. Those who don't, we kick out of the institution. If we are going to uphold certain expectations of success, then more effective and structured processes of orientation and socialization to the roles and expectations should be provided, so that *all* individuals have equal opportunities to be successful there. As one of the women of SRU put it, socialization to the academy often can feel "like I was in a sorority without being given the documents." With changing demographics, new technologies, new forms of education emerging every day, with the evolving role and perceived value of higher education within society, we can and should do better than that.

NOTE

1. Women outnumber men at the lecturer and instructor levels. U.S. Department of Education, National Center for Education Statistics, Integrated Postsecondary Education Data System (IPEDS), Winter 2007–08, Winter 2009–10, and Winter 2011–12, Human Resources component, Fall Staff section.

REFERENCES

Acker, J. 1992. "From Sex Roles to Gendered Institutions." *Contemporary Sociology* 21(5): 565–569. Retrieved from http://www.jstor.org/stable/2075528.

Aisenberg, N., and M. Harrington. 1988. *Women of Academe: Outsiders in the Sacred Grove*. Amherst: The University of Massachusetts Press.

Aronson, A. L., and D. L. Swanson. 1991. "Graduate Women on the Brink: Writing as 'Outsiders Within.'" *Women Studies Quarterly* 19(3&4): 156–173. Retrieved from http://www.jstor.org/stable/40003311.

Austin, A. E. 2002. "Preparing the Next Generation of Faculty: Graduate School as Socialization to the Academic Career." *The Journal of Higher Education* 73(1): 94–122. Retrieved from http://muse.jhe.edu/journals/jhe/summary/v073/73.1austin.html.

Becker, H. S. 1961. *Boys in White: Student Culture in Medical School*. University of Chicago Press.

Bensimon, E. A., and C. Marshall. 1997. "Policy Analysis for Postsecondary Education: Feminist and Critical Perspectives." In C. Marshall (ed.), *Feminist Critical Policy Analysis II: A Perspective from Post-Secondary Education*, 1–21. London: The Falmer Press.

Cawyer, C. S., C. Simonds, and S. Davis. 2002. "Mentoring to Facilitate Socialization: The Case of the New Faculty Member." *International Journal of Qualitative Studies in Education* 15(2): 225–242. doi: 10.1080/09518390110111938.

Christman, D. E. 2003. "Women Faculty in Higher Education: Impeded by Academe." *Advancing Women in Leadership Journal* 14.

Collins, P. H. 1991. "Learning from the Outsider Within: The Sociological Significance of Black Feminist Thought." In M. M. Fonow and J. A. Cook (eds.), *Beyond Methodology: Feminist Scholarship as Lived Research*, 35–59. Bloomington, IN: Indiana University Press.

Cross, C., and C. Armstrong. 2008. "Understanding the Role of Networks in Collective Learning Processes: The Experiences of Women." *Advances in Developing Human Resources* 10(4): 600–613. doi: 10.1177/1523422308320495.

de Janasz, S. C., and S. E. Sullivan. 2004. "Multiple Mentoring in Academe: Developing the Professorial Network." *Journal of Vocational Behavior* 64: 263–283. doi: 10.1016/j.jvb.2002.07.001.

de Janasz, S. C., S. E. Sullivan, V. Whiting, and E. Biech. 2003. "Mentor Networks and Career Success: Lessons for Turbulent Times [and Executive Commentary]." *The Academy of Management Executive (1993–2005)* 17(4): 78–93. doi: 10.5465/AME.2003.11851850.

Ehrich, L. C., B. Hansford, and L. Tennent. 2004. "Formal Mentoring Programs in Education and Other Professions: A Review of the Literature." *Educational Administration Quarterly* 40(4): 518–540. doi: 10.1177/0013161X04267118.

Forisha, B. L. 1981. "The Inside and the Outsider: Women in Organizations." In B. L. Forisha and B. H. Goldman (eds.), *Outsiders on the Inside: Women & Organizations*, 9–30. Englewood Cliffs, NJ: Prentice-Hall, Inc.

Glazer-Raymo, J. (ed.). 2008. *Unfinished Agendas: New and Continuing Gender Challenges in Higher Education*. Baltimore, MD: The Johns Hopkins University Press.

Harding, S. 1987. "Introduction: Is There a Feminist Method?" In S. Harding (ed.), *Feminism and Methodology: Social Science Issues*, 1–14. Bloomington, IN: Indiana University Press.

Hewlett, S. A., C. B. Luce, L. J. Servon, L. Sherbin, P. Shiller, et al. May 15, 2008. "The Athena Factor: Reversing the Brain Drain in Science, Engineering and Technology." *Harvard Business Review*, Report No. 10094.

Higgins, M. C., and K. E. Kram. 2001. "Reconceptualizing Mentoring at Work: A Developmental Network Perspective." *Academy of Management Review* 26(2): 264–288. doi: 10.5465/AMR.2001.4378023.

hooks, b. 2000. *Feminist Theory: From Margin to Center*, 2nd edition. Cambridge, MA: South End Press.

Johnson, B., and C. R. Ridley. 2008. *The Elements of Mentoring*. New York: Palgrave Macmillan.

Kram, K. E. 1985. *Mentoring at Work: Developmental Relationships in Organizational Life*. Lanham, MD: University Press of America, Inc.

Luke, C., and J. Gore. 1992. "Women in the Academy: Strategy, Struggle, Survival." In C. Luke and J. Gore (eds.), *Feminisms and Critical Pedagogy*, 192–210. New York: Routledge.

McWilliams, A. E. 2008. *Troubled Interpretations: Female Academics as Produced in Practice*. Doctoral dissertation, University of Georgia.

Monroe, K., S. Ozyurt, T. Wrigley, and A. Alexander. 2008. "Gender Equality in Academia: Bad News from the Trenches, and some Possible Solutions." *Perspectives on Politics* 6(2): 215–233. doi: 10.1017/5153792708080572.

Moore, G. 1988. "Women in Elite Positions: Insiders or Outsiders?" *Sociological Forum* 3(4): 566–585. doi: 10.1007/BF01115415.

Olsen, V. L., and E. W. Whittaker. 1977. "Five Characteristics of Professional Socialization." In R. L. Blankenship (ed.), *Colleagues in Organization: The Social Construction of Professional Work*, 157–165. New York: John Wiley and Sons.

Paglis, L. L., S. G. Green, and T. N. Bauert. 2006. "Does Adviser Mentoring Add Value? A Longitudinal Study of Mentoring and Doctoral Student Outcomes." *Research in Higher Education* 47(4): 451–476. doi: 10.1007/s11162-005-9003-2.

Ragins, B. R., J. L. Cotton, and J. S. Miller. 2000. "Marginal Mentoring: The Effects of Type of Mentor, Quality of Relationship, and Program Design on Work and Career Attitudes." *Academy of Management Journal* 43(6): 1177–1194. doi: 10.2307/1556344.

Ragins, B. R., and T. A. Scandura. 1999. "Burden or Blessing? Expected Costs and Benefits of Being a Mentor." *Journal of Organizational Behavior* 20(4): 493–509.

Reid, R. 1994. *Year One: An Intimate Look Inside Harvard Business School, Source of the Most Coveted Advanced Degree in the World*. New York: William Morrow and Company, Inc.

Rice, E. 1986. "The Academic Profession in Transition: Toward a New Social Fiction." *Teaching Sociology* 14: 12–23. Retrieved from http://www.jstor.org/stable/1318295.

Ropers-Huilman, B. 2008. "Women Faculty and the Dance of Identities: Constructing Self and Privilege within Community." *Unfinished Agendas: New and Continuing Gender Challenges in Higher Education*, 35–51.

Schleef, D. J. 2006. *Managing Elites: Professional Socialization in Law and Business Schools*. Lanham, MD: Rowman & Littlefield Publishers, Inc.

Schrodt, P., C. S. Cawyer, and R. Sanders. 2003. "An Examination of Academic Mentoring Behaviors and New Faculty Members' Satisfaction with Socialization and Tenure and Promotion Processes." *Communication Education* 52(1): 17–29. doi: 10.1080/03634520302461.

Tolar, M. H. 2012. "Mentoring Experiences of High-Achieving Women." *Advances in Developing Human Resources* 14(2): 172–187. doi: 10.1177/1523422312436415.

Van Maanen, J. 1977. "Experiencing Organization: Notes on the Meaning of Careers and Socialization." In J. V. Maanen (ed.), *Organizational Careers: Some New Perspectives*, 15–45. New York: John Wiley & Sons.

Van Maanen, J., and E. H. Schein. 1979. "Toward a Theory of Organizational Socialization." *Research in Organizational Behavior* 1: 209–264.

Weidman, J. C., D. J. Twale, and E. L. Stein. 2001. "Socialization of Graduate and Professional Students in Higher Education: A Perilous Passage?" *ASHE-ERIC Higher Education Report* 28(3).

Williams, J. 2000. *Unbending Gender: Why Family and Work Conflict and What to Do About It*. Oxford University Press.

Witz, A., and M. Savage. 1992. "The Gender of Organizations." In M. Savage and A. Witz (eds.), *Gender and Bureaucracy*, 3–62. Oxford: Blackwell Publishers. doi: 10.1111/j.1467- 954X.1991.tb03355.X.

Zellers, D. F., V. M. Howard, and M. A. Barcic. 2008. "Faculty Mentoring Programs: Reenvisioning Rather Than Reinventing the Wheel." *Review of Educational Research* 78(3): 552–588. doi: 10.3102/0034654308320966.

FIVE

A Novice Is a Novice at Any Level

*A Narrative of the Experiences of Two Female Academics
in Their Beginning Years of Teaching in a Higher
Education Institution in Jamaica*

Dian D. McCallum

Workplace mentoring is highly regarded as one of the best means of inducting new members into an organization, providing a number of benefits for the mentor and mentee as well as the organization as a whole. As places where teaching, learning and researching constitute their core functions, higher education institutions are not typically known for embracing workplace practices such as formal mentoring, as it might be commonly assumed. In other words, formal mentoring as an aspect of workplace socialization is not embedded in the organizational culture of these institutions of higher learning in a general sense and is therefore not an explicit means of acclimating new faculty members into most of these institutions. However in some countries such as the United States and Australia, formal mentoring for faculty in higher education is often a prominent feature of their induction activities and is becoming more common in other countries such as England. In small island states such as Jamaica, formal mentoring for new academics is not yet ingrained in the institutional practices at one of the chief institutions of higher education.

This chapter describes the 'induction' experiences of two female academics in their beginning years of teaching at a higher education institution in Jamaica and highlights the role of informal mentoring as the main institutional mechanism that these female academics experienced as a part of their ongoing socialization into the university, specifically at the departmental level. Though there is an organized set of activities for new faculty members, these are orientation-type activities to the university. Through a number of sessions, new staff members receive information on the university's regulations, supported by relevant extracts from the university's handbook which they are expected to access online to familiarise themselves with the rules and regulations set out therein. The handbook also provides information on all other matters relating to their employment at the university. They are also informed of the primacy of publishing and its role in career advancement and becoming tenured.

At the level of their respective departments however they found that their chief sources of information came mainly from one experienced member of the department in the case of one of the participant in this study, Thelma (pseudonym). With respect to the other female academic, Lenora (pseudonym), her informal support came from family members who were past faculty members, her former lecturer and her spouse, himself a member of staff in another department.

Irrespective of the fact that both female academics entered the university highly qualified in their subject disciplines, capped with their doctor of philosophy (PhD) degrees, and with a cumulative teaching experience of twenty-five years between them (twenty-two years in the case of one and three years in the case of the other), which included teaching at the college level, they were new to teaching in higher education. As one of the participants stated 'a novice is a novice at any level'. Besides learning the ropes of teaching at the university level, they also had to contend with a new requirement hitherto not demanded of them in the college setting. Specifically, they were expected to carry out research and to publish, a requirement which turned out to be a major challenge when considered against the heavy demands of teaching and other activities, as both Thelma and Lenora admitted.

The study takes a qualitative orientation to unearthing the 'induction' experiences of these two female academics utilizing the narrative interview supplemented by the episodic interview as the chief data gathering methods. This type of interview is integral to narrative inquiry which Clandinin and Connelly (2000) described as "a way of understanding experience . . . a collaboration between researcher and participants, over time, in a place or series of places, and in social interaction with milieus" (20). The study reveals essentially as Metros and Yang (2006) established that "College campuses, while expert at offering traditional education to a diverse student clientele, are not as skilled in identifying and supporting their own staff's professional development (PD) needs" (2). Perhaps the most fundamental revelation is that despite the universal rhetoric of gender equity, women academics are regarded as an underrepresented, disadvantaged, or minority group where access to informal or formal mentoring is concerned. This makes it more challenging for female academics to obtain senior leadership positions within academia.

MENTORING FOR WOMEN IN HIGHER EDUCATION: A RATIONALE

Mentoring is one concept that if not generally understood in a strictly formal and theoretical sense is more likely than not played out in every aspect of life. That is, mentoring is integrally wrapped up in child rearing given that many of its positive attributes are essential to parenting and in what children learn from their parents and even in what parents learn about their children. Mentoring is also embedded in the interactions children have with their peers and teachers at schools and in their interaction with other adults. In the workplace and other sites of social interactions mentoring is part of the informal, implicit and perhaps hidden process that takes place when novice employees are guided by, coached, supported and learn from their more experienced colleagues. In some cases, however, this learning is formally organized as in the case of certain traditional professions such as teaching, law, medicine and the clergy where neophytes learn about their professions in a clinical-type experience though the level of formality and support may vary within these professions. In one way or the other, we pattern the behaviour of some of those with whom we interact over a period of time and even call such person our mentor.

Though there are many definitions of mentoring, they tend to cohere around a core understanding that it is a process, generally confidential, reciprocal and affirmative in nature, involving, in the traditional sense, two individuals, who differ in ages and stages in their career or professional development with the more experienced and usually older of the pair being the mentor and the usually younger and less experienced being the mentee (Ragins and Kram 2008). Given the understanding that mentees are expected to learn from their mentors, Barlow's (2014) explanation of who is a mentor is useful in the context of the university. A mentor, she explains, is one who helps

> mentees acclimate to university life, offering information about the explicit and implicit aspects of surviving and thriving as a scholar and teacher at a particular institution. Mentors aid mentees in the process of learning about campus resources and opportunities, understanding departmental and institutional policies and procedures on tenure and promotion, balancing professional and personal responsibilities, and networking both within the university and the profession at large. (2014, 1)

Barlow also noted that mentoring is highly regarded as a critical component in the professional development of junior faculty and is beneficial to the institution in terms of staff productivity, staff satisfaction and success. In view of this, mentoring is thought to reduce staff turnover, engender greater retention and inspires commitment to university culture (Barlow 2014). The benefits of mentoring are regenerative as those who have been mentored tend to mentor others. As Barlow puts it "mentoring begets mentoring . . . those who are mentored well are significantly more likely to serve as active mentors for future junior colleagues, thus handing down a legacy of support to future generations of scholars and teachers" (2014, 2). Chandler (1996; citing Wright and Wright 1997) had observed similarly that "recipients of mentoring are more likely to subsequently mentor other professionals" (82). It is possible that the obverse of this observation could also be true.

The importance of mentoring for new faculty is evident in the consequences of its absence. Writing on this issue, Wunsch and Johnsrud (1992), argue that

> the major hindrance to women's success seems to be the lack of supportive, even hospitable climate. Faculty women report greater intellectual and social isolation . . . are more likely to have their scholarship discredited (Kritek 1984), although women publish as much as their male peers in refereed journals . . . [and] have greater difficulty obtaining resources to support scholarly activities required for tenure and promotion, such as professional travel funds, research monies, equipment for laboratories and released time for research activities. (176)

Wunsch and Johnsrud (1992; citing the Carnegie Foundation for the Advancement of Teaching 1990) also noted that "Female assistant professors often have heavier teaching loads, more students in large undergraduate classes, and more departmental committee assignments. Although women are good campus citizens, such citizenship is less valued for advancement than traditional research and publication" (176).

Nature of Higher Education Institutions

Higher education institutions across different cultural contexts have displayed one remarkable characteristic in that they have long been male-dominated institutions until female academics, arguably fewer in numbers in some disciplines, gradually began to gain some foothold within academe. Even as females continue to enter the higher education landscape across the globe in greater numbers, they are less visible in certain positions of leadership (Lunn 2007; Zellers, Howard, and Barcic 2008). That is, compared with their male counterparts only a far from representative few have succeeded in breaking through the so called "glass ceiling." The "glass ceiling," as Leo-Rhynie (2008) explained, "has increasingly been used to refer to the barriers to the advancement of women in various spheres of activity" (3). In the Malaysian context, the glass ceiling is substituted by the phrase 'concrete ceiling' to indicate the more complex and explicit nature of the challenges faced by female academics in higher education to move beyond the middle leadership level. In explaining this reality Luke (2001) stated:

> There is nothing hidden or transparent about women's inability to reach the most senior ranks of the university management because all senior executive positions in the sector are political appointments. (Luke 2001, 203; cited in Lunn 2007, 81)

Other factors such as religion and the realities of patriarchy also serve to restrict the roles of women.

In a general sense the literature on mentoring is consensual in the view that mentoring is the chief means by which female academics can be prepared to advance their careers in academia while noting too that they are likely to benefit from psychosocial mentoring (Kram 1985; cited in Zellers et al. 2008), given the fact that female academics are also faced with balancing academic and domestic life in ways which are dissimilar to their male counterparts given their care-giving roles in the home. In many cases, males are the chief beneficiaries of mentoring in light of the fact that higher education has always been regarded as male-dominated institutions where men have more access to the higher positions and are more easily mentored by male mentors (Quinlan 1999).

Traditionally, women were comparatively fewer in academia and so younger female academics are often not mentored by more experienced females. Even though more females have entered academia and continue to do so at a steady rate, they are nevertheless regarded as an underrepresented and minority group in leadership positions within academia. They are also seen as the group more likely to benefit from mentoring which can aid them in advancing in their career, experience greater levels of job satisfaction, increase their retention rates and provide psychosocial support in recognition of the fact that female academics are usually coping with care giving responsibilities which create some tension as they try to balance academic and family life (Gibson 2006).

The concept of the *token female* (Chandler 1996; citing Bolton 1980 and Kanter 1977) indicates that females in high positions are reluctant to provide mentoring support to others. In addition, the lack of senior women both at the full professor and administrative levels, according to Cullen and Luna (1993), meant that these token women experienced time restrictions which prevented them from providing adequate mentor support to their protégés. The role of mentoring for these senior women was further complicated by the "added responsibility of home and children. Primary caretaking roles confined women's mentoring activities" (Cullen and Luna 1993, 8). It is for these reasons that in many fields focus has been given to mentoring for academic women. Given the role that mentoring—in the affirmative—has played in the socialization of humankind from birth and throughout our schooling and working lives, it is not surprising that it's potential for improving the working lives of women in academia is seen as one way in which productivity and success in higher education can become more gender balanced.

There are a number of benefits that writers have identified in common with Quinn (2012) and captured in summary form. Drawing from research emanating out of the United States and Australia, he noted that the mentors, mentees and the higher education institutions all benefit from mentoring. The benefits for mentees are summarized:

- Career advancement, including a higher rate of promotion
- Increased opportunities and likelihood of staying at the institution
- Higher salaries
- Increased productivity and better time management
- Greater success in achieving external research grants
- Personal and professional development, including increased job related well-being, self-esteem and confidence and better work-life balance
- Preparation for the future and heightened career aspirations
- Developed networking skills (5).

As mentoring is a reciprocal process, it also entails some benefits for the mentors. In the act of providing guidance for their mentees, mentors tend to reflect on their own work and gain insights from the process itself. As such mentors are likely to experience professional growth as well. Quinn (2012) identifies career rejuvenation, increased confidence and personal fulfilment especially in seeing their mentee progress as benefits experienced by mentors.

THE RESEARCH PARTICIPANTS AND CONTEXT

This research was conducted with two women academics teaching in their second year in a higher education institution in Jamaica, subsequently referred to as *the university*. Both female were selected using the criterion sampling procedures, a type of purposive sampling. This sampling procedure is used in qualitative inquiry by researchers to select participants who satisfy certain criteria for inclusion in a research. The participants satisfied two main criteria: one relating to their gender in being female academics, the other to their status as early career academics, both in their second year of employment at the university.

Both female academics are qualified at the doctoral level in similar disciplinary areas but teach in different contexts: one in an academic department, the other in a professional education school. Both units are part of a larger faculty which consists of several departments which offer programmes in the humanities and education. The women, while novices to the academe, are both highly qualified in their respective fields but differ in terms of their experiences of teaching. One, named in this research as Thelma, worked across all the educational levels, accumulating twenty-two years of teaching experience in the process. The second, given the pseudonym Lenora, had accumulated three years of teaching experience before arriving at the academe though she also worked as a research assistant and spent one year in the private sector before entering higher education as a teacher educator.

Interestingly, both Thelma and Lenora worked at the same teacher education institution, Gabriel College (pseudonym), but in different departments before entering the university in the same academic year. One marked difference in the contractual employment, however, was that Thelma received a full-time three-year contract while Lenora was employed in a temporary position for one academic year in the first instance. She was subsequently employed on a full-time contractual basis at the end of her first year.

Profile of Thelma

Thelma is a full-time lecturer in a small department within the humanities and teaches in both the undergraduate and post-graduate programmes. Thelma has a PhD and a Master's degree in the field in which she currently lectures and is a professional teacher with a teaching diploma from one of Jamaica's Teachers Colleges. Thelma has over twenty years of teaching experience, having taught at the primary, secondary and tertiary levels before her entry into the university which is at the apex of the higher education sector. Thelma is married and is the mother of two children, a son and a daughter, both of whom are of school age at the secondary and primary levels, respectively. Thelma's arrival at the university level is for her a dream come true, having indicated to her mother after finishing high school that she wanted to be a teacher and wanted to teach at the university level someday. As Thelma shared, her mother, who was also a teacher, was far from touched by her daughter's decision to teach.

> When I finished high school and my mother said to me what do you want to do? Where you heading now? I had my O'levels and she said 'what must I do with you?' I said I wanted to teach and she said to me "you can't think of anything else?" You know my mother is a teacher [laughing . . .] She say "you going to suffer, you can't think of anything else?" But teaching was in my blood, it in my bone. I ate and breathe teaching. It was just . . . that was all I saw myself doing. And I said no I don't just want to be a teacher, I want to lecture at [the university level]. She said "oh so you planned to get your PhD?" So I said yes, I am gonna push as far up as I can go, and she said "Okay, sixth form

[grades 12 and 13 in Jamaica] don't make any sense for you, you going straight to Teachers' College to get your foundation."

From that conversation with her mother at the end of her high school preparation, it took Thelma over twenty years before she was to realize her dream of teaching at the university level.

Profile of Lenora

Lenora is an assistant lecturer in education with a PhD in her subject area as well as a Master's degree and a Diploma in Education. By the time she arrived at the university in a temporary lectureship position in the first year, she had accumulated three years of teaching experience, spending one year at the primary level after which she pursued her teaching diploma. Her most substantial teaching experience was obtained at Gabriel College on completion of her doctoral studies. She was employed at the College for two years before moving on to the university. In addition to her experience of teaching, Lenora worked as a researcher before pursuing doctoral studies in her area of specialization. Lenora is the mother of one child, a son, and is surrounded by family members who were once members of the university community as well as her spouse who is also a lecturer at the university. Lenora shared that her arrival at the university was a combination of good fortune and a risk at the same time. She was contacted by her former lecturer who needed to find a replacement for her position while she proceeded on leave. The risk factor was that she was on a yearly contract at Gabriel College and was not entitled to a secondment. She would have to resign. As she reasoned in reflecting on this aspect of her job shift she recalled:

> I decided to take the risk and come here. It was a risk in the sense that I was on a yearly contract at Gabriel College so I wouldn't get secondment. I would have to quit my job at Gabriel's and come to the university for a year not knowing what would necessarily happen after. But I decided to risk it because I think I have enough support family wise to do that. Other people don't necessarily have that because my husband works here . . . as well. . . . I decided to go ahead and accept the offer and tendered my resignation at Gabriel College.

DATA COLLECTION: THE NARRATIVE INTERVIEW

The data for the research was collected in three general stages. There was a preliminary exploratory interview with both Thelma and Lenora to explain the nature of the research and to obtain a general overview of their experiences to inform the proposal for this research. The second stage involved the long interviews which were conducted within the same week and lasted for two hours in the main with Thelma, with some degree of small talk before and after her main narrative and for fifty-eight minutes for Lenora, that time representing her main narrative and the preliminaries to remind her of the focus of the research and some information on narrative inquiry.

The narrative interview was the chief data-gathering device used in this research, though elements of the episodic interview (Flick 1997), was also used with Lenora. The narrative interview emerged as an alternative to the semi-structured interview in the quest for a more fulsome rendering of the subjective experiences of informants and as a means of controlling the influence of the researcher in structuring the informant's experience through the use of pre-structured questions. In the narrative interview as Hermanns (1995) outlined,

> the informant is asked to present the history of an area of interest, in which the interviewee participated, in an extempore narrative. . . . The interviewer's task is to make the informant tell the story of the area of interest in question as a consistent story of all relevant events from its beginning to its end. (183; cited in Flick 2009, 177)

The third stage of the data-gathering process involved the use of the episodic interview which enables the interviewer to "recurrently ask the interviewee to present narratives of situations" (Flick 2009, 186). This entails the use of an interview guide in order to focus the narrative on specific experiences.

DATA ANALYSIS

The analysis took place in a number of stages starting with the transcription of the data. Reading through the transcripts provided the opportunity to identify the themes that emerged from both narratives. Though I could have simply used the margins of the transcripts to write out the themes or ideas as I read through and highlighted specific segments of the text, I opted to adhere to the suggestion for analyzing narrative data provided by Jovchelovitch and Bauer (2000) based on the steps suggested by Schütze (1977; 1983). He identified six steps for analyzing narratives which includes transcription, separating the texts into indexical and non-indexical material, the former referring to texts which gives precise information, in terms of who, what, when, and why, while the latter refers to the passing of values, judgments, and justifications (Jovchelovitch and Bauer 2000).

The third step involves the ordering of the indexical statements into what Schütze refers to as trajectories while the fourth steps examines the non-indexical statements which are compared with operative theories and which represents the self-understanding of the informants. The fifth and sixth steps combined entails the clustering of and comparison between individual trajectories and is in essence what other writers on qualitative research generally refer to as the clustering of data into categories. The final step allows for the discernment of similarities between individual trajectories allowing for the recognition of collective trajectories. Based on the foregoing, but also based on the general procedures for unearthing themes inductively from the data, the analysis resulted two categories with themes:

- *Category 1:* Work experience before entry into higher education
  - *Themes:*
    - Thelma's journey into higher education
    - Lenora's stint in college teaching
- *Category 2:* Narrative of experience within the academe
  - *Themes:*
    - Orientation into the university and 'culture shock'
    - Thrown into the deep
    - Balancing family life and academia
    - The travails of publishing
    - Navigating the work culture at the department level

ETHICAL CONSIDERATIONS

The two female academics were selected on the principles of purposive sampling. That is, they satisfied the basic criteria for inclusion in this research, the gender-specific criterion of being female academics and the employment-status criterion of being junior faculty members both in their second year of employment within a higher education institution. The focus of the research is the extent to which they have benefitted or not from mentoring whether formal or informal and how the provision or lack of this vital form of institutional support has influenced their settling down into the rigours of life in the academe.

The participants are members of the same faculty within which I am also a staff member and are therefore my colleagues. I was privy to their status as junior faculty members because Thelma is a longstanding colleague and friend from our days as teachers in the same high school. We left that institution at different times and pursued our teaching careers at the college and university levels, respectively, before becoming colleagues again when she became a new faculty member at the university in 2012. Lenora, on the other hand, joined the staff of the university as a teacher educator in the same professional school of the faculty in which I am also a staff member. Teaching in different disciplinary fields did not provide much basis for us to work closely, but the practicum component of our teacher education programme provide the context for much inter-action. When I explained the nature of the research to her she expressed her own interest in narrative inquiry and graciously consented to partici-pate.

The ethical issues that I had to consider are not unlike those to be taken into consideration when conducting research of any kind. These issues loomed larger as I began the transcription of the recorded narra-tive data, but more so as I began the second phase of the analysis, in searching for themes or identifying individual trajectories in line with Schütze's terminology. There were two main issues/questions with which I had to grapple. The first was how could I invoke the principle of ano-nymity without making the institutions and participants too opaque, thereby rendering the work mythical? And, what 'violence' would I do to the narrative in view of the editorial work that had to be done to remove obvious identifiers? These identifiers included the disciplinary areas in which the participants teach and some specific incidents which character-ized the uniqueness of their 'induction' at the departmental levels.

In view of the above concerns, it became clear that some aspects of the narratives had to be suppressed in order to protect the identities of the participants as far as possible. At the same time, there was the concern to provide as faithful a representation as possible, even as I had to reorder the chronology of their narratives and leave out specific details. There was the need in other words, to re-present the stories with an ethic of care. Having done other qualitative-type research before, my engage-ment in narrative inquiry felt more confining in that more editorializing had to be done than in previous work, not so much to make the stories intelligible (for example deleting repetitions, some crutch words and contractions, false starts and recants) but largely to protect the identities of my participants. I drew inspiration then from Josselson's (2007) posi-tion about adopting an ethical attitude towards narrative research.

This attitude as she explained is essentially "a stance that involves thinking through . . . and deciding how best to honor and protect those who participate in one's studies while still maintaining standards for responsible scholarship" (2007, 538). Josselson also pointed to the ethical dilemmas which face narrative inquirers and which resonated with my own experience. She noted, "Ethics in narrative research . . . is not a matter of abstractly correct behaviour but of responsibility in human rela-tionship" (2007, 538). She stated in addition that

> The essence of the ethical conundrum in narrative research derives from the fact that the narrative researcher is in a dual role—in an inti-mate relationship with the participant (normally initiated by the re-searcher) and in a professionally responsible role in the scholarly com-munity. Interpersonal ethics demand responsibility to the dignity, pri-vacy, and well-being of those who are studied, and these often conflict

with the scholarly obligation to accuracy, authenticity, and interpretation. (Josselson 2007, 538)

Bloom's (2002) advice is handy in addressing if not resolving this 'ethical conundrum.' She suggests that novice researchers though it is just as applicable to the experienced ones, should "maintain humility and be ethically responsive to the research." More useful is her advice that:

> While qualitative researchers have general guidelines for ethical conduct, it is still the responsibility of each researcher to be continually aware of specific ethical problems that arise in each project and to respond not simply in ethical ways but in ethically situated ways. (Bloom 2002, 313)

NARRATIVE OF WORK EXPERIENCES BEFORE ENTRY INTO HIGHER EDUCATION

Thelma's Journey into Higher Education

Thelma's entry into higher education is a journey dotted with serendipitous moments. Her career moves, as she pointed out, were all well scripted and led her to the point which she had earlier in her life hoped to arrive. The experience of teaching at the College level seemed to have prepared her somewhat for the university, or so she thought. Having worked at Gabriel College (pseudonym) for nearly thirteen years in an environment where there was much camaraderie and warmth, she experienced a "culture shock" when she arrived in the academe. As Thelma recalled:

> In September of 1999, I started working at Gabriel College as a lecturer . . . which meant that I would have been would be lecturing and helping to run the library at the same time. I ended up in a department with only women. . . . I was a little apprehensive but I found the women took me in very readily and the head of department was very happy to have a "young bud" with my Master's in. . . . She didn't actually do her Master's [but] did a post-graduate diploma in it so she was happy to have me. . . . I found that she leaned a lot on me, a whole heap and I didn't mind it because it helped me. She took me to meetings with her even as a young member of staff. She exposed me at the administrative level to a lot of things which helped me later when I became head of department to function without even hitching because I knew exactly what to do and I had made the links already with senior members of staff. I had gained their respect and everything because of her response to my having come. I found that in general members of staff were very friendly, very warm, very welcoming. They would pass you on the corridor just knowing that you were a new member of staff they would stop and say is everything okay? What can I do to help? Have you done so and so yet? Did you do so and so? You need to talk

to so and so remember to talk to so and so about whatever whatever and that is the kind of experience I had; very loving, very warm, so the level of camaraderie at that place was just top of the line.

Thelma went on to share how that type of "induction" into the teaching staff at Gabriel College helped her to demonstrate a similar type of behaviour with new staff members recounting a specific experience of how she helped a new member of her department:

When I became head of department, and even before I became head of department but was a senior lecturer, I found that when new members of staff came in I was very, very welcoming, very warm. I went out of my way to help them. When I became head of department, I took on another member of staff, who to this day will tell you, will sing my praises, she came on without owning a car. Now you know that we had to go on teaching practice all over Kingston and St. Andrew and the outskirts and she was coming from a primary school with her Master's in. . . . She didn't own a car, she didn't have a driver's licence, she didn't have anything like that just her qualifications and I say to her no this isn't going to work you know and she said, I will take the bus and taxi man but I said no this isn't going to work and I took her with me I say you have to get you licence, and she am she say but I don't even know anything about. I walked her through the ropes, got her into a driving school, everything she got the driver's licence and I said so what about the car now, she say but the car, but I can't buy a car, no man, you not a credit union member or anything like that she say no she was a member of a Friendly Society so I say but they will help you to buy a car and I took her in my car up to the Friendly Society and I went with her and I said to them this young lady needs to buy a car, she has an account with you how can you help her? They worked with her and two twos she had her motor vehicle and when she got that car I remember the first day [laughing] she was terrified, she say she couldn't drive the car she was nervous and I drove behind her and said you follow back of me. I took her downtown where I knew there wouldn't be a lot of traffic and she drove behind me, I drove slowly the whole way and when I got her to a point caused she lived all the way in Spanish Town . . . and I said, when we got to a point, I drove her part of the way and I toot, I blew her and I said you can make it now, she went home she speaks about it everyday.

In concluding this aspect of her experience at Gabriel College, Thelma noted:

My response to her and to everyone who subsequently joined my staff was as a result of what happened when I went in. The tone was set for me and I saw that was happening around me generally speaking. I then became the librarian of the institution and I had thirteen members of staff working with me I took the same kind of approach . . . if I had a problem with anyone I would invite them into my office, close the door and have a closed-door meeting and we would be smiling coming out, no one would even know that there was a problem because that is how I saw them deal with other people; high level of professionalism and very good mentoring took place at that place. I am not saying it was a utopia, there were things that were not, you know, necessarily the way I would want, but in terms of mentoring, I believe, you know I learnt a lot there.

Lenora's Stint at College Teaching

Lenora commenced working at Gabriel College in 2010 and remained there until 2012. In describing her general experience at this tertiary-level teacher education institution, Lenora remarked on her informal orientation to the department of which she became a member, indicating that she had missed the formal orientation, having begun working immediately after the academic year had begun. In essence much of her informal orientation came at the hand of a member of the department who was herself a formed student of that institution. She knew 'the ropes' and enlightened Lenora as far as she could. Her head of department (HOD) also contributed to her understanding of her work context:

> Even though . . . I missed the formal orientation. I had the benefit of sharing an office with someone who was a past student [of the institution] and even though she was new she was able to help me through the ropes. . . . The difference with Gabriel's is that you had the leadership structure, you had a specific head of department I had . . . I worked with people who were within my age group so I felt a little more confident asking them questions. Our HOD had a very motherly and pastoral approach. The benefit of that is that I felt that she shielded us from some of the politics and she took that on herself. . . . At Gabriel's because the structure of the department was different . . . because we have a head of department, we knew exactly who to go to. Here [at the university] we have clusters . . . you not sure who is the head, who is responsible for what and the cluster changes because people have gone on leave. I don't know if it is a yearly thing, if it rotates, I don't know. Whereas at Gabriel's there was one person you know who go to, there was one administrative person who you know you go to for certain things.

Lenora drew some comparison between Gabriel College and the university which had different departmental organization or leadership structures. The chain of command or reporting relationships were more direct and seemingly personal than in her department at the university where the leadership structure, though more horizontally layered or not steeply hierarchical theoretically, is in practical terms more distant and diffused. Lenora also commented on the feeling of acceptance that she experienced at Gabriel College as a new member of staff especially in view of the fact that she was also an expectant mother:

The other benefit for me personally, they actually hired me at Gabriel's while I was pregnant and as I said the HOD, Mrs. Nelson was very motherly so she welcomed the fact that I was pregnant, and was very excited for me and I didn't get the feeling that I was going to be a bother and oh they going to have to find somebody to replace me, it was not a problem for her

NARRATIVES OF EXPERIENCE WITHIN THE ACADEME: COMMON ISSUES, UNIQUE EXPERIENCES

Thelma

Orientation into the University and "Culture Shock"

In narrating her experiences of the formal orientation she received to the university Thelma spoke of the generally informative nature of the orientation sessions that were held in the week prior to the commencement of her first year of teaching. In her summing up of the experience however, she concluded that the sessions were too frontloaded:

The orientation session for us, I think it lasted for a week. . . . I found it to be informative; to tell you the truth, although a lot of it was going over my head because I hadn't started working yet so I couldn't relate a lot of what I was hearing to the actual experience and by the time I started having the experience I forgot half of what I had heard. . . . Although it was informative the link that needed to have been made . . . was not made because it was given to me too early and in too huge a dose, the dosage was just . . . so one week and you stuck everything down my throat and expect that I am going to remember all of these things . . . in order to place them at the right point when I encounter that situation . . . so they are well intentioned and I appreciated what they did but you know much of it just went over my head, much of it. The only good thing that that did for me was to present persons who I could identify with as being new and "fool fool like myself," so I could put faces to inexperience so when I saw them on campus it is as though we had formed our own little survival group . . . so that one week helped us to be able to identify each other. . . . I haven't seen most of them for quite a while I guess they are as buried under the work as I am. Graduation we might see each other and stuff, but yeah that's basically how it was coming in.

The orientation sessions constituted the main programme of formal induction into the university. Other aspects of workplace socialization were largely informal and resulted in some culture shock for Thelma. Her description of her general experience of "induction" into the university culture left little doubt that the experience did not compare favourably with her experience at Gabriel College. She voiced that the culture at the university left her feeling isolated:

When I reached here it was like a culture shock. Having spent thirteen years at that institution and getting used to that way of doing things I couldn't handle the fact that members of staff would pass me on the corridor and look straight through me, no good morning, no smile, no nothing at all. And for a while that is what was happening until one and two would start to say, good morning, mutter a good morning and pass you and that kind of thing. Ahm I found it a little ah-ah-ah— what's the word, I am struggling to find the correct word, but it was off putting somewhat. Ahm then I found in my mind, I summed up the university as being a lonely place. I felt isolated, although I belong to a department but I am talking about the general response to my presence, I felt almost invisible, in the faculty for a while, ahm albeit that has changed somewhat now that people have become familiar with my face, people, will, most people, cause there are some people who look through me, but most people will pass and smile and say 'good morning', there are couple people on my block who, who will make an effort to say is everything okay, but it took a while for us to get there, you know.

Thrown into the Deep

Acclimating to the culture of the university as a whole was challenging in itself. At the departmental level, Thelma found that there were a number of expectations that she had to meet with very little formal guidance. She found solace, however, in the informal support and mentoring she received from one female staff member:

on a departmental level, I found that there were a number of things that I was expected to do that I got little or no instruction about, little or no heads up so I was just thrown into the deep. Ahm, "I am going to ask you to represent us on XYZ committee [laughing . . . she names the specific committee on which she was told she would represent the department]." I was told that I was supposed to represent the department on this committee. I don't have a clue what is [the committee] now, I don't know if I going look stupid by asking. . . . I don't know what the committee is, if it is not explained to me. I figure it is something I should know. So I don't want to look like a dummy asking what is [the committee] and then I hear "you don't know that?" So I just went and asked somebody else who was comfortable with being vulnerable before. I asked that person what it was, the person [told me the specific task of the committee]. I said okay, "so what's that?" [laughing] The person said, they meet once per month . . . she wasn't sure what to expect.

Not knowing what the committee was all about despite having being told by her colleague the specific task of that committee, Thelma was unprepared for the discussion that took place at the first meeting she attended on behalf of department. She described how she felt at that meeting:

I felt like a square peg in a round hole. I sat there and I was just totally [laughing], I felt stupid to tell you the truth, I was watching my watch and dying for the meeting to end, I felt uncomfortable.

Lenora

Arrival in the Academe: "Weighing the Risk against the Benefits"

Lenora's foray into university teaching came as I noted earlier, when she was asked to teach for her former lecturer during that lecturer's leave of absence for the academic year. As Lenora puts it, taking the job was a risk but one that she decided to take given the many benefits which she knew came with teaching at the university level in addition to the support structure she had in place. Nevertheless, leaving Gabriel College was 'bittersweet' for Lenora for though she was looking forward to the employee benefits she knew were offered at the university by virtue of her husband being a member of staff there, she was obviously attached to her working environment at the college. For as she noted, "the department at Gabriel's was pretty tight. I had good experiences with my other colleagues . . . yeah, I had good experiences and I had a good office mate that we worked very well together."

Though Lenora was looking forward to her new teaching assignment she also thought it would be a bit intimidating for as she mused "I was going to be teaching alongside persons who had taught me, ahm, so I felt quite intimidated by that fact." After two academic years at Gabriel College Lenora made the transition into higher education feeling that she had the basic preparation in her educational achievements and teaching experience, although limited, to take on the teaching assignments that would come her way.

Sources of Support in Transitioning into University Teaching

Lenora acknowledged that she was fortunate to have a support system in place as she transitioned into the university. She felt that she received sufficient support from her former lecturer to get her started in terms of the necessary instructional resources to facilitate her preparation for teaching.

What was good is that Megan [pseudonym for former lecturer] called me in before the start of the term and she went through the two courses that I was going to teach for her. . . . Megan went through . . . [materials available on the online delivery system] for me. . . . The two containers were pretty substantial, they had the PowerPoints, the lecture notes and so on, so that made the transition much, much easier for me. . . . I still felt overwhelmed because I think the depths of the contents that we provide here is deeper than say at Gabriel. For example here . . . we teach a lot more here through journal articles; at Gabriel they are trying to get to that point but they use more or less set texts. . . . So I was mentored formally in a sense through Megan and she has been a really, a good source of support for me. Nevertheless even though the course containers were, ahm had a lot of information, and my dissertation, the readings for my dissertation overlapped with the readings for one particular course. . . .

It took me nine hours of preparation because you know I am a beginning teacher and you know you want to be very well prepared so that in case students shoot a question you are able to answer . . . so I had the burden of preparation but I had the fortunes of my husband who had taught here at [the university] for two years I think by the time I started teaching here and so I kind of knew beforehand that I would have a lot of preparatory work, to make myself comfortable with the content and confidence especially as a novice teacher.

From all accounts, Lenora's early experiences of teaching at the university were just as hectic but not as "bumpy" it seems as was Thelma's. A similar trend is also obvious in the balancing act that both female academics had to work out with respect to family and work life.

Balancing Family Life and Academia

Thelma's Dilemma

Both Thelma and Lenora experienced in common the challenge involved in balancing family and work life as female academics. The issue, though common to both, was experienced in ways unique to their circumstances.

Thelma believed that her family is suffering because of the demands of her job. She confides that she has experienced a reduction in the quality time she gives to her family members.

I believe in family. I believe that family is very very important, I feel that I am short-changing my children and my husband. When I was at the other institution, I had a lot more time for family, ahm nobody was pressuring me, nobody was watching my time ahm, and so I, I had objectives that had to be met within a given time and I had my time to meet those objectives. What they wanted to know was that those objectives were met, they didn't care whether you were there from 8:00 the morning till 10:00 the night. Nobody really . . . you know . . . and I suspect that that is how it should be here, but it's not for me, let's leave it at that. Ahm and, I know that . . . nobody is telling you that you cant. There is the unwritten, the unsaid code and the unwritten code that you have to be able to listen to, you understand me?

. . . my family is suffering as a result of my having changed jobs. I have a son who is in third form . . . he is not intrinsically motivated. He needs to have you at him whatever. My son is not intrinsically motivated. . . . He is one of those children where you have to practically stand up in him back to get the work out of him. . . . When I finish lecturing [at] 8:00 clock sometimes, when I get home, he is watching TV, he is on his tablet, he is doing whatever, he does no homework, he does nothing. I feel guilty cause I am not there to ensure that these things [are done.] By the time I get home I am so tired I can barely do anything, I want to sleep; I head straight for my bed. My daughter is seven, she is in grade two . . . she is interested in her work, she is on the honour roll . . . but you still have to give her attention too. My husband has been asking me where is his wife . . . all of a sudden I am just another human being in the household. The university consumes my every second, my weekends, everytime!

Thelma recalled one of the seasonal holidays that is celebrated in Jamaica—Easter Monday—that her husband wanted to take the children to the beach. Thelma had hoped to use that day to complete the marking of some scripts. She told me how she arrived at a compromise.

Easter holiday . . . the Monday, my husband said, let's take the kids to the beach, now the coursework needed to be marked and I saw the holiday now as the period during which I was going to mark the coursework. He said no man we need to take them, we don't carry them anywhere and it's the perfect opportunity. You know what my compromise was? I took the work with me, to Fort Clarence beach and while my husband and the children were splashing about in the water, I was sitting on the beach in my jeans and T-shirts, watching the bags and towels . . . and marking like crazy. Now I felt very badly about it, but I couldn't do any better because I could not come back here the Tuesday morning without those papers graded, they had to be done and even when we got home . . . when we were on our way home, I said to him we have to buy dinner because I can't go home to cook, I had to finish this and my helper was off, you understand me? So it's like . . . I understand what he was saying, I am . . . the person who use to splash in the water with them, throwing ball and whatever I saw that as wasting time when I have my work to do and that kind of thing. It felt, it made me feel badly, but I just did not see myself doing any better than that, and ahm, so I find that my family life is suffering as a result but what, what, I don't understand is when I look around me at the other lecturers they don't look as stressed as I am, I am saying to myself what is it that I am.. is it the newness, is it that after a while it gets easier, why is it I am feeling so overwhelmed and so burdened down? Why can't I catch my breath?

At this point Thelma shared that the feeling of being overwhelmed has led her to consider "packing it in" on a number of occasions.

Several times I have come to the point where I say I am going to resign and go home, go sit down. Several times because my sanity is worth more than the job you know, it is very frustrating and I keep saying work is not suppose to feel like this, it's not suppose to feel like this, I am totally overwhelmed; I have never worked in a situation like this before, never in my life. You are supposed to be able to breathe when you are working, you are supposed to breathe, there is supposed to be a be a moment when you, you relax, you put back you back, you sit back in your chair and relax, I have not been able to do that for the two years since I have been here. I don't know when I have caught a breath, I don't know don't . . . I don't remember how it's done, you just going, going, going, the minute you jump a hurdle, ten more hurdles present themselves in front of you and higher hurdles than the ones you jumped. You just keep . . . it's like a constant . . . and you saying to yourself what on earth I have found myself in you know, it's crazy, crazy, crazy, Dian, it's absolutely crazy.

I love what I do, I am an educator, I am an educator. I am dedicated to the task of educating. I love my job but there is something about this particular job that I don't know, it is just absolutely overwhelming, I can't find another word to explain it. It is absolutely overwhelming and my family is suffering and I am afraid to speak of my family because I don't want people to think that . . . because of family I am not right for the job because ahm you know, family is going to get in the way of my performance . . . sometimes I feel like I am being tugged in many different directions; my husband tugging me there, my children tugging me there, my mother and father tugging me there, the university tugging me and the university seems to be always winning . . . you know. Me just feel like one day me husband will get frustrated and pack up him things and go 'bout him business . . . [laughs out loud].

Thelma's views on the effect of her academic life on her family life highlights the differences in the circumstances of herself and Lenora. Though Lenora also has a small family, that fact alone made a difference to how she experienced academic life. In addition, her spouse was also an academic. This too could have explained the comparative difference in how she experienced the tension between family and academic life.

Lenora's Luck

Having a husband in academia is very helpful, he understands completely what I have to do . . . both of us are in the same boat. He knows when I say, boy I need to write this paper, I need to stay up and so and so, he knows, he doesn't think about it, oh, teaching has ended you should have more time because he knows that even though teaching has ended you still have papers to mark, research to conduct, administrative things to do. So it helps to have a husband in academia and then because of that there are some little things for example he helps me with my mark sheet. Initially if I didn't have his help I would be clueless but he showed me and its funny afterwards now when they realise that the marks sheets were looking differently they had a workshop and I went to that workshop but it makes a big difference.

On another note with respect to the work-family life balance, Lenora related that while she felt a sense of unity between the work/family life spheres and support for her role as a mother at Gabriel College she did not experience that same feeling of care for the personal side of life at the university. She stated voiced in this regard that

> At the university, I didn't necessarily feel that I have that support, in a sense, it is more as if your personal life must be put aside and your professional life comes first and foremost. And . . . if it was only the demand of teaching and administration, but the demands of writing and research and how much they have been pushing us . . . makes it overwhelming and if you not careful . . . I for myself have made Saturday the day with my son and I just focus on him, for if I am not careful I would do work seven days a week just to fulfill the kind of mantra of research and whatever that is here.

While Lenora recognized the demands of the university with respect to the workload and the research culture that exists, she was aware that her temporary status in the first year shielded her somewhat from the pressure of research. On the question of feeling the pressure to research she acknowledged that "nobody expected me to research because I was just substituting . . . but in the second year now I got a renewed contract for two years [and] the pressure was definitely on. I felt it."

Both female academics had similar perspectives on the demands of university life on their family lives and have responded in their own way largely due to their circumstances. Thelma's husband has a career outside academia, and while he is not personally and experientially privy to the demands of life within the academy, he is vicariously engaged in the demands of university life. In a sense, Thelma has yet to find a way to feel that she has established some balance in both spheres because she still experiences the feeling of being overwhelmed and not having sufficient time for family members. Lenora is perhaps luckier than most female academics as her husband, also an academic, can relate personally to the demands of academia. She has also made a conscious decision to carve out time for her son. With respect to other aspects of their induction into university teaching they both had experiences which they singled out as particularly challenging for them. For Thelma it was her experiences of meeting the demands of research and publication while for Lenora the challenge was specific to the working and administrative culture of her department.

Unique Experiences in the Academe

Thelma: The Travails of Publication

> [On] the whole issue of publication heh woiee [laughing]. Now, I am coming from an environment where publication was not emphasized, the way it is emphasized at the university ahm we were encouraged to publish but it was just in words nobody really harassed you or had

anything much to, you know, nobody never ask me about publication to tell you the truth you know . . . but anyway, ahm when I came to the university . . . I knew I came in with a handicap because I had not published, but the publication thing, somehow started to feel like some kind of rope being pulled tight around my neck almost as if I was being hung from a tree that is the . . . I have started to have palpitation every time I think about publication I am having palpitation. . . .

When I just came in all I heard was you need to publish . . . and if you don't publish they not going to renew your contract. . . . I appreciate it, I understand, I am not a fool; if I want to hold my job, I have to publish . . . I don't have a problem with being reminded about it, because that is what drive you sometime, but the way you are reminded is almost as if you are being pounded with a beating stick and what frustrate me is that you trying. I sent out two articles now I didn't understand how hard it was . . . to "bruck you ducks" according to Jamaican people, to get your first work out there. I didn't understand it, so I did two articles, one, was a position paper and the another one was something I pulled from my PhD research paper. I sent them out, one of them came back with one long list of things that I was supposed to do, changes I should have made and the deadline I got was absolutely ridiculous. I couldn't do all of that given my workload within the period of time I was given for them to publish it so I gave up on that. I didn't understand that I could have asked for extension and it was long after that . . . I am hearing you should just ask them. . . . The second one, up to this day I have not heard a word from them. Not a word, so I have thrown that outside the door. I was very discouraged.

It was at this point in recalling how discouraged she became when her first article was returned with the editorial comments and which she was unable to resubmit given the time constraints that she recounted the assistance and advice that she received from a colleague in the department with respect to another article which she eventually succeeded in getting published.

One member of staff had been holding my hand through this research process, she has really been a tower of strength to me. . . . The other influences outside of that have been so strong and negative, that if it was not for her, I would probably have just handed in my resignation and gone home to sit down. It's been that stressful and I finally did a research paper when I finished it she said to me who is your editor? I said what? She said "you need to get an editor, somebody to go through it for you" . . . "I am going to put you on to who I use." She did that for me [and] the young lady checked it everything, the style that they asked for [because] I haven't even heard of it before in my life. She did her research, she put in the references in the style, in text citation, everything, she fixed it up for me, tidied it up nicely, sent it back to me and I did my finishing touches and send it off to one of the biggest [named the disciplinary field] journal . . . out of Britain and . . . they accepted it. . . . That was when I got confidence and I said to myself, "but you can do this, you can do this girl." So that is where I started feeling now all is not lost.

In addition, to her feeling that she would have given up but for the support she obtained from her colleague, Thelma also gushed at the feeling of belonging she experienced when a senior academic at the level of the professoriate, took the time to ask her about her progress and to give her some words of encouragement. In sharing this experience she recounted:

> somebody else, in very very high position saw me just about the time I was struggling to finish the research paper. He saw me along the corridor and he said "what's going on? How are things with your research?" That was just before I sent it off and I told him what the situation was and that I had sent off two and . . . I am about to send off another. He said "don't give up." He does not know how I appreciated that talk and you know it shocked me because I didn't expect that he would stop and talk to a pleb like me. I mean . . . his attitude was so different from what I was getting from other quarters that I said you know if he could talk to me like that, then maybe all isn't lost. You can imagine how I felt when I realize that [the journal] had accepted my research. I went straight to him and I said "thank you so much" . . . and he was genuinely happy for me . . . he said "you have made my day so go after the next one" . . . I appreciated it so there are people who now that they becoming familiar with me have really been taking me in and trying to you know walk with me along the way but when I just came here, it was such a lonely, lonely . . . it was lonely. I . . . just locked up inside my office, I just locked up, locked away myself so the only time you would see me was when I am going to classes or going for lunch. You know but ahm yah, it's been two years and I think I am beginning to find my feet.

Lenora: Navigating the Working Culture at the Departmental Level

For Lenora, her experience in the university were integrally related to the structure of the department in which she worked and the nature of her contractual arrangement in the first year. Unlike Thelma who began working on a three-year contract and which therefore mean she would have been expected to teach, research and publish among other requirements for full-time academic staff, Lenora began teaching at the university on a temporary one-year contract. She was therefore not faced with the same pressure for publication and research in the same way as Thelma. Her first year therefore saw her trying to navigate the teaching culture in her department especially as it related to understanding the administrative structure and how the practicum, a key aspect of her job, operated. Lenora found herself making a lot of comparisons between her former job and the new one at the university.

At Gabriel College . . . the structure of the department was different. First of all we had a head of department, and Mrs. Nelson has a very motherly, pastoral persona . . . and because we have a head of department we knew exactly who to go to. Here [at the university] we have [disciplinary based teaching groups headed by a coordinator] . . . you not sure who is the head, who is responsible for what and the [teaching groups] change because people have gone on leave. I don't know if it is a yearly thing, if it rotates, I don't know. Whereas at Gabriel College there was one administrative person who you know you go to for certain things. I know it was smaller. . . .

The difference with Gabriel College is that you had the leadership structure, you had a specific head of department . . . I worked with people who were within my age group so I felt a little more confident asking them questions. Our HOD had a very motherly and pastoral approach. The benefit of that is that I felt that she shielded us from some of the politics and she took that on herself.

Because of the [teaching groups] and many people not understanding how [they] work, I think you don't necessarily know who to go to, you kind of find out by the way for there is no specific orientation that says "oh Dr X is [responsible for this programme] . . . you just find out by the way." A student comes and asks you a question and you go to [the administrative staff members] . . . and they send you to Dr. X who handles it and eventually you pick up, oh she is the [named position] . . . coordinator or you might see it in the minutes of a meeting. Then in terms of administrative support . . . you don't know what to ask [the administrative staff assigned to your teaching group] to do. Is it okay for me to ask her to photocopy, to go to [photocopying centre] and do that? You don't kind of know the operations and an email sometimes is not sufficient, you do need a formal orientation. So not having a traditional administrative leader — a head of department] is challenging but, as [the overall leader of the unit] says, [the new administrative structure] needs time to work out.

Lenora shifts to speak of her experience in the supervision of the practicum. She had worked in this capacity at Gabriel College and recounts that the experience was different. She felt that the organization of the field experience at the university was not as efficient.

in terms of my experience with the practicum, I think an orientation in terms of — I think they had some orientation but I think I missed it, I think . . . compared to Gabriel College it's a different practicum culture here and it would have been good to have had some more support in terms of how this thing really operate in terms of the expectations of the supervisor. I don't know if that was formally done, I know I did not, I can't remember why but I may have missed it if they had one. . . . I think I could have had more support . . . the practicum at Gabriel College helped me tremendously. . . . If I just came into the university without having gone to Gabriel College, I would have been lost. The two practicum delivery systems . . . are similar, but Gabriel College runs a more efficient process.

While Lenora stated that she could have received some more support in matters to do with administrative student matters, teaching of new courses and in the supervision of the practicum, it was Thelma who provided a fuller discourse on how she felt about her experiences as a new member of staff at the university and issued the call for more support for new staff members. In expressing her views and thus her judgment on how new academics are treated she coined her experience as a "bumpy" one. She was highly critical of the lack of support for her irrespective of the experiences and qualifications with which she entered this new, unfamiliar cultural and working environment. She remarked on the time it took for her to adjust.

> It took a while and I settled in. I caught my rhythm and stuff but I had to learn on my feet, I had to . . . my brain had to be doing overtime. I had to be trying to figure out okay this is this, this is that, okay, alright so next time I must remember that so and so and after a while I found my feet but believe me, it was a bumpy, [chuckling] bumpy landing, where that was concerned and that is the case with a number of other things. I feel that while I am not a student, neither am I a child.
>
> When you come into a new environment there are going to be some things that are cultural as they relate to that environment, so you need, you need some kind of acculturation; somebody needs to walk you through, so yes you have been working in a tertiary institution for thirteen years it does not mean, things are done differently here, so you need somebody, some kind of cushioning, you know, you don't need it in an environment where people are going to mock you and say, you mean say she no know that? You want a situation where you can be vulnerable, you can feel free to be vulnerable to say "Lord have Mercy is wha dat?" . . . you can trust the people not to go and whisper to somebody else to say you want to tell me she come her with PhD and she don't know so and so? You see what I am saying? So because you are afraid of being vulnerable, you don't trust who is in your environment you end up not asking critical questions and it makes settling in much more difficult than it had to be.

On the whole matter of being mentored and supported, Thelma expressed the view that

> I believe to a great extent there is some personality thing has to do with one's ability to mentor. Some people are just naturally giving people, naturally nurturing people and you have other people who are cold and not necessarily accommodating of other people and of their shortcomings . . . they [are] not patient with the people they perceive to be not knowing as much as they do and they don't realise that it is experience that taught them the wisdom and this person is going to get his or her experience as well…you just have to appreciate that about people

and after a while you learn to navigate through the system and navigate through the personalities. You have to interact with and navigate through the workload and navigate through everything. . . . It's really rough.

LEARNING FROM THE NARRATIVES OF LENORA AND THELMA: MENTORING FOR ENHANCED PRODUCTIVITY AND FACULTY JOB SATISFACTION

Thelma and Lenora entered the university with differences in their accumulated teaching experiences, but they shared one common experience in being formerly employed at Gabriel College. Though faculty mentoring is not formally established at Gabriel College, it is evident that a strong culture of informal mentoring and support exists. The literature shows that informal mentoring is more typical in academia than is formal mentoring. In addition, Thelma's experience confirm the view expressed in the literature that mentoring begets mentoring and that those who benefit from such support are more than likely to provide similar support themselves. In addition, the feeling of isolation that Thelma experienced is not uncommon in an organizational setting where no standard form of socialization outside the initial orientation exercise exists to provide support for newcomers. It is likely that Lenora's experience in this regard differed substantially from Thelma's because of the support network that she had.

The fact that both Thelma and Lenora entered their higher education teaching positions on different terms of employment played a not too insignificant role in how they experienced their very first year of teaching at the university level. Of more profound significance is how they both experienced different levels of tension between their work and family lives. This certainly, as the literature shows, is more unique to female academics and no doubt hampers their progress and career advancement within the university. It brings into sharp relief the justification for a support system to cater to female academics.

Thelma's experience of "induction" into higher education is typical enough of the experience of women faculty in other higher education fields especially outside Jamaica where race issues add another layer of complexity. Her experience is not too dissimilar from Lenora, who though teaching within the same faculty, experienced challenges of being new to academe, but challenges which highlighted the vast differences in work culture amongst and between departments of the same institution. Lenora's experiences also underscore the uniqueness of experiences which can make transitioning into new position relatively uncomplicated given the right combination of factors. Not everyone is likely to benefit from such a mix of favourable circumstances. If nothing else, there seems to be a need for some common starting point for new academics which will pave the way for them to begin and advance in their careers while understanding and appreciating the differentials that will exist between and amongst them with respect to paths taken, challenges faced, opportunities presented and destinations reached.

Thelma's success in getting her article accepted for publication after she received some guidance from her colleague and her feeling of satisfaction with that achievement and the talk of assurance to which she referred helped to boost her spirit. It goes without saying that mentoring, whether formal or informal, or other form of collegial support can have a positive effect on staff productivity and job satisfaction.

CONCLUDING THOUGHTS

The experiences depicted here of Thelma and Lenora represent a significant part of the totality of their first two years of teaching within a higher education setting in Jamaica. Their experiences differed very little from beginning teachers in the secondary system in Jamaica or from the experiences of junior female faculty in other higher education institutions outside Jamaica. The single most important policy implication of this research is that formal processes need to be adopted to see to the professional well-being of new members of the academic staff. The mentoring literature provides sufficient insights into why formal mentoring is desirous, how such programmes should be organized and the different formats they can take (group, peer mentoring, mentoring circles alongside traditional format such as the experienced mentor paired with the generally less experienced mentee). The need for new members to understand the culture of the organization is self-evident. It reduces the likelihood that they will be socialized only into the toxic elements of organizational culture usually by informal sources. At the same time the informal processes cannot be ignored and will be strengthened by the formal structures which will complement its existence.

In addition, formal mentoring would establish the protocols to guide mentoring relationships while helping those involved in the process to be mindful of the concerns that new members will have, especially new female academics who will likely have concerns relating to balancing work and family life. For mentoring to become ingrained in the culture of the academy, its development would need to be seen as a central part of the policy imperatives of the administration and given explicit approval and support by the administration. Mentoring must be seen to be valued and taken into consideration during tenure and promotion reviews so that it can be regarded as a worthwhile endeavor by those who will commit themselves to this largely voluntary effort.

As with the main policy implication arising from this study, my main recommendation is that the organizational culture of the university be examined with a view to making it more conducive to mentoring and infused with a culture of support for junior faculty as well as faculty at various stages of their professional career ladder. It seems that there can be no loser in this policy shift as the research output for which the university is already known will only be enhanced. Before a worthwhile mentoring policy can be established and the organizational culture gradually transformed, an institutional audit must first be conducted on a faculty by faculty basis, but done at the various levels—the units, centres, departments, schools—to establish empirically the extent to which gender is a factor in how staff members are mentored and promoted. The questions I still seek to be answered are the following: 1) To what extent does the token woman syndrome exist within the university setting? 2) Real or imaginary, based on the experiences of female academics becoming tenured or moving up the academic ladder, is there a glass ceiling?

REFERENCES

Barlow, M. 2014. "Junior Faculty Mentoring: A Report on the National State of the Art and a Best Practices Document for the University of Colorado." Retrieved from https://facultyaffairs.colorado.edu/a-z.../BestPracticesmentoring.pdf.

Bloom, L. R. 2002. "From Self to Society: Reflections on the Power of Narrative Inquiry." In S. Merriam and associates (eds.), *Qualitative Research in Practice: Examples for Discussion and Analysis*, 310–313. San Francisco, CA: Jossey-Bass.

Chandler, C. 1996. "Mentoring and Women in Academia: Reevaluating the Traditional Model." Retrieved from https://web.mit.edu/cof/12/www/Diversity/MentoringandWomeninAcademia.pdf. doi: 10.2979/NWS.1996.B.

Clandinin, J. D., D. Pushor, and A. Murray Orr. 2007. "Navigating Sites for Narrative Inquiry." *Journal of Teacher Education* 58(2): 21–35. doi: 10.1177/0022487106296218.

Clandinin, D. J., and F. M. Connolley. 2000. *Narrative Inquiry: Experience and Story in Qualitative Research*. San Francisco, CA: Jossey-Bass.

Cullen, D., and G. Luna. 1993. "Women Mentoring in Academe: Addressing the Gender Gap in Higher Education." *Gender & Education* 09540253, 5(2): 1–14. Retrieved from http://web.a.ebscohost.com.rproxy.uwimona.edu.jm/ehost/detail?vid=8&si.

Flick, U. 2009. *An Introduction to Qualitative Research*, 4th edition. SAGE Publications Ltd. Retrieved from https://LIVRO_UWEFLICK-An_Introduction_to_Qualitative_Research.

Flick, U. 1997. *The Episodic Interview: Small Scale Narratives as Approach to Relevant Experiences*. Retrieved from http:/www./lse.ac.uk/methodology/pdf/QualPapers/Flick-espisodic.pdf.

Gibson, S. K. 2006. "Mentoring of Women Faculty: The Role of Organizational Politics and Culture." *Innovative Higher Education* 31(1): 63–79. doi: 10.1007/s10755-0069007-7.

Josselson, R. 2007. "The Ethical Attitude in Narrative Research: Principles and Practicalities." In D. J. Clandinin, *Handbook of Narrative Inquiry*, 537–566. Thousand Oaks, CA: SAGE Publications. doi: http://dx.doi.org/10.4135/9781452226522.

Jovchelovitch, S., and M. Bauer. 2000. *Narrative Interviewing* [online]. London: LSE Research Online. Retrieved from http://eprints.lse.ac.uk/2633.

Leo-Rhynie, E. 2008. *The UWI Glass Ceiling: Splinters, Cracks and Scratches*. Kingston, Jamaica: Centre for Gender and Development Studies, University of the West Indies, Mona.

Lunn, M. 2007. "Women Academicians: Gender and Career Progression." *Jurnal Pendidikan* 32: 77–90. Retrieved from www.ukm.my/jurfpend/journal/vol%2032%202007/.../Jpend32[05].pdf.

Metros, S. E., and C. Yang. 2006. "The Importance of Mentors." In C. Golden (ed.), *Cultivating Careers: Professional Development for Campus IT*. Retrieved from www.educase.edu/cultivating-careers.

Quinlan, K. M. 1999. "Enhancing Mentoring and Networking of Junior Academic Women: What, Why, and How?" *Journal of Higher Education Policy and Management* 21(1): 31–42. Retrieved from http://dx.doi.org/10.1080/1360080990210103.

Quinn, J. 2012. *Mentoring: Progressing Women's Careers in Higher Education*. United Kingdom: Equality Challenge Unit London. http://www..ecu.ac.uk/publications.

Ragins, B. R., and K. E. Kram. 2008. "The Roots and Meaning of Mentoring." In B.R. Ragins and K. E. Krams, *The Handbook of Mentoring at Work: Theory, Research and Practice*. SAGE Publications, Inc. Retrieved from http://www.corwin.com/upm-data/17419_Chapter_1.pdf.

Wunsch, M. A., and L. K. Johnsrud. 1992. "Breaking Barriers: Mentoring Junior Faculty Women for Professional Development and Retention." *To Improve the Academy*. Paper 269. Retrieved from http://digitalcommons.un.edu/podimproveacad/269.

Zellers, D. F., V. M. Howard, and M. A. Barcic. 2008. "Faculty Mentoring Programs: Reenvisioning rather than Reinventing the Wheels." *Review of Educational Research* 78(3): 552–588.

SIX

The Courage to Give, the Courage to Receive

Mentor-Protégé Relations with Women of Color

Lillie Ben

Growing up and being the only girl in the family, everyone was telling me what to do. I'm the youngest in my family with two older brothers. I was born and raised in the Midwest—in Omaha, Nebraska—and I grew up working in my family's restaurant business. Nothing is unusual about this story except that my parents were Koreans who immigrated to America in the late 1940s and bought a restaurant shortly after arriving. It was located in the forest area of Omaha on fourteen acres of land, and I started working there at the age of four. The establishment specialized in Korean and Chinese cuisines and it became a popular five-star restaurant by the 1980s and remained this way throughout the 1990s until it closed around 2000. We initially lived above the restaurant, and our neighbors and the neighborhood kids were few and far between; so mostly, my interactions were with my family. I remember as a child always being told what to do—by my parents, by my two older brothers, even by the restaurant help.

Unlike some people who resent having others telling them what to do, I got used to it. I internalized listening to examples of what and how to do things . . . it grew on me. Later in life, I came to appreciate listening to others who were wiser than me because I realized that their words could help me to cut wasted time and save me from having to experience the frustrations of trial and error. In hindsight, I equate those yesteryears as life's lessons from which I learned and experienced . . . like being an apprentice or a "protégé."

While I had no intentions of running the family business, the family culture disempowered me, and I had no choice but to stay in the family environment longer than most grown children who tend to leave home at early ages to be on their own. While my childhood and young adulthood were harsh, on the upside, the experiences that I gained as a "protégé" provided me with the tools to gain more knowledge and wisdom about people and about business and work ethics, that today, I see my past as priceless . . . it's why I'm so passionate about mentoring.

Fast-forward to the twenty-first century, I've noticed that over the past five or more years, there is a reoccurring theme that seems pervasive especially among professional women/professional women of color: a discerning and yearning for available and qualified mentors to guide the women towards leadership and other value-added roles in their business career.

MENTOR-PROTÉGÉ DESCRIPTION

I begin this section by providing an operational definitions of the mentor and protégé for both the settings in business and academia. According to Hamilton and Hamilton (1990):

> A mentor is an older, more experienced person who seeks to further the development of character and competence in a younger person by guiding the latter in acquiring mastery of progressively more complex skills and tasks in which the mentor is already proficient. The guidance is accomplished through demonstration, instruction, challenge, and encouragement on a more or less regular basis over an extended period of time. In the course of this process, the mentor and young person develop a special bond of mutual commitment. In addition, the young person's relationship to the mentor takes on an emotional character of respect, loyalty, and identification. (358)

In this regard, an "ideal" mentor differentiates from that of a coach or teacher because the latter generally advises through demonstrative "instrumental" skills based on a particular subject matter or domain that is more narrowly focused; whereas a mentor addresses content and concepts with greater breadth and depth while the interactions may also assimilate the teachings of personal development, social competence, and character development through the psychosocial perspective (Haggard, Dougherty, T. W., Turban, and Wilbanks 2011; Lerner and Steinberg 2009).

An "ideal" protégé is described as the youth who focuses on challenging- and goal-directed activities and who [sooner vs. later] comes to appreciate the mentoring relationship as a means through which s/he has the opportunities to master skills, explore outside-the-box thinking, and attain instrumental goals that the youth learns to value as s/he undertakes her/his transformational journey (Allen and Eby 2007; Chun, Litzky, Sosik, Bechtold, and Godshalk 2010). O'Neil and Wrightsman (2001) described the mentor-protégé in academe as:

> A mentor is much more than an academic advisor. The mentor's values idealized norms that can have considerable influence on how mentees see themselves and the profession. Mentees have various emotional responses to their mentors, aberration, awe, fear, and idealization. Experiences with mentors can be impactful and remembered for many years. The mentor's power and influence on the mentee approximates the intensity that parents and children have on each other. (112)

Regardless of the specific mentoring environment (for example, academic or business), an "ideal" interactive relationship must honor the values that underlie reciprocity and respect from/by both parties over the course of their interactions (Allen and Eby 2007; Fletcher and Ragins 2007; Haggard, Dougherty, T. W., Turban, and Wilbanks 2011; Hunt and Michael 1983). The driving force that directs the relational development and gives the mentorship its direction primarily originates from the mentor's perspective as a result of his/her vision and wisdom; whereas the momentum and energy that underlies the dyadic interactions are primarily derived from (for example, energized by and is the foundation of) the protégé as s/he promotes and pulls-through the agenda that is, by necessity, protégé-centric.

GENERALIZED POINTS OF VIEWS ON MENTORING IN ACADEMIA

The low ratio of women to men who are holding upper-level management positions in the academic setting is not drastically different from the gender ratio respectively found in the business setting. The practice of advocating the "good-old-boy networks" or the "boys' club" in academe insures that the majority share of those higher-career-level positions are held by men (Aspan 2013; Franklin 2005; Kalb 2006; Paoline 2003). The "boys' network" makes it difficult for women to advance to the level of career positions that are heavily male-dominated. The outcome of this is coined "the glass ceiling" —an invisible (un-breachable) barrier that limits women from achieving high ranking positions (Cullen and Luna 1993; Franklin 2005; Giscombe and Mattis 2002; Hofmans, Dries, and Pepermans 2008; Paoline 2003). Thus, there is a gender mismatch in academia, such that the numbers and the status indicate that men are primarily positioned at the upper levels of management.

It has been determined that women mentoring women is both immensely practical and highly impactful (Fletcher and Ragins 2007; Turner, Viernes, Gonzalez, and Wood 2008). Studies have also shown that same-gender mentorships are invaluable for women with similar career interests (Burke and McKeen 1990; Eby 2011, Gilbert 1985; McKeen and Bujaki 2007). Women in senior level positions who have the status and the power can enable their female protégés to succeed with all the benefits that an "ideal" mentorship relationship can. Unfortunately, in reality, women experience what is referred to as an "accumulative disadvantage" where over the years, opportunities for women to work with a role model decreases as she climbs the career ladder; whereas this outcome affects men to a lesser degree because men network continuously and together with role models as they climb their career ladder (Adya 2008; Reskin and Bielby 2005; Trauth, Nielsen, and von Hellens 2003; Xia and Kleiner 2001). With the scarcity of women who are positioned at the top-levels of management, the collaborative relationships with other women at the top levels are greatly diminished. Thus, for women in academe, there are limited collaborative relationships and networking opportunities which places them at a disadvantage for securing impactful mentorship relationships (Clark and Corcoran 1986; Kalb 2006; Xia and Kleiner 2001).

No doubt, women protégés could/would benefit from women mentors who are positioned in upper-level management. Unfortunately, in a male-dominated hierarchy, there are fewer women mentorships from women in upper management because of the paucity of women administrators who are positioned at the top. It should be noted, however, that simply having a women mentor who is positioned at the level of a senior executive does not guarantee that her protégé will reach higher levels even with a mentor's glowing recommendation (Cullen and Luna 1993; Lentz and Allen 2009; Tharenou 2005; Tong and Kram 2013).

A concern that limits the quantity of women in positions in upper management is referred to as the "Queen Bee" syndrome—whereby women at the top may not (be able to) support a women's advancement from below (Cullen and Luna 1993). The term, "Queen Bee syndrome" refers to women in senior-level positions who distant and dissociate from and derogate their gender and, as a result, block fellow women employees from similarly ascending the ranks within their organization (Rindfleish 2000; Sheppard and Aquino 2013). Albeit, there is a dearth of research evidence that both support and negate the observations and outcomes. There also exists biases based on the perspectives of what and who are the object and objectives of the observers' study and the segments of industries that support gender discrimination (Derks, Ellemers, van Laar, and de Groot 2011; Sheppard and Aquino 2013). As well, there are double standards that society imposes on women employees who are assumed and expected to support their fellow employees compared to the understanding and acceptance that men employees are expected to compete with their fellow employees (Sheppard and Aquino 2013). Hence, within the context of gender discrimination and the workplace environment, working females versus the working males have conjured the "Queen Bee syndrome." Real or imagined, this phenomenon is more about the consequence of gender discrimination rather than the cause of it (Derks et al. 2011; Rindfleish 2000; Sheppard and Aquino 2013) and the results of this syndrome "make it more likely that low identified women turn against their own group" (Derks et al. 2011, 533).

Research studies that have focused on "interpersonal styles" have shown disparaging acceptance of character between the male faculty and the female faculty/female faculty of color (Shollen, Bland, Taylor, Weber-Main, and Mulcahy 2008). Faculty women/faculty women of color may be viewed with double standards of characterization. For example, white men faculty who spoke boisterously and with a firm delegation were viewed as "authoritative" and as "leaders"; whereas the same behavior expressed by females/females of color were viewed as "bitchy" and "un-feminine" (2008). Also, if a faculty woman/faculty woman of color was perceived as being less likable, there was less likelihood that the woman/woman of color would receive recommendations for a higher salary and special opportunities as compared to her male counterparts (Heilman, Wallen, Fuchs, and Tamkins 2004).

While there is a shortage of tenured women, and especially tenured women of color, these women are also overburdened with committees and advising responsibilities in addition to their involvement with traditional academic activities (Kulis and Miller 1988). Because of their commitments, tenured women/tenured women of color are more limited in their time to volunteer for mentorship positions. Additionally, the stereotype that tenured women/tenured women of color are [seemingly] negatively perceived by others can also raise limitations on women's abilities to participate in group social networks—opportunities that might, otherwise, expose women to further options and opportunities toward their career advancements (Bradley 2000; Wyche and Graves 1992).

MENTORING IN ACADEMIA

Women's opportunities at network building do not afford them the same level of effectiveness that is afforded to men (Bradley 2000; Kemelgor and Etzkowitz 2001). As a consequence, the outcomes negatively impact women in ways that they have greater difficulty establishing research collaborations, securing tenure track faculty positions, and securing grants. And previously stated, faculty women/faculty women of color are usually not invited to participate in social functions and informal communications that would otherwise allow them more opportunities for career advancements (Bradley 2000; Kemelgor and Etzkowitz 2001).

Some faculty women/faculty women of color are positioned as mere academic "tokens" (that is, individuals who are primarily hired to fill gender or race quotas). As a result, "token" women are marginalized as being (perceived as) less qualified when compared to their male European-American counterparts (Wyche and Graves 1992). Even if "token" women were tenured, their image might be perceived as having less status/power and prestige; and with that perception, protégés—especially male prospective protégés—might be reluctant to work with a "token" faculty woman as a prospective mentor because of her (perceived) diminished power/status (Shollen, Bland, Taylor, Weber-Main, and Mulcahy 2008; Wyche and Graves 1992).

Cross-gender, as the name implies, is a mentor-protégé relationship between genders while cross-ethnicity is the relationship between people of different color. Regarding the latter relationship, research findings suggest that some protégés experience discomfort and uncertainty around their interactions due to the lack of knowledge, experiences, values, and behaviors about cultural differences (Shollen, Bland, Taylor, Weber-Main, and Mulcahy 2008; Weisinger and Tarauth 2003). At times, cross-gender and/or cross-cultural communications are sufficiently uncomfortable that the differences can lead to sensitive discussions around issues that ultimately result in a diminished or a dissolution of the dyadic relationship (Weisinger and Tarauth 2003; Shollen, Bland, Taylor, Weber-Main, and Mulcahy 2008).

Based on gender differences and from the protégés' experiences, female student protégés who were cross-gender mentored (that is, female student protégés' who were paired with male faculty mentors) experienced greater focus on career functions regarding structure and directions while also experiencing less focus on psychological functions regarding personal development (Portillo 2007; Weisinger and Tarauth 2003). By contrast, female student protégés who were paired with female faculty mentors/female faculty mentors of color experienced greater focus on psychosocial functions that provided the protégés with greater personal support. It was also reported that student protégés of color required greater psychological support (Weisinger and Tarauth 2003; Portillo 2007). Because female student protégés of color had expressed more need for confidence-building and because so few in reality receive the opportunity to work with female faculty mentors/ female faculty mentors of color, female student protégés of color required more focus on their psychosocial needs than compared to their white male counterparts (Reid and Wilson 1999).

MENTORING IN BUSINESS

In the business setting, there are a number of research reports that positively correlate mentorships with the protégés' productions regarding career satisfaction, higher paid promotion, higher income, overall job satisfaction, increased organizational commitment with colleagues and supervisors, and positive interactions with agents of socialization (Eby 2011; Ghosh, Reio, and Haynes 2012; Kram and Ragins 2007; Wanberg, Kammeyer-Mueller, and Marchese 2006). Douglas and Schoorman (1988) agreed with other generalized studies on mentorship; in their study, the researchers sampled 109 registered nurses and concluded that there was a positive correlation between the protégés' dyadic experiences and the increases in their job performances, career commitments, and interpersonal competence. However, not all research findings reported that mentorships have positive outcomes (Melymuka 2008; Reskin and Bielby 2005; Xia and Kleiner 2001). Cullen and Luna (1990) concluded that though there were advantages with same-gender mentorship programs in that women protégés received greater psychosocial support, the women mentors also revealed having greater intentions to leave their organization than compared to their male counterparts (Cherniss 2007; Chun, Litzky, Sosik, Bechtold, and Godshalk 2010; 1990; Kram 1985).

Research focused on mentorships in business conclude that positive mentoring relationships do enable protégés to gain greater access to senior managers in ways that advances the protégés' career (Blake-Beard, O'Neill, and McGowan 2007; Kram and Ragins 2007; Weinberg and Lankau 2011). The mentorship process encourages bonding through the company's social networking. These networking opportunities, allow protégés are able to build alliances and coalitions with upper-level decision makers while also allowing them to gain greater access to information as a repository of formal communications (Dreher and Ash 1990). However, these social networks appeared to provide greater advantages for male protégés than for their female counterparts (Leck, Orser, and Riding 2009; Lemons and Parziner 2007; Lentz and Allen 2009).

How does a mentorship program impact an organization? Research studies have focused on a specific type of employee behavior referred to as "organizational citizenship behavior" (OCB). The findings reveal a positive correlation between the organization and their protégés (Ghosh, Reio, and Haynes 2012; McManus and Russell 1997). The employees' behaviors depicted performances that were above and beyond their job descriptions along with an overall lowering of employee turnover rate and tardiness (Eisenberger, Karagonlar, Stinglhamber, Neves, Becker, and Gonzalez-Moralex 2010; Gakovic and Tetrick 2003; Zagenczyk, Gibney, Kiewitz, and Restubog 2009). Further findings suggested that mentors became better role models and supportive leaders (Sumner and Niederman 2004; Tharenou 2005; Tong and Kram 2013). Moreover, studies that focused on high-quality mentoring relationships showed a higher positive correlation between protégés and the quality of the protégés' behavior than compared to lower quality mentorship relationships/programs (Donaldson, Ensher, and Grant-Vallone 2000). Thus, the studies suggested that employees—as protégés of mentorship relationships—

showed longer-lasting positive effects among their diverse workforce, a stronger relationship in accepting their organization's goals and values, and a greater willingness to speak more highly about their organization; they were more motivated and involved with their organization, and they displayed greater organizational efficiency and effectiveness (Donaldson, Ensher, and Grant-Vallone 2000; Ghosh, Reio, and Haynes 2012; Tepper and Taylor 2003).

BUSINESS SETTING: WOMEN AND WOMEN OF COLOR IN COMPANIES

As a very broad generalization about businesses and organizations, employees who volunteer as mentors are perceived as having higher company status because they provide extra value-add when compared to the employees who do not volunteer as mentors (Allen, Eby, Poteet, Lentz, and Lima 2004; Collins and Holton 2004; Fletcher and Ragins 2007; Ragins and Scandura 1994). The status ranking was especially true for mentors in upper-management positions. However, as was noted in the academic setting, in the business setting, women's presence in upper-level management positions is sparse . . . consequently; the availability of women mentors at that level is also sparse.

Women mentors/women of color mentors carry higher visibility with greater performance pressures than do their male counterparts (Ragins and Scandura 1994). As a result, the cost/benefits of the mentorship outcomes likely differ between the genders. Inevitably, there are associated higher consequential costs for women mentors/women of color mentors if their protégés perform less than expected (that is, women experience higher consequential costs for their performance than compared to the performance of their white male counterparts). Additionally, the reports indicated that women mentors might avoid mentoring other women to avoid the label of being a "feminist troublemaker" (Ragins and Scandura 1994). Additionally, studies on same-gender and cross-gender mentorship programs for women in management positions reported that women mentors attained less organizational power, status, and influence than their male counterparts. The findings suggested that the outcomes of mentorship relationships differed based on the gender composition of the dyads (Ballenger 2010; Burke and McKeen 1990; Vieito 2012).

Compared to men, women, in general, face greater barriers to career advancement, and as such, they require greater time to focus on advancing their careers rather than taking the time to help others—including mentoring other women (Nieva and Gutek 1981; Vieito 2012; Xia and Kleiner 2001). Regarding the concept of status and power, women employees and especially women of color employees, in general, carry less (perceived) status than compared to their male counterparts (Nieva and

Gutek 1981; Paoline 2003; Schaubroeck and Lam 2002). As such, female mentors and their cross-gender protégés face greater risk regarding "succession outcomes" as compared to male-male mentoring dyads (Ragins and Sundstrom 1989).

In 1981, researchers Nieva and Gutck concluded that men employees focused more on career-oriented attributes (viz., organizational networking) than compared to women employees who were more likely to focus on hard work, perseverance, and determination . . . and paying less attention to forming ties with upper management through social networks (1981). As well, male employees tended to move through the corporate ranks in "packs," whereas female employees tended to move alone (Neal 2007). Corporate social networks facilitated stronger bonding through male-male mentorships in that the networks allowed male protégés to reap greater returns from their influential relationships than compared to the bonding relationships through female-female mentorships (Buckalew, Konstantinopoulos, Russell, and Seif 2012; Matsa and Miller 2011; Noe 1988).

Thus, research findings concluded that an employee's success in securing management and higher professional career positions depended to a large part on the employee's ability to gain access to senior members within their organization via their company's social networks and company's mentoring relationships (Eagly and Carli 2007; Gilbert 2003; Pillai, Prasad, and Thomas 2011). In business, as in academe, women employees/women employees of color experienced less access to senior members of their organizations that prevented them from achieving the same quality of networking relationships as that experienced by their male counterparts (Dreher and Ash 1990).

Interestingly, in their book, *The Managerial Women*, Haning and Jardim (1977) interviewed women in the United States and all executives reported that they had reached their highest level of career position, in part, due to their protégé-mentor relationship—in which all mentorships were cross-gender (that is, the mentors were all men). The women interviewees who did not reach their highest career position lacked the protégé-mentor experience (Haning and Jardim 1977).

MY PERSONAL EXPERIENCE

Presently, I voluntarily serve as the executive director of the Colorado Chapter of "WIN!" (Women-in-NAAAP [National Association of Asian-American Professionals]), a national Asian American women's organization. The organization's primary purpose is to provide a safe sistership and mentorship environment that supports confidential discussions around shared values, beliefs, and experiences among our women protégés who learn leadership skills for their personal and professional growth and development. Since assuming the executive role, I have personally mentored over thirty professional Asian women protégés through our monthly group and monthly one-on-one mentoring programs that lasts six to eighteen months — depending on the program.

I passionately serve women as their mentor primarily because of my familial up-bringing. I grew up experiencing blatant gender discrimination with limited career options and life opportunities. Today, I've come to firmly believe that every woman has the inherent *right* to realize her full potential (that is, devoid being marginalized or discounted and internalizing the negative repercussions). I firmly believe in presenting women with opportunities so they may discover and own their full potential; I also firmly believe that some women need some guidance and a gentle nudge to move them along their journey; and I firmly believe that I can help.

My underlying philosophy on mentoring is based on my definition of "leadership," *"I would want for the other that which I would want for myself."* That is, I would want to be mentored by an effective and impactful mentor; and therefore, I also mentor my protégés with this same conviction that underlies my own philosophy.

My criterion for working with protégés is based on two prerequisites. The first is based on the conceptualization of a "student" . . . such that, "when the student is ready, the teacher will appear." In short, I only work with students — individuals (women with professional careers) who are eager and willing to learn about their own personal and professional growth and development. The second prerequisite is based on an imperative stipulation that the protégé is willing to "keep an open mind." In fact, I use the acronym, KOM (keep (an) open mind) and insist that all my protégés keep KOM at all times.

The level of an interactive relationship is primarily dependent on the level of the interactive skill sets that the mentor "brings to the table," and to a lesser degree, on the interactive skill sets of the protégé. As well, the quality of mentorship interactions depends to a large degree on the ability that both mentor and protégé commit to keeping KOM.

There is an important principle that underlies an individual's abilities/ skills that applies primarily to mentors, and it entails the concept of "lack." Simply stated, a mentor cannot effectively apply skills that s/he does not effectively internalize. In other words, if the mentor has not truly experienced the skill set to the degree that s/he has effectively internalized these, then the mentor may likely be less effective (that is, have less impact) at influencing the protégé. This principle is especially true for mentoring on leadership skills.

The primary value-add that underlies the purpose of my mentoring professional women protégés/professional women protégés of color (for example, Asian women) is in developing their leadership skills for this twenty-first century. The standard by which I judge my interactions as a mentor is based on best practices in serving as an "ideal" mentor for my protégés. To achieve this level of standard requires *courage* for several reasons that will soon become apparent. The "ideal" mentor must first have knowledge about "who" and "what" is the protégé, followed by the courage to implement the "what" and the "how" of the mentoring process in order to nudge forward (that is, push) the protégé to her/his outer limits of her/his current boundaries—always with the intentions of moving the protégé to the next level of her/his potential growth and at the protégé's pace. An effective mentor/mentorship requires the skills as listed above in order to have knowledge about the protégé's present outer limits—limits that are at a lesser level than the protégé's overall realized potential. As a mentor, I keep my resolve to implement the mentoring process at the level of best practices that is based on my definition of "leadership": *"wanting for the other that which I would want for myself "* (that is, I would want a mentor to altruistically counsel me [as a protégé] and to encourage me even when I am emotionally pushing back).

Likewise, on the part of the protégé, it takes courage for her/him to acknowledge her/his limitations that s/he must overcome in order to advance the process to the next level. For most protégés, coming to that self-realization is scary such that *fear* is the primary cause and reason for the emotional pushback. The degree to which the protégé overcomes her/his resistance will depend upon on a) the healthiness of her/his own self-efficacy and b) the mentor's leadership skills to instill sufficient trust and ensure safety through understanding and inspiring her/his protégé to keep the process moving forward.

To display the appropriate level of courage that is necessary to achieve an effective mentorship outcome requires a good understanding about the art and science of implementing and internalizing EQ/EI (emotional quotient/intelligence). Mentoring women protégés/women protégés of color (for example, Asian women protégés)—requires an understanding that women, in general—as compared to men, in general—lack the confidence and competence on a personal and professional level. These attributes (confidence and competence) are essential to skillfully compete in this twenty-first century. It takes courage for mentors to nudge women to strengthen their confidence and competence, and it takes even more courage for women protégés/women of color protégés—especially Asian women protégés—to overcome their perceived lack of confidence/competence because in many cases, this "lack" may be culturally driven.

CONCLUSION

Mentorship necessitates the courage to commit and to resolve to the act of mentoring at the level of "best" practices. It is far too easy for a mentor to allow the protégé to be dropped through the cracks or to allow the mentorship to wane to dissolution. In today's business environment, mentorships are an essential partnering resource without which it is difficult especially for women/women of color to single-handedly climb and reach the top of the corporate ladder. And given the complexities of the local and global business environments, it takes a broad degree of skills (that is, technical and psychosocial) to maneuver the different philosophies and biases in today's workplace. Hence, the phrase, *"Begin with the end in mind"* is most appropriate as a reference resource to begin with "mentorship" (in mind) as a means to attain one's goals. When the decision is made by two parties to engage in the mentorship process that assimilates the "ideal" mentor and the "ideal" protégé, both parties efficiently and effectively work in tandem to increase the likelihood that the dyadic relationship will attain a positive outcome. Finally, when one views a committed mentor-protégé relationship, one should realize that *courage* plays a fundamental role by both (mentor and protégés) to ensure that the dyadic relationship will be truly sustainable.

REFERENCES

Acker, S., and C. Armenti. 2004. "Sleepless in Academia." *Gender and Education* 16: 3–24.

Adya, M. P. 2008. "Women at Work Differences in IT Career Experiences and Perceptions between South Asian and American Women." *Human Resouce Management* 47(3): 601–635. doi: 10.1002/hrm.20234.

Allen, T., and L. Eby. 2003. "Relationship Effectiveness for Mentors: Factors Associated with Learning and Quality." *Journal of Management* 29: 469–486.

Allen, T., L. Eby, and E. Lentz. 2006. "The Relationship between Formal Mentoring Program Characteristics and Perceived Program Effectiveness." *Personnel Psychology* 59: 125–153.

Allen, T. D., and L. T. Eby, eds. 2007. *The Blackwell Handbook of Mentoring: A Multiple Perspectives Approach.* Malden, MA: Blackwell Publishing.

Allen, T. D., L. T. Eby, M. L. Poteet, E. Lentz, and L. Lima. 2004. "Career Benefits Associated with Mentoring for Protégés: A Meta-Analysis." *Journal of Applied Psychology* 89(1): 127–136. doi: 10.1037/0021-9010.89.1.127.

Aspan, M. 2013. "Citigroup Boys' Club Highlights Industry Gender Gap." *American Banker* 178(7): 1–11. Retrieved from Business Source Complete website: http://eds.b.ebscohost.com.ezp.waldenulibrary.org/eds/delivery7sl.

Ballenger, J. 2010. "Women's Access to Higher Education Leadership: Cultural and Structural Barriers." *Forum on Public Policy Online* 2010(5).

Blake-Beard, S. D., R. M. O'Neill, and E. M. McGowan. 2007. *The Handbook of Mentoring at Work: Theory, Research, and Practice.* Thousand Oaks, CA: Sage Publishing.

Bradley, K. 2000. "The Incorporation of Women into Higher Education: Paradoxical Outcomes." *Sociology of Education* 73: 1–18.

Buckalew, E., A. Konstantinopoulos, J. Russell, and E.-S. Seif. 2012. "The Future of Female CEOs and Their Glass Ceiling." *Journal of Business Studies Quarterly* 3(4): 145–153.

Burke, R. J., and C. A. McKeen. 1990. "Mentoring in Organizations: Implications for Women." *Journal of Business Ethics* 9(4/5): 317–332.

Campbell, T. A., and D. E. Campbell. 1997. "Faculty/Student Mentor Program: Effects on Academic Performance and Retentions." *Research in Higher Education* 38: 727–742.

Cherniss, C. 2007. *The Role of Emotional Intelligence in the Mentoring Process*, eds. B. R. Ragins and K. E. Kram. Thousand Oaks, CA: Sage.

Chun, J. U., E. B. Litzky, J. J. Sosik, D. C. Bechtold, and V. M. Godshalk. 2010. "Emotional Intelligence and Trust in Formal Mentoring Programs." *Group & Organization Management* 35: 421–455.

Clark, S. M., and M. Corcoran. 1986. "Perspectives on the Professional Socialization of Women Faculty." *Journal of Higher Education* 56: 20–43.

Collins, D. B., and E. F. Holton. 2004. "The Effectiveness of Managerial Leadership Development Programs: A Meta-Analysis of Studies from 1982–2001." *Human Resource Development Quarterly* 2(2): 217–248.

Covey, S., Z. Ziglar, and B. Tracy. 2013. "Begin with the End in Mind." Retrieved 04/17/2004, from http://www.usadojo.com/articles/end-goals.htm.

Cronan-Hillix, T., W. S. Davidson, W. A. Cronan-Hilix, and L. K. Gensheimer. 1986. "Student's View on Mentors in Psychology Graduate Training." *Teaching of Psychology* 13: 123–127.

Cullen, D. L., and G. Luna. 1990. *A Comparative Study of Female Mentors in Academe and Business*, ed. A. D. J. P. Mroczek. Dekalb, IL: Northern Illinois University Press.

Cullen, D. L., and G. Luna. 1993. "Women Mentoring in Academe: Addressing the Gender Gap in Higher Education. *Gender & Education* 5(2): 125.

Davidson, M. J., and C. L. Cooper. 1986. "Executive Women under Pressure." *International Review of Applied Psychology* 35: 301–326.

Davies-Netzley, S. A. 1998. "Women above the Glass Ceiling: Perceptions on Corporate Mobility and Strategies for Success." *Gender and Society* 12: 339–365.

Day, R., and T. D. Allen. 2004. "The Relationship between Career Motivation and Self-Efficacy with Protégé Career Success." *Journal of Vocational Behavior* 64: 72–91.

Derks, B., N. Ellemers, C. van Laar, and K. de Groot. 2011. "Do Sexist Organizational Cultures Create the Queen Bee?" *British Journal of Social Psychology* 50(3): 519–535. doi: 10.1348/014466610X525280.

Donaldson, S. I., E. A. Ensher, and E. J. Grant-Vallone. 2000. "Longitudinal Examination of Mentoring Relationships on Organizational Commitment and Citizenship Behavior." *Journal of Career Development* (4): 233.

Douglas, C. A., and F. D. Schoorman. 1988. *The Impact of Career and Psychosocial Mentoring by Supervisors and Peers*. Paper presented at the 48th Annual Meeting of the Academy of Management, Anaheim, CA.

Dreher, G. F., and R. A. Ash. 1990. "A Comparative Study of Mentoring among Men and Women in Managerial Professional and Technical Positions." *Journal of Applied Psychology* 75: 539–546.

Eagly, A. H., and L. L. Carli. 2007. "Women and the Labyrinth of Leadership." *Harvard Business Review* 85(9): 63–71.

Eby, L. T. 2011. *APA Handbook of Industrial and Organization Psychology*, Volume 2. Washington, DC: American Psychological Association.

Eby, L. T., T. D. Allen, S. C. Evans, T. Ng, and D. L. DuBois. 2008. "Does Mentoring Matter? A Multidisciplinary Meta-Analysis Comparing Mentored and Non-Mentored Individuals." *Journal of Vocational Behavior* 72: 254–267.

Eby, L. T., J. R. Durley, S. C. Evans, and B. R. Ragins. 2006. "The Relationship between Short-Term Mentoring Benefits and Long-Term Mentoring Outcomes." *Journal of Vocational Behavior* 69: 424–444. doi: 10.1016/j.jvb2003.07.001.

Eisenberger, R., G. Karagonlar, F. Stinglhamber, P. Neves, T. E. Becker, and M. G. Gonzalez-Moralex. 2010. "Leader-Member Exchange and Affective Organizational Commitment: The Contribution of Supervisor's Organizational Embodiment." *Journal of Applied Psychology* 95: 1085–1103.

Ennis, S. R., M. Rio-Vargas, and N. G. Albert. 2011. "The Hispanic Population: 2010." Retrieved April 17, 2014, 2014, from www.census.gov/prod/cen2010/briefs/c2010br_04.pdf.

Fletcher, J. K., and B. R. Ragins. 2007. *Stone Center Relational Cultural Theory: A Window on Relational Mentoring*, eds. B. R. Ragins and K. E. Kram. Thousand Oaks, CA: Sage.

Franklin, C. 2005. "Male Peer Support and the Police Culture: Understanding the Resistance and Opposition of Women in Policing." *Women & Criminal Justice* 16(3): 1–25.

Gakovic, A., and L. E. Tetrick. 2003. "Psychological Contract Breach as a Source of Strain for Employees." *Journal of Business and Psychology* 18: 235–246. doi: 10.1023/A:1027301232116.

Ghosh, R., T. G. Reio, and R. K. Haynes. 2012. *Mentoring and Organizational Citizenship Behavior: Estimating the Mediating Effects of Organization-Based Self-Esteem and Affective Commitment*, Volume 23. John Wiley & Sons, Inc.

Gilbert, L. A. 1985. "Die Mentions of Same-Gender Student-Faculty Role-Model Relationships." *Sex-Roles* 12(1/2): 111–123.

Gilbert, J. 2003. "Lonely at the Top." *Sales & Marketing Management* 155(7): 46–49.

Giscombe, K., and M. Mattis. 2002. "Leveling the Playing Field for Women of Color in Corporate Management: Is the Business Case Enough?" *Journal of Business Ethics* 37: 103–199.

Gooty, J., M. Gavin, P. D. Johnson, M. L. Frazier, and D. B. Snow. 2009. "In the Eyes of the Beholder: Transformational Leadership, Positive Psychological Capital, and Performance." *Journal of Leadership and Organizational Studies* 15(4): 353–367.

Greenhaus, J. H., and R. Singh. 2007. *Mentoring and the Work-Family Interface*, eds. B. R. Ragins and K. E. Kram. Thousand Oaks, CA: Sage.

Haggard, D. L., T. W. Dougherty, D. B. Turban, and J. E. Wilbanks. 2011. "Who Is a Mentor? A Review of Evolving Definitions and Implications of Research." *Journal of Management* 37(1): 280–304.

Hamilton, S. F., and M. A. Hamilton. 1990. *Linking Up: Final Report on a Mentoring Program for Youth*, ed. D. o. H. D. F. Services. New York: Cornell University.

Hamlin, R. G., and L. Sage. 2011. "Behavioral Criteria of Perceived Mentoring Effectiveness. An Empirical Study of Effective and Ineffective Mentor and Mentee Behavior within Formal Mentoring Relationships." *Journal of European Industrial Training* 35(8): 752–778.

Heilman, M. E., C. J. Block, R. F. Martell, and M. C. Simon. 1989. "Has Anything Changed? Current Characteristics of Men, Women, and Managers." *Journal of Applied Psychology* 74: 935–942.

Heilman, M. E., A. S. Wallen, D. Fuchs, and M. M. Tamkins. 2004. "Penalties for Success: Reactions to Women who Succeed at Male Gender-Typed Tasks." *Journal of Applied Psychology* 89: 416–427.

Hennig, M., and A. Jardim. 1977. *The Managerial Women*. Garden City, NY: Anchor Press/Double Day.

Higgins, M. C., and K. E. Kram. 2001. "Reconceptualizing Mentoring at Work: A Developmental Network Perspective." *Academy of Management Review* 26: 264–288.

Hoeffel, E. M., D. Rastogl, O. M. Kim, and H. Shabid. 2010. "The Asian Population: 2010." Retrieved April 17, 2014, from www.census.gov/prod/cen2010/briefs/c2010br-11.pdf.

Hofmans, J., N. Dries, and R. Pepermans. 2008. "The Career Satisfaction Scale: Response Bias among Men and Women." *Journal of Vocational Behavior* 73: 397–403.

Hollingsworth, M. A., and R. E. Fassinger. 2002. "The Role of Faculty Mentors in the Research Training of Counseling Psychology Doctoral Students." *Journal of Counseling Psychology* 49: 324–330.

Holmes, S. L., L. D. Land, and V. D. Hinton-Hudson. 2007. "Race Still Matters: Considerations for Mentoring Black Women in Academe." *Negro Educational Review* 58(1/2): 105–129.

Hunt, D. M., and C. Michael. 1983. "Mentorship: A Career Training and Development Tool." *Academy of Management Review* 8: 475–485.

Kalb, C. 2006. "A New View of the Boy's Club." *Newsweek* 148: 40–41.

Kemelgor, C., and H. Etzkowitz. 2001. "Overcoming Isolation: Women Dilemmas in American Academic Science." *Minerva: A Review of Science, Learning and Policy* 39: 239–257.

Kram, K. E. 1985. *Mentoring at Work*. Illinois: Scott, Foresman.

Kram, K. E., and B. R. Ragins. 2007. *The Handbook of Mentoring at Work: Theory, Research, and Practice*. Thousand Oaks, CA: Sage Publishing.

Kulis, S., and K. A. Miller. 1988. "Are Minority Women Sociologists in Double Jeopardy." *American Sociologist* 4: 323–339.

Leck, J. D., B. Orser, and A. Riding. 2009. "An Examination of Gender Influences in Career Mentoring." *Canadian Journal of the Administrative Sciences* 26(3): 211–229.

Lemon, M. A., and M. Parziner. 2007. "Gender Schemas: A Cognitive Explanation of Discrimination of Women in Technology." *Journal of Business Psychology* 22(1): 91–98.

Lentz, E., and T. D. Allen. 2009. "The Role of Mentoring Others in the Career Plateauing Phenomenon." *Group & Organization Management* 34: 358–384.

Lerner, R. M., and L. Steinberg. 2009. *Handbook of Adolescent Psychology*, 2nd edition. New York: Wiley.

Matsa, D. A., and A. R. Miller. 2011. "Chipping Away at the Glass Ceiling: Gender Spillovers in Corporate Leadership." *American Economic Review* 101(3): 635–639. doi: 10.1257/aer.101.3.635.

Mayer, H. 2006. *Frontiers in Entrepreneurship*, ed. A. Zacharakis. Babson Park, MA: Babson College.

McKeen, C. A., and M. Bujaki. 2007. *The Handbook of Mentoring at Work: Theory, Research, and Practice*. Thousand Oaks, CA: Sage Publications.

McManus, S. E., and J. E. A. Russell. 1997. "New Directions for Mentoring Research: An Examination of Related Constructs." *Journal of Vocational Behavior* 51: 145–161.

Melymuka, K. 2008. "Why Women Quit Technology Careers." *Computerworld*. Retrieved from Why Women Quit Technology website, http://www.computerworld.com/s/article/319212/why_women_quite_technology.

Morrison, A., R. White, and V. Velsor. 1987. *Breaking the Glass Ceiling*. Reading, MA: Addison-Wesley.

Mullen, E. J. 1994. "Framing the Mentoring Relationship as an Information Exchange." *Human Resource Management Review* 4: 257–281.

Neal, A. 2007. "Women Mentoring Women: Tapping the Wisdom in Networks to Navigate Career Obstacles and Opportunities." *Global Business and Organizational Excellence* (1): 49.

Nieva, V. F., and B. A. Gutek. 1981. *Women and Work*. New York: Praeger.

Noe, R. A. 1988. "Women and Mentoring: A Review and Research Agenda." *Academy of Management Review* 65: 65–78.

O'Neil, J. M., and L. S. Wrightsman. 2001. "The Mentoring Relationship in Psychology Training Programs." In S. W. A. K. Hess (ed.), *Succeeding in Graduate School: The Career Guide for Psychology Students*, 111–127. Mahwah, NJ: Lawrence Erlbaum Associates Publishers.

Orser, B., A. Riding, and J. Stanley. 2012. "Perceived Career Challenges and Response Strategies of Women in the Advanced Technology Sector." *Entrepreneurship & Regional Development* 24(1/2): 73–93. doi: 10.1080/08985626.2012.637355.

Panteli, A., J. Stack, and H. Ramsay. 1999. "Gender and Professional Ethics in the IT Industry." *Journal of Business Ethics* 22(1): 51–61.

Paoline, E. I. 2003. "Taking Stock: Toward a Richer Understanding of Police Culture." *Journal of Criminal Justice* 31: 199–214.

Payne, S. C., and A. H. Huffman. 2005. "A Longitudinal Examination of the Influence of Mentoring in Organizational Commitment and Turnover." *Academy of Management Journal* 48(1): 158–168. doi: 10.5465/ajm.2005.15993166.

Pazy, A. 1987. "Sex Differences in Responsiveness to Organizational Career Management." *Human Resources Management* 26: 243–256.

Pillai, K. R., S. Prasad, and J. Thomas. 2011. "Why Do Women Still Experience Downward Gravitation in the Corporate Ladder? A Close Look at Glass Ceiling in Bahrain." *Research & Practice in Human Resource Management* 19(1): 1–10.

Portillo, S. 2007. "Mentoring Minority and Female Students: Recommendations for Improving Mentoring in Public Administration and Public Affairs Programs." *Journal of Public Affairs Education* 13: 103–114.

Ragins, B., and E. Sundstrom. 1989. "Gender and Power in Organizations: A Longitudinal Perspective." *Psychological Bulletin* 105: 51–88.

Ragins, B. R., and J. L. Cotton. 1991. "Easier Said than Done: Gender Differences in Perceived Barriers to Getting a Mentor." *Academy of Management Journal* 34: 939–958.

Ragins, B. R., and T. A. Scandura. 1994. "Gender Differences in Expected Outcomes of Mentoring Relationships." *Academy of Management Journal* 37: 957–971.

Ragins, B. R., and T. A. Scandura. 1999. "Burden or Blessing? Expected Costs and Benefits of Being a Mentor." *Journal of Organizational Behavior* 20: 493–509. doi: 10.1002/(SICI)1099-1379.

Rastogl, S., T. D. Johnson, E. M. Heoeffel, and M. P. Drewery. 2010. "The Black Population: 2010." Retrieved April 17, 2014, from www.census.gov/prod/cen2010/briefs/c2010br_06.pdf.

Reid, P. T., and L. Wilson. 1999. "How Do You Spell Graduate Success?" NETWORK. *Black Issue in Higher Education* 10(10): 100.

Reskin, B. F. 1979. "Academic Sponsorship and Scientists' Careers." *Sociology of Education* 52: 129–146.

Reskin, B. F., and D. Bielby. 2005. "A Sociological Perspective on Gender and Career Outcomes." *Journal of Economic Perspectives* 19(1): 71–86.

Rindfleish, J. 2000. "Senior Management Women in Australia: Diverse Perspectives." *Women in Management Review* 15(4): 172.

Rosen, B. 1982. *Career Progress of Women: Getting In and Staying In*. New York: Praeger.

Russell, J. E. A. 1994. *Career Counseling for Women in Management*. Hillsdale, NJ: Eribaum.

Scandura, T. A., and E. A. Williams. 2004. "Mentoring and Transformational Leadership: The Role of Supervisory Career Mentoring." *Journal of Vocational Behavior* 65: 448–468. doi: 10.1016/j.jvb.2003.10.003.

Schaubroeck, J., and S. Lam. 2002. "How Similarity to Peers and Supervisors Influences Organizational Advancement in Different Cultures." *Academic of Management Journal* 45(6)" 1120–1136.

Sciences, I. o. E. 2008, 2007. "Post-Secondary Education." Retrieved April 17, 2014, fromhttp://nces.ed.gov/pubs2009/2009020_3b.pdf.

Sheppard, L. D., and K. Aquino. 2013. "Much Ado about Nothing? Observers' Problematization of Women's Same-Sex Conflict at Work." *Academy of Management Perspectives* 27(1): 52–62. doi: 10.5465/amp.2012.0005.

Shollen, S. L., C. J. Bland, A. L. Taylor, A. M. Weber-Main, and P. A. Mulcahy. 2008. "Establishing Effective Mentoring Relationships for Faculty, Especially Across Gender and Ethnicity." *American Academic*, 131–158.

Singh, V., D. Bains, and S. Vinnicombe. 2002. "Informal Mentoring as an Organizational Resource." *Long Range Planning* 35(4): 389–405. doi: 10.1016/s0024-6301(02)00064-x.

Sosik, J. J., and V. M. Godshalk. 2000. "The Role of Gender in Mentoring: Implications for Diversified and Homogenous Mentoring Relationships." *Journal of Vocational Behavior* 57(1): 102–122. doi: 10.1006/jvbe.1999.1734.

Sosik, J. J., and V. M. Godshalk. 2005. "Examining Gender Similarity and Mentor's Supervisory Status in Mentoring Relationships." *Mentoring and Tutoring* 13: 41–54.

Spencer, R. A., J. V. Jordan, and J. Sazama. 2004. "Growth-Promoting Relationships between Youth and Adults: A Focus Group Study." *Families in Society* 85(3): 354–362.

Styles, M. B., and K. V. Morrow. 1992. *Understanding How Youth and Elders Form Relationships: A Study of Four Linking Lifetimes Programs*. Philadelphia, PA: Public/Private Ventures.

Sumner, M., and F. Niederman. 2004. "The Impact of Gender Differences on Job Satisfaction, Job Turnover, and Career Experiences of Systems Professionals." *Journal of Computer Information Systems* 44: 29–40.

Tepper, B. J., and E. C. Taylor. 2003. "Relationships among Supervisors' and Subordinates' Procedural Justice Perceptions and Organizational Citizenship Behaviors." *Academy of Management Journal* 46: 97–105.

Tharenou, P. 2005. "Does Mentor Support Increase Women's Career Advancement more than Men's? The Differential Effects of Career and Psychological Support." *Australian Journal of Management* 30(1): 77–109.

Tharenou, P., S. Latimer, and D. Conroy. 1994. "How Do You Make It to the Top? An Examination of Influences on Women's and Men's Managerial Advancement." *Academy of Management Journal* 37: 899–931.

Thile, E. L., and G. E. Matt. 1995. "The Ethnic Minority Undergraduate Program: A Brief Description and Preliminary Findings." *Journal of Multicultural Counseling and Development* 23: 116–126.

Tong, C., and K. E. Kram. 2013. *The Efficacy of Mentoring—The Benefits for Mentees, Mentors, and Organizations*, eds. D. B. P. J. Passmore and F. Freier. West Sussex, UK: Wiley-Blackwell & Sons.

Trauth, E. M., S. H. Nielsen, and L. A. von Hellens. 2003. "Explaining the IT Gender Gap: Australian Stories for the New Millennium." *Journal of Research and Practice in Information Technology* 35: 7–20.

Turban, D. B., T. W. Dougherty, and F. K. Lee. 2002. "Gender, Race, and Perceived Similarity Effects in Developmental Relationships: The Moderating Role of Relationship Duration." *Journal of Vocational Behavior* 61(2): 240–262.

Turner, C., S. Viernes, J. C. Gonzalez, and J. L. Wood. 2008. *Faculty of Color in Academe: What 20 Years of Literature Tells Us*, Volume 1. *Journal of Diversity in Higher Education*.

Underhill, C. M. 2006. "The Effectiveness of Mentoring Programs in Corporate Settings: A Meta-Analytical Review of the Literature." *Journal of Vocational Behavior* 68(2): 292–307.

Vieito, J. P. 2012. "Gender, Top Management Compensation Gap, and Company Performance: Tournament versus Behavioral Theory." *Corporate Governance: An International Review* 20(1). doi: 10.1111/j.1467.2011.00878.x.

Wanberg, C. R., J. Kammeyer-Mueller, and M. Marchese. 2006. "Mentor and Protégé Predictors and Outcomes of Mentoring in a Formal Mentoring Program." *Journal of Vocational Behavior* 69: 410–423.

Weinberg, F. J., and M. J. Lankau. 2011. "Formal Mentoring Programs: A Mentor-Centric and Longitudinal Analysis." *Journal of Management* 37(6): 1527–1557.

Weisinger, J. Y., and E. M. Tarauth. 2003. "The Importance of Situating Culture in Cross-Cultural IT Management." *IEEE Transactions in Engineering Management* 50(1): 26–30.

Wrightsman, L. S. 1981. *Research Methodologies for Assessing Mentoring*. Paper presented at the American Psychological Association, Los Angeles.

Wyche, K. F., and S. B. Graves. 1992. "Minority Women in Academia: Access and Barriers to Professional Participation." *Psychology of Women Quarterly* 16(4): 429–437.

Xia, A., and B. Kleiner. 2001. "Discrimination in the Computer Industry." *Equal Opportunities International* 20(5–7): 117–120.

Zagenczyk, T. J., R. Gibney, C. Kiewitz, and S. L. Restubog. 2009. "Mentors, Supervisors and Role Models: Do They Reduce the Effects of Psychological Contract Breach?" *Human Resource Management Journal* 19: 237–259. doi: 10.111/j.1748.8583.2009.00097x.

SEVEN

The Role of a Mentor in Supporting Early Career Academics

The Relationship Is More Important Than the Label

Julie Haddock-Millar and Chandana Sanyal

Before we share our stories, we begin with a little background information. All United Kingdom (UK) universities undertake research and teaching, although the mission focus and balance of activities varies. Some institutions concentrate primarily on teaching while others are more research intensive. Universities also increasingly transfer knowledge through their formal and informal relationships with businesses and other organisations. More recently, universities are also seeking to use their expertise and facilities to develop thriving social and business communities in their region. Some universities have formed groups with common interests; these include the various regional university associations and also the so-called "mission groups" such as Russell Group and the University Alliance. Million+ is a university think tank working to help solve complex problems in higher education and to ensure that policy reflects the potential of the UK's world-class university system. It mainly comprises post-1992, new universities. The Russell Group is an association of twenty major research-intensive universities in the UK, and the University Alliance consists of member institutions that have a balanced portfolio of research, teaching, enterprise and innovation as integral to their missions.

Middlesex University (MU or Mdx) based in Hendon, North London, England, is a member of Million+ working group. As is the case with many former polytechnics, Middlesex was formally organised as a teaching institution in 1973, yet can trace its history back to the nineteenth century. In 2012, the university restructured its academic schools in order to align them more closely with the needs of industry. Courses at Middlesex are now delivered by the School of Business, Law, Art and Design, Health and Education, Media and Performing Arts and Science and Technology, alongside the university's Institute for Work Based Learning. Also following a successful recruitment campaign during 2012, seventy outstanding academics joined MU, half at Professor and Reader levels. In the UK a professor is a highly accomplished and recognized academic, and the title is awarded to senior academics only after significant scholarly work. The title of reader denotes an appointment for a senior academic with a distinguished international reputation in research or scholarship. It is an academic rank above senior lecturer or principal lecturer, recognising a distinguished record of original research. By 2013, one hundred new academics across all levels of seniority joined the university. In September 2014, the university implemented a new academic staffing structure which offered three career pathways, focused on teaching and learning, research and knowledge transfer or professional practice. This signalled a shift towards a "research-led" university which represents a significant change in strategic direction for all academic staff.

JULIE'S STORY

Julie was educated in the UK, having grown up in a "traditional" English family in the armed forces. Prior to joining MU in 2008, Julie trained as a lawyer, joined the civil service and then moved to the private sector for ten years. She held a variety of senior leadership and management positions, including the role of Regional/Cluster Human Resource (HR) Manager, responsible for the strategic talent management and delivery for over 10,000 employees. During this time, Julie found that she had a real passion and flair for supporting others in their developmental journey, where mentoring and coaching became a core feature of a talent management framework. To provide the theoretical foundation to underpin the role, Julie decided to gain a formal HR qualification through the MA Human Resource Development (HRD) with MU, joining as a mature student. Shortly after joining the university as a full-time student, Julie was given the opportunity to become a Lecturer and make the transition to a full-time permanent member of the Human Resource Management (HRM) team. At the time, life was changing dramatically; Julie's mother, in her early fifties, was diagnosed with cancer and passed away shortly thereafter. Julie and her husband were planning their wedding and the purchase of their first home to start a family together. Julie's mother had always said to her that she would make a great teacher and a people-focused role would suit her personality and capabilities.

Looking back, the changes in her personal life influenced her decision to join the university to become a teacher and pursue a career which would fulfil her potential to develop and nurture talent. She held the position of Lecturer for three years and was promoted to Senior Lecturer via the accelerated route in September 2011. Since joining the university and gaining her appointment as a Senior Lecturer, Julie has completed a Postgraduate Certificate in Higher Education (PG Cert HE), a Doctorate in Professional Studies (DProf) and has been appointed to a variety of external positions, such as Fellow of the Higher Education Academy (HEA), Academic Assessor with the Chartered Institute of Personnel and Development (CIPD), and External Examiner with the University of Surrey and Leeds Metropolitan University. Since commencing her journey with MU, Julie has had the opportunity to work with several internal and external colleagues whom she refers to as her "mentors." They have all been instrumental in her continuing personal and professional development.

JULIE'S MENTORS

In this next section, Julie shines a light on two mentors that have had the greatest impact on her, identifying the nature of the relationship, her perception of their key strengths and the reasons why Julie believes these relationships have been successful.

In 2009, Julie met Dr Barbara Workman, who at the time was the Director of the Centre of Excellence for Teaching and Learning (CETL). Barbara provided "seed money" to develop and grow innovative projects, and Barbara awarded Julie a grant of £3,000 to develop a mentoring network—Middlesex University Mentoring Network (MUMN). Barbara is an ex-nursing practitioner, leader, manager, teacher, researcher and mother. Barbara came into academia through the teaching route. She had successfully navigated her way through a number of career transitions and now had the role of developing teaching and learning excellence across the University. Over the following five years, Julie has come to regard Barbara as a close friend and mentor; she has championed Julie's ideas and shared her passion for mentoring, encouraging Julie to continue to develop projects both internal and external to the university. Barbara has taken on both "formal" and "informal" roles: formally, by university appointment, Barbara mentored Julie through her application to become to a University Teaching Fellow, in recognition of her outstanding performance in teaching and supporting learning. Informally, Barbara has been a constant advisor, acting as a sounding board, giving her insight, and sharing her knowledge and many years of experience. Barbara has often coached Julie, helping her to reach her own conclusions, through reflection and critical dialogue. Since embarking on the small-scale project in 2009, the design, implementation and evaluation of multi-stakeholder mentoring programmes has become a core feature of Julie's role both within and outside of the university. Barbara has developed Julie's confidence and self-esteem through mutual respect and acceptance, successfully moving between the role of sponsor, advisor, counsellor, and friend (Clutterbuck 2004).

It was through Julie's involvement in the MUMN that she met Professor David Clutterbuck, a successful practitioner academic, entrepreneur, author, mentor, coach, father and granddad. Attending a small-scale conference at MU in 2010, David invited Julie to co-author her first case study book chapter in his publication entitled *The Diversity Mentoring Casebook*. This provided a fantastic opportunity for Julie to develop her technical skills and knowledge specifically around research, inquiry and publishing. This has led to further opportunities to publish within David's network. David provided the catalyst for her to forge her academic research interests in mentoring practice, completing a DProf, with mentoring at the heart of the thesis and ultimately leading a "professional development" research cluster within the university and the facilitation the university's first international mentoring conference. Since 2010, David has provided numerous opportunities for Julie to become involved in conferences, research and publications. He has introduced Julie to his networks, guided her, coached and counselled her. David has acted as Julie's advisor and consultant on a number of mentoring projects she has developed, sharing his knowledge and experience to improve and develop the content. David invited Julie to co-write *The Talent Wave Fieldbook*, which will be her first opportunity to write a book. David recognises Julie's keenness to want to continue to develop her research skills and build a successful career as a Practitioner Academic. The relationship mutually benefits David and Julie; he has a willing and competent partner to support the production of the book. Alongside this, he can progress other publications, and Julie can develop her academic writing skills from an expert in the field. David and Julie have a developed a successful informal relationship because the support and commitment is reciprocated, freely given and mutually beneficial.

CHANDANA'S STORY

Chandana's entry into academia was not through the traditional route, that is, through doctoral studies at the university with professorial guidance and support. Chandana came into academia through the practitioner route when she was encouraged to join the faculty as a senior practitioner in Human Resource Development (HRD) to teach on the Master's programme on Human Resource Management.

Chandana is of Asian origin, and her formal education up to post-graduate level was completed in India. In 1983 she got married and moved to the United Kingdom. Chandana worked briefly in the Civil Service before the birth of her first child; she then spent the next five years bringing up her two children. Chandana returned to work when her children started school and soon found herself working in the arena of HRD in local government in the UK. Over the next ten years she built up her expertise in this field both through gaining experience in a range of learning and development roles and acquiring the relevant qualifications.

CHANDANA'S MENTORS

In 2003, Chandana stepped into the academic arena in the UK. When working as Learning and Development Manager her line manager encouraged her to undertake an MA in HRM as a part of her development at MU, her local university. Initially, Chandana was apprehensive about undertaking this study due to her family commitments, work pressures, and also a lack of understanding of the academic standards and expectations in the UK. However, she had a very positive learning experience and a personal sense of achievement when she successfully completed her study with a distinction in 2005. Soon after, Chandana was invited by the Head of the Department in HRM at her university to join the department as an Associate Lecturer. She continued in this role while still working as a full-time Workforce Development Manager for the next four years. In 2009, she decided to move into academia, and Chandana joined the university in a permanent Lecturer post.

The first couple of years of this transition from a practitioner to an academic, Chandana has been fortunate to be supported and guided by two colleagues: the Head of the Department, Dr Mary Hartog, and the then Director of Programmes, Professor Derek Miles, who acted as a confidential advisor and guide; they were her trusted advisors, friends, teachers and wise counsellors (Shea 1997; Klasen and Clutterbuck 2004). Mary provided both sponsorship by recommending Chandana for roles such as module leader and programme leader within her department and offered development opportunities such as participating in assessment moderation and academic validation. Mary encouraged Chandana to co-facilitate lectures and seminars with her, and they marked and moderated coursework together which helped Chandana enormously to familiarise herself with the academic grading structure. Her informal coffee chats with Derek provided an insight into the dynamics of the institution and helped her to understand how to engage and build relationships with key people in the department. It was through these relationships that Chandana learnt how to adapt in the academic role; the term mentoring was not used, but the ethos of mentoring was applied (Clutterbuck 2004). Chandana believes that these informal "mentors" may have invested in her because they thought that she could benefit from their help or they may have selected her based on her potential. In their studies, Singh, Ragins, and Tharenou (2009) and Allen and Eby (2007) suggest that mentors select their protégés based on their performance and potential. Therefore, Chandana's background, ethnicity and age were of no consequence here; it was about her ability and capabilities. Their support was invaluable in helping Chandana to become confident in her role as a Lecturer.

Early last year, Chandana was offered a coach-mentor as a part of her career development. This was a random opportunity offered by Mary, her Head of Department; the coach-mentor, Dr Barbara Workman, needed the experience as a part of her qualification, and Chandana was a willing colleague. At this stage, Chandana had just started her DProf and also a shift towards a "research" focus. This was a totally new experience for Chandana, and therefore the support was very timely. Over the last two years Chandana had encountered some strong comments and views from seniors and professors in leadership roles about the rigour of academic research, professional scholarship and the challenges of publishing; this created a picture of the "world of academia" as elitist, traditional, and exclusive. Chandana had six sessions with Barbara to discuss her concerns and challenges, particularly her anxiety around her research work. Barbara helped Chandana to put this area of her work in perspective to her overall role as an academic lecturer. The relationship with Barbara was successful in large part due to her skills in listening, creating structure, providing a positive attitude, sharing experiences and offering feedback (Freedman 2009). During this time, she successfully completed the first phase of DProf and delivered four conference presentations, including two papers. Chandana humbly gives credit to Barbara for helping her to take her first steps into the research arena.

More recently, Chandana had another positive "mentor" experience; in this case the official "mentor" title did apply. As a part of the application process for a teaching fellowship within the university, Chandana was allocated a "mentor," Dr Sheila Cunningham. This was a developmental relationship in which Sheila shared her experience and knowledge to support and guide Chandana through the application process, including submission of the supporting application statement. Here, Chandana was able to experience and observe the approach and the style of the mentor in helping her to address the gaps in the application statement. Sheila was constructive, emphasising that Chandana had a lot of strong evidence to support her application but she needed to work on the presentation of this information. Although Chandana needed to put in a lot of work, she never for a moment felt undermined or negatively challenged. In fact, she was positively challenged and energised by this mentoring experience. This demonstrated to Chandana how as a mentee she was able to take the initiative, regularly reflect on the process, respect her mentor and be open to change and new ideas (Allen et al. 2007; Clutterbuck 2011).

JULIE AND CHANDANA'S SHARED EXPERIENCE

Julie and Chandana work closely together on a number of projects and interrelated activities. Therefore at times they have experienced working with the same mentor. This section explores their experience of being mentored by a male professor.

Part of Julie and Chandana's job role remit is to collaborate with a range of organisations to explore research interests and educational development. In this respect, they are actively involved in Green Human Resource Development (HRD) research. This is a new research area and is one which they integrate into their teaching practice, incorporating the role of HR practitioners and the corporate social responsibility agenda. In 2009, Julie collaborated with a number of colleagues to write a paper developing the concept of Green HRD and received an award from the Chartered Institute of Personnel Development. It was at this point that Julie met Professor Michael Muller-Camen, a leading academic in the field of sustainable human resource management, at Middlesex University. Alongside a number of colleagues, Michael was very keen to conduct some empirical research to "test" some of the ideas/concepts that the team had developed. At the time, McDonald's had introduced a new environmental initiative, "Planet Champions." With Michael's encouragement, Julie approached David Fairhurst, McDonald's U.K., Chief People Office, Europe. David agreed to develop a research project, and in 2011, with the support of a number of colleagues, Michael and Julie conducted a small-scale piece of research in the UK. Alongside Professor Derek Miles, Michael and Julie successfully published a book chapter based on the research conducted in the UK (Haddock-Millar, Muller-Camen, and Miles 2011). Following this success, Michael and Julie secured a British Academy Grant to continue the research in Sweden and Germany, with McDonald's full support. At this point, Chandana joined the team; since this time Michael, Chandana and Julie have been developing an empirical paper, based on the data gathered from the UK, Sweden and Germany for the *International Journal of Human Resource Management*. Michael has since joined Vienna University of Economics and Business and retains a position at MU. Michael's support is primarily at a distance; communication is through email. What works with the relationship Julie and Chandana have developed with Michael is that they both have high regard for his scholarly knowledge in the research domain and have a deep appreciation of his drive to develop research which advances theory and practice in this area. Michael, Julie and Chandana are developing work which they hope to publish in high-ranking academic journals. The first article is near completion; it would be fair to say that it has been a tough journey. Notwithstanding this, Michael has used his mentoring skills to coach, guide, counsel and develop network opportunities for Julie and Chandana. In the coaching space, Michael has helped Julie and Chandana to develop their research writing competence which is absolutely essential in their role as a Senior Lecturer wanting to progress to Associate Professor. He has set goals to develop the paper, which has ensured that Julie and Chandana have continued to shift the paper from a draft to a completed piece of work. In the counselling space, Michael has given Julie invaluable career advice. An editorial role was recently brought to Julie's attention, and she approached Michael to seek his advice. Michael advised Julie to speak to her key career stakeholders to seek their view around the timing and value of the role, within the context of her career aspirations. This was sound advice; she did not apply for the role as the timing would have been premature. In a networking role, Michael has introduced Julie and Chandana to people within the Green HRM network, most recently suggesting they submit an abstract to the International HRM conference in Poland, which was accepted. This opportunity provides Julie and Chandana with the opportunity to see and hear colleagues with similar research interests and develop their subject knowledge. This will be crucial if Julie and Chandana are going to be successful academics within the new organisational structure. Very few if any academics write alone; finding colleagues who wish to co-investigate and co-write is important. As a guardian, Michael's feedback is always thoughtful and comprehensive, sufficiently challenging and nurturing at the same time. He is a role model to Julie and Chandana; on occasions when Julie and Chandana have had face-to-face sessions with Michael, he has energised them with his knowledge, warmth and praise.

WHY WERE THESE CONNECTIONS SO SUCCESSFUL?

Julie and Chandana's positive experiences demonstrate that whether formal or informal; whether labelled a mentor or without this title, when experience and knowledge is passed from one to another it can be a highly effective intervention, offering opportunities for learning and career development. An early definition of mentoring, provided by the European Mentoring Centre (now the European Mentoring and Coaching Council) defines mentoring as an off-line help by one person to another in making significant transitions in knowledge, work or thinking. A broad definition of mentoring is provided by Parsloe and Wray (2000) where mentoring is presented as a process that supports and encourages learning to happen, while the UK Chartered Institute of Personal Development's 2013 fact sheet defines mentoring as a learning opportunity for both sides, the more experienced mentor and the less or inexperienced mentee. Thus, these three definitions imply that mentoring is a process of engagement between two people who are committed to bringing about a change—in either the knowledge, skills, attitudes or abilities of the mentee. In a recent email exchange with Julie, Clultterbuck defined mentoring as "helping someone with the quality of their thinking about issues (and particularly career and medium to long-term development issues) that are important to them." The informal mentors who supported Julie and Chandana in their early period of transition from a practitioner to an academic did exactly this; assisted them to move from one stage of development to another, which made the phenomenon a rewarding experience (Wallace and Gravells 2007; Clutterbuck and Ragins 2002).

What do the "mentors" have in common? The mentors Julie and Chandana have described are skilled in developmental and sponsorship mentoring, positioning their style and approach as appropriate to the context and situation. They each have expansive internal and external organisational networks and are established in their fields of expertise. They are significantly more experienced than Julie and Chandana and have trodden a path which gives them the expert knowledge to coach, guide and counsel "mentees." Julie and Chandana's mentors had a strong sense of their own self-awareness and behavioural awareness, they are committed to their own learning and other people's learning, and they are able to develop meaningful relationships. All of these developmental or sponsorship relationships have helped Julie and Chandana to progress in their career from a Lecturer to Senior Lecturer.

CURRENT AND FUTURE CHALLENGES

Julie and Chandana's experiences in mentoring so far focus on teaching and learning and early career academic outputs, rather than the "traditional" academic outputs such as ABS (Academic Journal Quality guide) journal articles. It is in this area that both the relationship and the label of "mentoring" get more confusing. Julie and Chandana now explore their impressions and encounters with "educational leaders" and how this has shaped their thinking and views on the type of mentoring that is required to support them through the next stage of their career development journey to Associate Professor or a leadership role with the institution.

Selecting a "professional practice career track" rather than the "research fellow" career track can be seen as narrowing down the range of career network and academic publication opportunities by those on the traditional research route. Both Julie and Chandana were told very early on in their academic career by a number of colleagues that they would find it difficult to successfully navigate a career path in academia if they selected the DProf route, some claiming "it is the worst thing you can do" and "it is the wrong choice if you want to be an academic." As described, both Julie and Chandana came from a practitioner background. Therefore, the DProf made sense, building on their existing strengths and knowledge to inform their developing practice. From the mentoring context, there are only a handful of academics that have opted for this route so this narrows the mentoring options for Julie and Chandana greatly. Furthermore, within their own academic department, there is one female professor and ten male professors, only one of which is known for his work in the professional practice arena. In Cullen and Luna's (2006) study, they claim that there are too few female mentors, and those females in senior leadership positions in academia are too stretched and overburdened to mentor. As early career researchers, Julie and Chandana could benefit from mentorship from those with experience in their practitioner academic field, however, these females might be even fewer. As such, this would require the exploration of mentoring networks beyond each department, school and institution.

Other challenges exist, such as the challenges of having a young family and committing whole-heartedly to a successful academic career. As mature students, Julie and Chandana had entered academia later in their career, and this also can be seen as a limitation; developing an academic career at a senior level is a life-time commitment, and therefore mentors might be more willing to invest in those at the beginning of their journey as their research assistant. Allen et al. (1997) point out that mentoring relationships are often formed because individuals have common interests or when the juniors remind the seniors of themselves. This will mean that men will often gravitate towards sponsoring men with whom they connect more naturally.

Julie and Chandana wanted to be mentored by someone who could relate to them on a personal level; they wanted and still want someone who understands their constant priorisation of work, family, and community. Julie has two young children, aged three and eighteen months, and is the primary carer for both. Chandana has an extended family and very strong ties with her local community, regularly hosting events and religious ceremonies. Julie aspires to be mentored by a mentor in a similar situation who has successfully navigated his/her career to the level of Professor, whilst supporting a young family. Chandana would ideally like to work with a mentor that can relate to her cultural and community commitments. But are there such women in academic roles? Within Julie and Chandana's immediate reach, this is not the case. Therefore, if women like Julie and Chandana are to succeed in academia, the institution needs to move from informal mentoring that relies on individual initiatives to more formal mentoring programmes. This might be achieved through formal mentoring networks with proactive partner institutions to accommodate the diverse needs of early career professionals wishing to aspire to upper level and leadership roles.

REFERENCES

Allen, T. D., and L. T. Eby. 2007. *The Blackwell Handbook of Mentoring: A Multitude Perspective Approach.* Chichester, UK: Wiley-Blackwell.

Allen, T. D., M. L. Potect, and J. E. A. Russell. 2000. "Protégé Selection by Mentor, What Makes the Difference?" *Journal of Organisational Behaviour* 21(3): 271–282.

Allen, T. D., M. L. Potect, and S. M. Burroughs. 2000. "The Mentor's Perspective: A Qualitative Inquiry and Future Research Agenda." *Journal of Vocational Behaviour* 51(1): 86.

Clutterbuck, D., and B. Ragins. 2002. *Mentoring and Diversity: An International Perspective.* Oxford, UK: Reed Educational and Professional Publishing Ltd.

Clutterbuck, D. 2004. *Everyone Needs a Mentor: Fostering Talent on Your Organisation,* Fourth Edition. London: CIPD.

Clutterbuck, D. 2011. *Mentoring for Diversity.* Buckinghamshire, UK: Clutterbuck Associates.

Cullen, D. L., and G. Luna. 1993. "Women Mentoring in Academe: Addressing the Gender Gap in Higher Education." *Gender and Education* 5(2): 125–137.

Freedman, S. 2009. "Effective Mentoring." *IFLA Journal.* Sage publications, www.ifl.sagepub.com.

Haddock-Millar, J., N. Onyiuke, H. Villalobos, R. Asumadu, G. Gabor, and T. Derodra. 2011. "Middlesex University Mentoring Network: Student Perspectives of Their Learning Journey and Opportunities for Impact." *Enhancing Graduate Impact,* BMAF / HLST.

Haddock-Millar, J., N. Onyiuke, H. Villalobos, R. Asumadu, G. Gabor, and T. Derodra. 2011. "Middlesex University Mentoring Network: Leveraging Diversity." *The Diversity Mentoring Casebook,* Clutterbuck Associates.

Haddock-Millar, J., M. Muller-Camen, and D. Miles. 2011. "McDonald's Achieving Environmental Sustainability." *Managing Human Resources for Environmental Sustainability,* eds., S. Jackson, D. Ones, and S. Dilchert.

Haddock-Millar, J., C. Sanyal, and C. Rigby. 2014. *Blended Approaches to Mentoring Programmes.* International Mentoring Association 26th International Conference on Learn, Share and Grow 2014, March 8–10, Phoenix, AZ.

Haddock-Millar, J., C. Sanyal, and C. Rigby. 2014. *Mentoring for Employability: A Three Dimensional Framework.* 15th International Conference on Human Research Development Research and Practice Across Europe, University Forum Human Resource Development Conference (2014), June 4–6, UK.

Haddock-Millar, J., C. Rigby, and C. Sanyal. 2013. "*Developing a Public Sector Mentoring Scheme: A Multi-Stakeholder Perspective.*" Brightside 1st Annual Conference, London, UK.

Haddock-Millar, J., C. Rigby, and D. Clutterbuck. 2012. "*Developing a Public Sector Mentoring Scheme: A Multi-Stakeholder Perspective.*" European and Mentoring Coaching Council 19th Annual Conference, Bilbao, Spain.

Klasen, K., and D. Clutterbuck. 2004. *Implementing Mentoring Schemes: A Practical Guide to Successful Programmes.* London, UK: Elsevier Butterworth-Heinemann.

Parsloe, E., and M. J. Wray. 2000. *Coaching and Mentoring.* UK: Kogan Page Publishers.

Sanyal, C., and C. Rigby. 2013. "Does E Mentoring Work? The Effectiveness and Challenges of an International Professional Mentoring Scheme." European and Mentoring Coaching Council 3rd Annual Research Conference, Dublin, Ireland.

Shea, G. F. 1997. *Mentoring,* revised edition. USA: Crisp Publications Inc.

Singh, R., B. R. Ragins, and P. Tharenou. 2009. "Who Got a Mentor? A Longitudinal Assessment of the Rising Star Hypothesis." *Journal of Vocational Behaviour* 74(1): 11–17.

Wallace, S., and J. Gravells. 2007. *Mentoring*, 2nd edition. Exeter: Learning Matters.

III

Steps toward Successful Mentoring

EIGHT

Beyond Sisterhood

*Using Shared Identities to Build Peer Mentor Networks
and Secure Social Capital in the Academy*

Tamara Bertrand Jones, JeffriAnne Wilder, and La'Tara Osborne-Lampkin

As the twenty-first century forges ahead, black women in the academy continue to move forward. The research documents two distinctive, yet parallel narratives shaping the experiences of black women in higher education: one story highlights the steady progression of black women's attendance, retention, and overall presence in colleges and universities since the 1940s (McDaniel, DiPrete, Buchmann, and Shwed 2011). The other story reveals the trials as well as the triumphs facing many black women at all levels in academe (see Wilder, Bertrand Jones, and Osborne-Lampkin 2013).

For black female faculty, many obstacles often impede their job satisfaction, scholarly productivity, and overall success in academic environments. These challenges encompass personal, organizational, and political realms that inhibit black female success (Wilder, Bertrand Jones, and Osborne-Lampkin 2013). Black faculty often experience isolation and alienation in academic departments, micro-aggressions from peers, and professional jealousy (Johnsrud and DesJarlais 1994; Phelps 1995; Thompson and Louque 2005). For black women, race coupled with gender creates even more barriers in academic environments (Johnson-Bailey and Cervero 2008).

We acknowledge that these challenges are not experienced by all black women in academia. However, these issues do point to the need for black women academics to establish and maintain strong support systems (Gregory 1999). A community of scholars, comprised of other black female scholars, is integral to the professional development of black women in academia (Bertrand Jones and Osborne-Lampkin 2013; Turner 2002). Yet, chances of developing such connections on most American campuses are limited due to the low numbers of the population in these predominately white settings. Black, non-Hispanic women comprise only 3.6 percent of all full-time faculty in the United States (NCES 2009). These small numbers often necessitate that black females look outside their home institutions for mentors to build social capital necessary for success in academia.

In this chapter, we share our experiences in connecting with one another as black women and creating a strong peer network. The commonality that we share as three black women in the academy brings us together as sisters in the struggle of the professoriate. Yet, this chapter describes how we have been able to move beyond sisterhood. We discuss the role of peer mentoring in facilitating the development of social capital necessary for success in the academy. As scholars with similar research interests of mentoring, advising, and faculty development, we have benefited from the collective brain trust that comes from a group with similar goals and interests. Our collaboration has not only served to strengthen our current and future collaborative scholarship, but it has influenced our individual development as scholars and women.

We begin the first section of this chapter with our individual stories on the pathway to the professoriate, detailing how and why we decided on careers in academia—and the various challenges and triumphs associated with our journeys. We move into a discussion on how the three of us came together to form a professional research partnership. The latter portion of this essay engages a discussion of social capital and the importance of peer mentoring as a critical factor in our success and in the development of black female scholars in general. Lastly, we examine how our participation in the Sisters of the Academy (SOTA) Institute has influenced our scholarly productivity and contributed to our overall professional and personal development.

SHARING OUR STORIES

Storytelling is a focal aspect of the African American cultural tradition (Gates 1989; Goss and Barnes 1989). Historically, stories reflected the shared identity and cultural values of African American people, and they were told to preserve heritage, offer inspiration, and foster empowerment (Banks-Wallace 2002). This oral tradition was especially valuable during the time in which African Americans were struggling for emancipation from slavery in the 1800s and for civil rights in the twentieth century. As Banks-Wallace (2002) explains, "African American storytelling affirms the ongoing commitment of a people determined to nurture a unique, spiritually based culture in the midst of an oppressive environment" (413).

For African Americans in the academy—especially women of color—storytelling stands at the center of both our lived experiences and theory building. Many black women have employed a subjective standpoint to examine the various ways in which their race, gender, and other aspects of their identity shape their lives inside the ivory tower. As historian Stephanie Y. Evans (2007) notes, narrative accounts and personal anecdotes are key features of the black feminist tradition:

> many Black women educators kept their social standpoint and cultural identity at the fore of their treatises. They used dialogue rather than monologue as part of the teaching and learning process. (9)

The stories of black women academics provide a deeper comprehension of the complexity of issues at the intersection of race and gender, and how these complexities contribute to the often mysterious world of academia. Collins (1986) stated "the act of insisting on Black female self-definition validates Black women's power as human subjects" (S17). She furthers that black women have a commonality of experience and these voices need to be heard.

Most importantly, storytelling is vital to the growth and preservation of women of color in academe today. Because we live in a society that has purportedly transcended race, it has become easier to dismiss thoughts or feelings of prejudice and discrimination as ungrounded and irrational. Oftentimes, as black women we may believe that our experiences with racism, sexism, and other forms of inequality are isolated and unique. However, when we begin to speak up and share our struggles—and more importantly, our successes over those challenges—we can effectively grow as scholars, teachers, mentors, and individuals. In the same way that stories are told within the African American community, stories can be shared among black women in the academy for the purposes of expression, resistance, and empowerment.

We recognize that coming into voice—particularly for underrepresented minorities at predominately white institutions—is a privilege that not every black woman in academe holds. Having ownership over one's voice is something that many black women scholars have to attain gradually, carefully, and strategically. At many higher educational institutions, a culture of silence and passivity can make storytelling a considerable risk. So, we share our stories here for those women who (for a variety of legitimate reasons) have to remain silent. Our journeys are valid and are useful as "data" to facilitate a better understanding of other black women's experiences, as well as generate future areas of inquiry.

JeffriAnne's Journey in the Academy

The majority of women in my family are educators, so in many ways, I always knew that I would follow in the path of the footsteps laid before me. Watching my mother, aunts, and other relatives achieve advanced degrees showed me that black women's intellectual capacity and educational attainment was both valuable and boundless. Making the decision to pursue my doctorate in sociology, however, was resolved when I started college and immediately noticed no one who looked like me at the front of the classroom. I have had a host of wonderful professors and mentors throughout the course of my undergraduate and graduate career. However, in a span of the ten years I spent on the path to the PhD, only one of my professors was a black woman. Similarly, I encountered just as few black women enrolled in my master's and doctoral programs. At each step of the process, this disappointment only fueled my drive and motivation to be a recognizable face for the next black woman—and any other student (race and gender notwithstanding) needing to benefit from the diverse voices and perspectives of black female faculty in higher education.

I attended a private, liberal arts institution for my undergraduate education, and it was there that I discovered my passion for sociology and women's studies. I had caring and compassionate professors who showed genuine care and concern about my well-being, and they encouraged me to pursue graduate studies. Although the vast majority of my professors were white, I was introduced to many black women and other women of color via the literature in the classroom. This exposure only piqued my interest and reinforced my desire to study and learn more about the unique experiences of women of color.

Several years later when I enrolled in my doctoral program in sociology, I had an equally rewarding experience. I had nurturing professors, a supportive cohort of PhD students inside my department, and a peer network outside of my department through my institution's Office of Graduate Minority Programs (OGMP). It was there that I met a large number of minority students who were also pursuing their doctorates. Undoubtedly, this organization stood at the core of my personal and professional survival throughout graduate school. OGMP offered graduate students of color like me mentorship, professional development opportunities, and an abundance of knowledge on how to best navigate the oftentimes-rugged terrain of the doctoral process. And perhaps most importantly, I gained friends and peer mentors for life.

As a faculty member, I have had a much more difficult experience in building relationships and connecting with other colleagues at my institution. Since the start of my tenure-track position, I have been the only underrepresented minority faculty member in my department, and my status as an "only" has significantly impacted my experience. While I have warm colleagues, I am regularly frustrated by the absence of female faculty of color on my campus. Like much of the literature documents, I spent much of my pre-tenure probationary period managing my identity, emotions, and impressions. Almost every moment of my life at work (especially in my first year after graduate school) was carefully organized and scripted. In many ways, I likened the relationships and alliances I built at my institution to the reality show *Survivor*. I was always on guard, did not completely trust anyone, and felt that in many ways, my race and gender haunted me in ways that my white and black male colleagues did not have to consider.

La'Tara's Journey in the Academy

The pursuit of an advanced degree was considered the next "logical step" in terms of my academic and professional development. This "logical step" was largely impacted by the expectations set forth by my mother who was the first from her family to graduate from college and was an educator. I chose to attend an HBCU for my graduate studies where I met my friend Dawnette. After realizing that we had attended the same undergraduate institution, sharing our great individual experiences while at the institution "across the street," we developed an in-class relationship. After realizing that we had some common interests and held the same high expectations for the quality of our work, we developed a close friendship and support system for each other throughout our graduate program. It was also during this graduate program that I met one of my mentors who was a long-standing and highly regarded adjunct professor. Similar to my co-authors, I have had some outstanding professors during through the course of my PhD; however, it was during my graduate program that I first encountered faculty, one in particular, who would mentor and inspire me to pursue a doctoral degree.

My pursuit of a terminal degree, in the area of educational policy in particular, was largely centered on my desire to have a "seat at the table" to influence educational policy and practices for at-risk student populations. This desire was largely due to my early professional experience as a corrections administrator. Within this capacity, I was responsible for monitoring contract compliance of all aspects of facility operations for six private correctional facilities—ranging from food service to security. However, it was my oversight and evaluation of the educational policies and programs designed to reduce inmate recidivism that I found most intriguing and would serve as, perhaps, one of the largest influences in my desire to pursue my doctoral studies. So, I began the pursuit of a doctoral degree in educational policy, with the "intended purpose" of examining educational policy and reform efforts designed to improve educational outcomes for marginalized populations.

During my doctoral program, I was fortunate to have two friends whom I met prior, one, the only black male in the program at the time, and the second, a black woman who started the semester after, to go through the program, at least through coursework. We developed a close network to support each other through our studies, largely holding each other accountable for both academic and personal decisions that might impact our academic success. While I had great faculty members throughout the program who supported me as a scholar, two women in particular would become my mentors. One navigated me through the application process, provided me with my first assistantship, and explained the importance of becoming associated with the faculty member whom she believed was the "most up and coming faculty member in the department." The other, coincidentally the "the most up and coming faculty member," was my program and doctoral advisor, mentor, and later colleague. I was provided academic and professional opportunities, largely centered on research, which was to a degree uncommon to most students in our department, which made me a highly competitive candidate for the assistant professorship.

As an entering assistant professor, I entered a department in which I was highly respected as a scholar and was embraced and supported as a junior scholar and colleague. While I had not experienced any of the challenges that I had heard plagued other minority colleagues, it was during this time that I was intimately introduced to the literature surrounding these issues by one of colleagues and co-authors of this chapter, Dr. JeffriAnne Wilder. Unfortunately, as I transitioned from the assistant professorship and took on other faculty roles in the academy, my experience has been different and some of the challenges, I had only read or heard about emerged.

Tamara's Journey in the Academy

I knew I wanted to attend graduate school after attending the National Black Graduate Student Conference (NBGSC) in North Carolina while a junior in college at the flagship university in Texas. I attended school there during the Hopwood years, so being surrounded by five hundred black graduate students from around the country and some international students as well, was supremely validating after experiencing the doubt that came from perceived slights or questions about my academic competency. During the conference, I met a doctoral student completing his studies in African American studies at Temple University. I wanted to become just like him. I wanted to sound intellectual, able to articulate my knowledge about the black experience, and become an accomplished scholar.

Not long after returning to campus after the conference, I met with an advisor who asked me what I wanted to pursue after graduation. I told him I planned to attend graduate school. "To study what?" he asked. I shrugged my shoulders. By the time I'd gotten back home the reality of the distance between Temple and Texas, along with the prospect of knee-deep snow during the winter months, made me rethink my plans for pursuing African American studies. Unfortunately, I did not know enough about the graduate school process to search for similar programs in warmer climates or programs that were closer to home. Instead I just abandoned those hopes. After some conversation, my advisor and I realized that I had a passion for working with students, developing student programming, and overall engagement in student life on campus. That day I learned about student affairs, or higher education administration. Shortly thereafter, through a series of events that was surely divinely inspired, my family and I attached a U-Haul to the back of my car and moved me to Florida for graduate school.

During graduate school while at Florida State University (FSU) I developed a network of other black women. In my master's cohort there were four other black women and one black man. That year the program admitted three other black males for doctoral study. As a result, I had a built-in network within my cohort. Because of my exposure to the National Black Graduate Student Association (NBGSA), I joined the local Black Graduate Student Association (BGSA). Through BGSA I met other black women and men, some of whom became my core support system.

As I assumed leadership in NBGSA and the local BGSA, I attended more conferences; I heard the stories of alienation, isolation, and misunderstanding that plagued other black graduate students throughout their education. It was largely due to these stories that I became involved in recruiting for the college of education, assisting with visiting days for underrepresented prospective students to help increase the numbers of these students throughout the college, not just in my program. It was through these stories that I heard at professional conferences of women who did not have support systems, on or off campus. Those stories led me and six other black women to create Sisters of the Academy Institute (SOTA).

We will provide more historical background on SOTA in a subsequent section of this chapter, but I'd like to share how SOTA has influenced my journey to the academy. I write about the specific aspects of my graduate school journey in "Me-Search Is Research: My Socialization as an Academic" (Bertrand Jones, in press). However, for this chapter I focus on my experience as a faculty member.

After ten years as an administrator I transitioned to a tenure-track faculty position. Because I was involved in SOTA and was instrumental in developing and implementing SOTA's signature program, the Research BootCamp, I assumed I knew what a faculty position entailed. At the time I was engaged in research and evaluation work, I had undergraduate and graduate teaching experience, and service was my middle name. So, I knew what being an academic was all about. I remember writing to my administrative colleagues on my first day in my new office that I felt like a freshman moving into the residence hall. My office furniture had not arrived yet, so I had piecemeal old furniture. My office was about half the size of the office I'd left. There was no welcome sign on my door or colleagues waiting to take me to lunch to celebrate my first day. Honestly, the other faculty were not present, which only intensified my feelings of bewilderment.

Later, I would understand the culture of our department—that most faculty worked from home and no one had been "properly" welcomed when they arrived. It wasn't just me. After acknowledging the reality of my new situation, my knowledge of the importance of professional networks kicked in, and I started to look for friendly faces to begin developing my "work relationships." I went to lunch with one colleague and lunch with her shook my confidence and added to the angst I already felt. All of the negative aspects of her experience I took on as if they were mine. While I attributed my feelings to being unaware previously, I began to question my worth and contribution as a scholar. As a result I remained paralyzed, unable to full embrace my new role for a year and a half. I couldn't adequately articulate my feelings to anyone else; because I was too busy trying to balance all of my new responsibilities and expectations.

DEFINING SOCIAL CAPITAL AND CHALLENGES TO BUILDING SOCIAL CAPITAL FOR BLACK FEMALE SCHOLARS

As we have learned as minority female students and now faculty, our success was not happenstance nor did it occur in isolation. Gaining access to critical knowledge, networks, and other professional development opportunities can sometimes be a challenge for individuals who have not acquired sufficient amounts of social capital. A term advanced by sociologist Pierre Bourdieu (1986), social capital refers to resources, benefits, or added value as a result of membership within a particular group. Within the academy, social capital equates to concrete resources (for example, funding, co-authorship opportunities, and research collaboration). However, these benefits, such as emotional support, collegial relationships, and political alliances, are equally intangible.

For marginalized and underrepresented minority populations, the acquisition of social capital can be a daunting task, particularly for junior faculty members who are new to an institution and may not feel comfortable enough to initiate the development of such important cultural assets. Oftentimes, building social capital begins with seeking a mentor who shares "common ground": individuals with shared norms, values, and overall belief systems. For others, finding someone with shared social identities is the first step in building social capital. However, for black female faculty, finding someone who meets the "common ground" criteria may be a challenge.

THE ROLE OF MENTORING IN BUILDING SOCIAL CAPITAL

Mentoring has been described as a dynamic, mutually beneficial process between two individuals that consists of a range of formal and/or informal activities and interactions that may be related to work, skill acquisition, and social or emotional aspects of the mentor or protégé (Davidson and Foster-Johnson 2001; Gibson 2006). Mentoring activities can range from a mentor providing feedback on teaching and research (Haines 2003; Kram 1988) to helping the protégée "navigate the often-treacherous waters of spoken and unspoken rules and codes of academe" including those associated with expectations for tenure and promotion and identifying and becoming involved in the "right" opportunities (Kram 1988, 94).

Jean-Marie and Brooks (2011) offer a conceptual understanding of mentoring for women faculty of color based on the mentoring literature. They, along with others, also identify many benefits of mentoring. Several studies suggest informal/formal mentoring and supportive networks can enhance socialization (Davis 2008; Gibson 2006; Bertrand Jones and Osborne-Lampkin 2013; Peña and Wilder 2011), impact scholarly productivity, and increase persistence in women faculty of color (Fries-Britt and Kelly 2005; Holmes, Land, and Hinton-Hudson 2007). For newly minted faculty, mentoring can play an important role in their academic development and career trajectories, particularly for women and faculty of color (Dixon-Reeves 2003; Sorcinelli and Yun 2007; Tillman 2001). For example, mentors can help socialize protégés to life in the professoriate. In fact, some scholars assert that the degree they successfully learn the ins and outs of the academy hinges on the types of mentoring relationships they establish (Cawyer, Simonds, and Davis 2002). Tillman (2001) notes that in addition to facilitating the social adjustments, mentoring can also facilitate emotional and cultural adjustments to institutions in which women faculty of color often face alienation and isolation.

While the benefits of mentoring are uncontested, scholars note that the particular quality and nature of mentoring can influence the retention of women faculty of color (Diggs et al. 2009; Jean-Marie and Brooks 2011; Tillman 2001). For example, moving from a "one-size-fits-all model" for mentoring relationships can potentially improve the quality of mentoring and better meet the needs of the protégé (Peña and Wilder 2011). Brown, Davis, and McClendon (1999) wrote about mentoring in higher education, cautioning that "in order for mentors and mentoring programs to reach their potential, they must debunk and confront several myths,"

myths that can arguably impact the quality and nature of the mentoring relationship. The myths identified include: (1) The myth that any senior person can mentor any junior person; (2) the myth that if mentors engage with protégés during formal meetings, they have made a sufficient commitment; (3) the myth that mentoring is entirely formal; (4) the myth that faculty of color can only be mentored by faculty of color; and (5) the myth that a mentor and protégé's research interests, must be a perfect match (Brown et al. 1999, 96). Brown and colleagues debunk each of the myths and present options for engaging in successful mentoring relationships. They remind us that the likelihood of the perfect storm, or all the expectations for mentoring aligning perfectly in all relationships, is slim. Instead, peer mentoring offers an opportunity for mentoring that meets the needs of faculty of color, black female faculty in particular.

Peer Mentoring and Black Women

Lack of a critical mass of senior black scholars limits opportunities for same race-same gender mentoring relationships for black women (Stanley and Lincoln 2005). Fortunately, a greater number of black female peers are available for mentoring, thus developing peer mentoring relationships becomes particularly important for black women in academia (Thomas, Hu, Gewin, Bingham, and Yanchus 2005). Peer relationships offer an alternative to conventional mentoring relationships, with many of the same functions and benefits (Kram and Isabella 1985; Thomas et al. 2005). Peer relationships not only provide greater access to mentoring (Thomas et al. 2005), these relationships often last longer, are more intimate, and have higher levels of self-disclosure and trust than conventional mentoring relationships (Kram and Isabella 1985). Additionally, these relationships provide confirmation, emotional support, and friendship. As a result, the mutuality of these relationships, the notion that both individuals experience being a receiver and a giver in the relationship, helps individuals develop "a sense of competence, responsibility, and identity as experts" (Kram and Isabella 1985, 118).

Faculty of color receive less social support than their white counterparts (Jackson 2004; Ponjuan, Martin Conley, and Trower 2011). This socio-emotional bonding in organizations, as described by Denton (1990), includes relationship building within and outside of the work setting. In organizations, black women are less likely to participate in this type of bonding and subsequently are excluded from networks where these exchanges occur. In order to mitigate the consequences of foregoing the information-sharing that occurs in these networks, Denton argued that black women create opportunities for their own socio-emotional bonding with other black women.

In a study of over seventy black professional women, Denton (1990) identified three types of bonding activities that helped to shape their relationships with other black women. These activities included social companionship—social activities and sharing feelings; instrumental bonding—problem-solving and networking; and supportiveness—encouragement and emotional support. Of the three types of activities, the supportiveness bonding behavior was indicative of more influence on personal growth as compared with the other two types. In essence, when encouragement and emotional support were identified as a central component of their relationships, the women experienced greater personal and professional growth. The relationships with other black women confirmed and validated experiences for these women that others, non-black and/or non-female, may not understand (Denton 1990).

OUR COLLECTIVE JOURNEY: THE INFLUENCE OF PEER MENTORING

Despite the almost twenty-five years since Denton's study, based on our reflection, our relationships indicate that the encouragement and emotional support provided by the group, or peer mentoring relationships, is invaluable and has resulted in personal and professional growth. From our personal narratives is it clear that we are at different stages in different positions in the academy. Two of us are in traditional faculty positions, one recently tenured and the other on the tenure track, with another in a research faculty position. Despite these different locations, our collective is a "cadre of supportive colleagues who have equal or complementary work styles and values, but also in which reciprocity is clearly an integral element in the peer relationship" (Henderson, Hunter, and Hildreth 2010, 35).

JeffriAnne's Reflection on Our Collective Journey

Although I have been quite successful in my career thus far, I have greatly missed the opportunity to connect regularly with faculty counterparts from a shared cultural background. Since the start of my career as a sociology professor, one of the greatest difficulties I have managed is the absence a strong cohort of black female faculty at my institution who can readily understand the general stressors of the professoriate but also relate to the specific nuances of being a woman of color. While I do have a small group of colleagues at my current institution, who offer guidance and mentorship, developing relationships with other faculty who share my racial and gender background has been challenging. Thus, I have relied heavily on my friends from my doctoral program, and others who serve as my confidants, peer mentors, and trusted ear in times of need.

I met La'Tara in the fall of 2008 when we joined the faculty at the same university. Because she was the only other black woman at the New

Faculty Orientation, I noticed her immediately. We became cordial in our first year but did not really develop a friendship until the fall of 2009. After we recognized that we had similar research interests and were part of the same sorority, we connected more often and formed a research partnership with another African American faculty member who was a full professor and at the time, La'Tara's department chair. The three of us co-authored a paper and later collaborated on a National Science Foundation (NSF) grant. La'Tara and I began to exchange ideas, offer advice, and solidified a real peer mentoring relationship. In 2010, La'Tara transitioned to another institution, and I was saddened to be losing a good friend, colleague, and mentor. Fortunately, our friendship and relationship as peer mentors continued and flourished when she introduced me to Tamara Bertrand Jones.

My research partnership and mentoring alliance with La'Tara and Tamara has greatly improved my sense of efficacy and worth as a scholar in the academy. Because of my connection with them, I have acquired both tangible and intangible forms of social capital that have made a real difference in my life and career. Although neither of them is at my home institution, we talk on a regular basis, affirm each other personally and professionally, and have been very productive in publishing quality research in top journals. Further, I have leaned on both of these women as I have pondered the next steps in my career, took the journey to tenure and promotion, and needed sound professional advice in making career-making (or breaking) decisions. Most importantly, La'Tara and Tamara offered encouragement and support when I recently took a considerable risk in stepping forward about my experience with prejudice and discrimination at my institution. They were there to weigh the pros and cons of such a bold move and have continued to be there for me as I have managed the positive and negative consequences of this deeply political act. All told, my relationship with La'Tara and Tamara really is more than just an academic sisterhood; we are each other's advocates, mentors, and teachers. We have learned a great deal from one another and will continue to thrive and grow together as friends as scholars.

La'Tara's Reflection on Our Collective Journey

As noted, I met JeffriAnne when I joined the faculty of the University of North Florida (UNF) where we developed a collaborative research partnership. JeffriAnne and I would eventually develop a peer mentoring relationship and friendship in which I become to rely on heavily as I transitioned into a research faculty position at another institution. It was at my "new" institution that I had the opportunity to formally meet Tamara, whom I had been informally introduced to by a colleague who had been my department chair at UNF and a mentor to Tamara both as a student and faculty member. Shortly after I arrived at FSU in the fall of

2010, Tamara introduced herself and invited me to lunch. Although I was cordial to Tamara, I did not make any effort to solidify lunch plans. Due to Tamara's efforts, we eventually met for lunch and this meeting served as the foundation for what would later develop into a peer mentoring relationship that would be built on candor, trust, and respect in which we would see our individual and collective scholarship flourish.

It wasn't until the fall of 2012, after I had transitioned to another department, that Tamara and I began to work together as scholars when she invited me to co-author a publication, surrounding graduate student development. It was during this time, that I recognized how Tamara's interests and the work that JeffriAnne and I had begun intersected a great deal. So, the three of us began a journey engaging in scholarly activities that generated three scholarly publications within a year in top-tier journals. Our partnership not only has resulted in a clearly defined research agenda in a particular line of inquiry but has developed into a genuine relationship that has transcended our professional careers.

In 2010, for both professional and personal reasons, I decided to leave a tenure-track position to pursue a research faculty position that I believed would greatly enhance my research agenda and professional career. JeffriAnne was instrumental in helping me to think through this decision. While this decision has resulted in many additional outstanding opportunities, I found myself questioning my decision due to number of reasons. As such, I have relied on both of these women a great deal as I continued to evaluate this decision, navigated this new territory, and pondered my next career moves. This level of genuine peer support among colleagues was foreign to me prior to meeting JeffriAnne and Tamara. Moreover, our professional and personal relationships have mitigated feelings of isolation and the need to legitimize my work-indeed, new experiences. Lastly, while I have had great professional success, thus far, prior to meeting JeffriAnne and Tamara, I had essentially navigated my professional journey, largely, without the benefit of having a connection with colleagues who shared my cultural background. Through our individual and collective work, we seek to enhance these opportunities for other black women in the academy.

Tamara's Reflection on Our Collective Journey

With my experience in SOTA, connecting with another black woman in the same space was natural for me. I never knew that our lack of a lunch date meant that La'Tara was actually questioning my motives. Despite the initial mistrust, our mentoring relationship developed because of our professional experiences and research interests. My relationship with La'Tara was the beginning of rebuilding my confidence in my ability to succeed as a faculty member. Adding JeffriAnne to the collective only strengthened our relationship and bolstered my own confidence.

My work with JeffriAnne and La'Tara reminded me to believe in myself and trust that my development as a scholar was indeed a process. Despite the toxic environments that many black women encounter, I found myself in a space where I could flourish as a scholar within a community of other black women who believed in and supported me. I wondered how many other black women were like me in that the difference, both in professional productivity and personal growth, from one semester to the next centered on a support network of colleagues who understood. Not just understood me as a black woman, but could relate to me as a black female scholar. Our peer mentoring relationship extended beyond sisterhood. Our conversations initially centered on building upon our mutual interests for advancing our individual research agendas and shifted to crafting ways to shape a shared agenda making the most of our individual strengths and current positions in the academy. All with the end goal of equipping other women with the tools they need to be whole in the academy.

LOOKING FORWARD: CREATING A NETWORK OF BLACK FEMALE SCHOLARS

In 2001, Sisters of the Academy (SOTA) Institute was created to help facilitate the success of black women in academia by providing a support network. SOTA's motto, scholarship through collaboration, provides the guiding framework for the organization's mission and programming. Through professional development programs like the signature Research BootCamp©, Writing Clinic and Retreat, and Intensive Grants Workshop, SOTA addresses black women's need for accessible information centered on the black woman's experiences. SOTA's network of graduate students, junior and senior faculty, and other women in academia provide a ready source of mentors, both peer and senior.

Our collaboration, with its serendipitous beginnings, is the embodiment of SOTA's mission and motto. By building a supportive network, we are all successfully negotiating the university environment and producing scholarship as a result of our collaboration. In this chapter, we shared our individual and collective experiences as black female faculty in the academy. Here, our purpose and intended outcome was twofold. First, drawing from our own experiences we provide further evidence to support some of the professional challenges black female faculty encounter. Two, and perhaps more important in this context, we highlight a mechanism we used to combat these challenges, a contribution and a testament to the individual and collective resilience of scholars and practitioners in moving us along the research continuum. Essentially, scholars have been successful in identifying "the problem," developing research questions, and using an array of research methodologies for inquiries surrounding these issues. Scholars have also generated substantial and significant findings that have provided insight into the multi-faceted issues surrounding black female faculty. As we continue to move forward, indeed, we must continually pose the questions: What are the lessons we have learned along the way? How have these lessons informed the exploration of these issues, and how might they inform future inquiry? Most importantly, how have policies and practices changed as a result of our prior inquiry into these issues, and where are the opportunities to shape policy and practice as we move forward?

Over the past few decades, there has been much discourse and research surrounding the challenges plaguing minority women faculty in the academy, including black female faculty. In fact, viable platforms have been created to not only promote and engage scholars and practitioners alike in meaningful discourse surrounding these issues; but scholars have also engaged in a range of scholarly activities to accurately reflect and document the experiences of black women in the academy. Research surrounding these issues has also generated numerous strategies and mechanisms to support underrepresented minority women faculty and to mitigate some of the challenges black female faculty face. As such, the barriers and challenges that confront black female faculty and the need to implement policies and programs to ameliorate these issues have been established and is essentially uncontestable.

From the collective work in this area, we know that there remain, in some instances, deeply rooted institutional, organizational, departmental, and individual values, beliefs, and perceptions that perpetuate issues surrounding race and gender that inhibit the success of minority female faculty, including black female faculty. We also know that we have continued to see increasing numbers of black female faculty in the academy, and some have experienced great professional and personal success. With that being said, there are continued opportunities to enhance policies and practices that will continue to promote the representation and advancement of women faculty of color.

Our individual and collective experiences, along with other empirical evidence, suggest that informal mentoring experiences can be extremely effective tools to build social capital for minority scholars, and to potentially mitigate some of the challenges they face. Through a peer mentoring network, we were able to create a space where we could flourish as scholars within a community of other black women where we believed in and supported each other. However, the benefits of formal policies and programs that provide formal, structured mentoring experiences cannot be overlooked. For example, Sisters of the Academy (SOTA) has been successful in providing proven, effective formal networking and professional development opportunities for black women scholars and practitioners on a larger, national scale.

So, while it is equally important to promote ongoing dialogue and research around the potential obstacles to success for black female faculty, we are certainly positioned to highlight the increasing success we have had in creating mechanisms and supports, both informal and formal, to combat these issues. Exploration of these networks are also worthy of further exploration to continue to impact policy and practice. Specifically, we propose that we continue to identify and examine exemplar policies and programs, and promising practices to refine and/or redefine policy and to scale up and replicate programs and practices to expand these opportunities to further support and advance women faculty of color.

REFERENCES

Banks-Wallace, J. 2002. "Talk That Talk: Storytelling and Analysis Rooted in African American Oral Tradition." *Qualitative Health Research* 12(3): 410–426.

Bertrand Jones, T. Forthcoming. "Me-search Is Research: My Socialization as an Academic." In D. J. Davis, R. J. Brunn, and J. L. Olive (eds.), *Intersectionality in Education Research*. Sterling, VA: Stylus.

Bertrand Jones, T., and L. Osborne-Lampkin. 2013. "Early Career Professional Development: Enhancing Black Female Faculty Success." *Negro Educational Review* 64(1–4): 59–75.

Bourdieu, P. 1986. "The Forms of Capital." In J. G. Richardson (ed.), *The Handbook of Theory and Research for Sociology of Education*. New York: Greenwood Press.

Brown, M. C., G. L. Davis, and S. A. McClendon. 1999. "Mentoring Graduate Students of Color: Myths, Models, and Modes." *Peabody Journal of Education* 74(2): 105–118.

Cawyer, C. S., C. Simonds, and S. Davis. 2002. "Mentoring to Facilitate Socialization: The Case of the New Faculty Member." *Qualitative Studies in Education* 15(2): 225–242.

Collins, P. H. 1986. "Learning from the Outsider Within: The Sociological Significance of Black Feminist Thought." *Social Problems* 33: 514–532.

Davis, D. J. 2008. "Mentorship and the Socialization of Underrepresented Minorities into the Professoriate: Examining Varied Influences." *Mentoring & Tutoring: Partnership in Learning* 16(3): 278–293.

Davidson, M. N., and L. Foster-Johnson. 2001. "Mentoring in the Preparation of Graduate Researchers of Color." *Review of Educational Research* 71(4): 549–574.

Denton, T. C. 1990. "Bonding and Supportive Relationships among Black Professional Women: Rituals of Restoration." *Journal of Organizational Behavior* 11(6): 447–457.

Diggs, G. A., D. F. Garrison-Wade, D. Estrada, and R. Galindo. 2009. "Smiling Faces and Colored Spaces: The Experiences of Faculty of Color Pursuing Tenure in the Academy." *Urban Review* 4(1): 312–333.

Dixon-Reeves, R. 2003. "Mentoring as a Precursor to Incorporation: An Assessment of the Mentoring Experience of Recently Minted Ph.D.s." *Journal of Black Studies* 34(1): 12–27.

Evans, S. Y. 2007. *Black Women in the Ivory Tower, 1850–1954*. Gainesville, FL: University Press of Florida.

Fries-Britt, S., and B. T. Kelly. 2005. "Retaining Each Other: Narratives of Two African American Women in the Academy." *The Urban Review* 37(3): 221–242.

Gates, H. 1989. "Introduction: Narration and Cultural Memory in the African American Tradition." In L. Goss and M. Barnes (eds.), *Talk that Talk: An Anthology of African American Storytelling*, 15–19. New York: Simon & Schuster .

Gibson, S. K. 2006. "Mentoring of Women Faculty: The Role of Organizational Politics and Culture." *Innovative Higher Education* 31(1): 63–79.

Goss, L., and M. E. Barnes, eds. 1989. *Talk that Talk: An Anthology of African-American Storytelling*. New York: Simon and Schuster.

Gregory, S. T. 1999. *Black Women in the Academy: The Secrets to Success and Achievement*. Lanham, MD: University Press of America.

Henderson, T. L., A. G. Hunter, and G. J. Hildreth. 2010. "Outsiders within the Academy: Strategies for Resistance and Mentoring African American Women." *Michigan Family Review* 14(1): 28–41.

Holmes, S. L., L. D. Land, and V. D. Hinton-Hudson. 2007. "Race still Matters: Considerations for Mentoring Black Women in Academe." *Negro Educational Review* 58(1–2): 105–129.

Jackson, J. 2004. "The Story is Not in the Numbers: Academic Socialization and Diversifying the Faculty." *NWSA Journal*, 172–185.

Jean-Marie, G., and J. S. Brooks. 2011. "Mentoring and Supportive Networks for Women of Color in Academe. Women of Color in Higher Education: Changing Directions and New Perspectives." *Diversity in Higher Education* 10: 91–108.

Johnson-Bailey, J., and R. M. Cervero. 2008. "Different Worlds and Divergent Paths: Academic Careers Defined by Race and Gender." *Harvard Educational Review* 78(2): 311–332.

Johnsrud, L. K., and C. D. Des Jarlais. 1994. "Barriers to Tenure for Women and Minorities." *The Review of Higher Education* 17(4): 335–353.

Kram, K. E. 1988. *Mentoring at Work: Developmental Relationships in Organizational Life*. Lanham, MD: University Press of America.

Kram, K. E., and L. A. Isabella. 1985. "Mentoring Alternatives: The Role of Peer Relationships in Career Development." *Academy of Management Journal* 28(1): 110–132.

McDaniel, A., T. A. DiPrete, C. Buchmann, and U. Shwed. 2011. "The Black Gender Gap in Educational Attainment: Historical Trends and Racial Comparisons." *Demography* 48(3): 889–914.

National Center for Education Statistics. 2009. *Digest of Education Statistics: 2009*. Retrieved from http://nces.ed.gov/programs/digest/d09/.

Peña, M., and J. Wilder. 2011. "Mentoring Transformed: When Students of Color See Diversity in Leadership." *Diversity in Higher Education* 10: 345–363.

Phelps, R. E. 1995. "What's In a Number: Implications for African American Female Faculty at Predominantly White Colleges and Universities." *Innovative Higher Education* 19(4): 255–268.

Ponjuan, L., V. M. Conley, and C. Trower. 2011. "Career Stage Differences in Pre-Tenure Track Faculty Perceptions of Professional and Personal Relationships with Colleagues." *The Journal of Higher Education* 82(3): 319–346.

Sorcinelli, M. D., and J. Yun. 2007. "From Mentor to Mentoring Networks: Mentoring in the New Academy." *Change* 39(6): 58–61.

Stanley, C. A., and Y. S. Lincoln. 2005. "Cross-Race Faculty Mentoring." *Change* 37(2): 44–50.

Thomas, K. M., C. Hu, A. G. Gewin, K. Bingham, and N. Yanchus. 2005. "The Roles of Protégé Race, Gender, and Proactive Socialization Attempts on Peer Mentoring." *Advances in Developing Human Resources* 7(4): 540–555.

Thompson, G. L., and A. C. Louque. 2005. *Exposing the "Culture of Arrogance" in the Academy: A Blueprint for Increasing Black Faculty Satisfaction in Higher Education*. Sterling, VA: Stylus.

Tillman, L. C. 2001. "Mentoring African American Faculty in Predominantly White Institutions." *Research in Higher Education* 42(3): 295–325.

Turner, C. S. V. 2002. "Women of Color in Academe: Living with Multiple Marginality." *The Journal of Higher Education* 73(1): 74–93.

Wilder, J., T. Bertrand Jones, and L. T. Osborne-Lampkin. 2013. "A Profile of Black Women in the 21st-Century Academy: Still Learning from the 'Outsider-Within.'" *Journal of Research Initiatives* 1(1): 27–38.

NINE

Surviving the Academy

Reflections on Mentoring Female Faculty in Higher Education

Isaac A. Blankson, Venessa A. Brown, and
Ayşe Y. Evrensel

Institutions all over the world have a responsibility for providing a clear set of guidelines regarding their expectations from employees through inclusive and effective support mechanisms. Such guidelines and support mechanisms are expected to ensure that the institution functions at its highest level while promoting a sense of community among its employees. Independent of the nature of the institution, the fundamentally important part of providing professional support to employees is being intentional about this support. This chapter describes the support activities provided by a university for its faculty with an emphasis on female faculty. The Peer Consulting and Mentoring Program (PCMP) at Southern Illinois University Edwardsville (SIUE) is a grassroots support program for all faculty members, which is confidential and non-evaluative. Most important, it is provided by faculty for faculty. Being intentional about a mentoring program requires the identification of the challenges faced by faculty members. In academia, the variety of tasks that a faculty member needs to accomplish with success (such as teaching, research, and service) puts a significant pressure on the faculty member especially during the non-tenured years. As Mentor guides Odysseus's son Telemachus in Homer's *Odyssey*, mentors help faculty members to put the latter's current challenges in perspective.

Especially in the case of mentoring female faculty members, challenges come from different directions. First, while women have stronger representation in academia compared to half a century ago, there are still field-related variations in the representation of female faculty. This is not just a simple representation problem. Relevant academic structures have been formed by male academics for centuries and women have found these structures not necessarily conducive to thriving in academia. Second, trying to solve the riddle of the academic life coupled with their family-related responsibilities puts an additional pressure on female academician vis-à-vis their male counterparts. Third, anyone who has ever had female mentees knows that women tend to incessantly reflect on what is going on, what is being said, how they are being perceived, and so on. These are some of the female-specific pressures that need to be addressed when mentoring women in academia. Therefore, this chapter describes the approach of an academic peer consulting program to mentoring female academics. We suggest that being mindful and reflective on one's own experience in academia is an important ingredient of meaningful mentoring.

Our chapter is organized as follows. The following section presents an administrator's perspective of mentoring female faculty members reflecting her own experiences through the steps of academic career. The third section highlights the special position in which female academics find themselves at the beginning of their academic career and also shows that being mindful of the structural issues in academia is the first step toward successful mentoring of women. The fourth section highlights Southern Illinois University Edwardsville's (SIUE) Peer Consulting and Mentoring Program and shares the feedback from its female mentees. Finally, the last section concludes with our recommendations on how to effectively mentor female faculty members.

RELEVANCE OF MENTORING IN HIGHER EDUCATION: FROM A UNIVERSITY ADMINISTRATOR'S PERSPECTIVE

I will never forget the first day I walked into the classroom. My mind was focused on the children and families which I had served for over ten years while in practice. I was committed to ensure that the students that cross my path or took my classes would definitely be prepared for serving "my clients." You see I had a personal investment in ensuring that new social workers who entered the field of child welfare or the social work profession was equipped with the knowledge, skills, abilities and more important the passion to serve hurting families. So I opened my classes with "My name is Dr. Venessa Ann Brown. . . . I have a support system and none of you are in it." My point by making that statement was to say to my students that it is not about you. You do not look to your clients to take care of you. You do not expect to receive a thank you for all of the advocating that you will do. I sincerely was motivated to get this message across and prepare them for the journey ahead. As far as I was concerned, I could provide anyone who was not prepared for class a withdrawal slip. I had no problem with this approach, because I was set to prepare my students to become strong, caring, and effective social workers.

One day I sat and had coffee with a seasoned faculty member who had informally decided to mentor me. I never asked him, but our conversation and my respect for him led to a very healthy mentoring relationship. Our conversations led me to question whether I was frightening the students in my attempt to prepare them for the hurt and disappointments of so many of my clients. So, I invited him to sit in on my class and later he told me that he so enjoyed the class and wondered if the students would ever measure up to my expectation of commitment and passion for the profession. He stated that casually a few students came up to him and said "Wow, Dr. Brown really has the passion for the profession, and she wants us to be the best, but I wonder if we ever could." I went home and thought "Venessa, you are not doing protective services right now, and the students need to know you care."

I tell this story because it was my mentor who was able to assist me in transforming my perspective and bringing my passion to the classroom. I may not have learned the early lessons without having a mentor whom I respected and who wanted to see me be successful in higher education. He assisted me in transferring my social work skills, people skills, and passion from direct practice to the classroom. I have never forgotten our many conversations over coffee and the times we went over my student evaluations when he helped me process the information and develop strategies to make positive changes. My mentor helped me to grow as a passionate professor with high expectations who is also able to effectively communicate with her students without being so hard on them or myself. You see, my passion stemmed from a sense of conviction when I left child welfare practice. I left child welfare practice with the feeling that I owed a debt to families and children from whom I had learned how to be a good social worker. I was not about to let them down. My mentor helped me to put my passion for social work in perspective so that I can instill my passion in my students in a positive way.

My mentor was with me all the way through tenure and ultimately to a full professor. He listened to me, shared his experiences, challenged me to have a broader perspective, laughed with me and at me and taught me to laugh at myself. During those twelve years I became a better professor and went on to mentor my students and other colleagues. After taking an administrative role, I was committed to ensure that there was an institutional commitment to peer consulting and mentoring. There is no doubt that there is an administrative role in building an institutional mentoring structure in academia, where the administrator sets the stage for a confidential, supportive, and non-evaluative peer mentoring program and faculty mentors fellow faculty at every level of their academic journey. In addition to institutional buy-in, it is important to understand the needs, opportunities, and challenges facing female faculty

WHAT DO FEMALE MENTEES WANT? CHALLENGES AND OPPORTUNITIES OF MENTORING FEMALE ACADEMICS

What did I want when I started out as a female academic? Honestly, I didn't even know for which goals and outcomes to strive. I was a newly arrived female and relatively younger foreign faculty member. I learned at that time that things get really complicated when you start teaching at a university in a different country. In Turkey, where I came from, professors stood in front of the class and provided their lecture as a monologue. I was not aware of teaching styles and techniques, considerations as to how the material is received by students, and so on. The first course I taught in the United States was an utter shock. I did not understand why my students were behaving in a way as if I was not providing them with what they expected. They did not understand what I was trying to do. When the stories of my culture shock reached the department chair, he preferred the bossy approach and not one that of a mentor, I realized years later. He pretty much told me to shape up; I wondered how. I also realized for the first time what it means to have a foreign name and be female in the classroom with students whose customs and expectations were not clear to me.

Of course, later on I realized that this experience was not unique. One does not have to be a younger, foreign, and female faculty member to get lost in academia. Experiences of feeling alone and not being understood apply to female faculty in general and African American or Hispanic female academics as well. In other words, any of these groups of academics can identify themselves with the feelings of uncertainty, inadequacy, and isolation. The shortest but not so informative answer to the above question of what female mentees want is not to remain alone and know that someone would understand their challenges and care enough to assist. While this answer incorporates the ultimate goal of mentoring, there are countervailing structures in academia that would weaken or even inhibit effective mentoring of female academics. As such, I provide an explanation as to what makes mentoring female academics a unique subject. Following, I discuss the possibilities for providing a female-centered approach to mentoring.

What Is So Special about Female Mentees in Academia?

Academia is still a male-dominated workplace in the twenty-first century both in the United States and elsewhere in the world. In the United States and as of 2010, the percent of female faculty in bachelor, master's, and doctorate institutions are 45.5 percent, 46.1 percent, and 38.1 percent, respectively. U.S. statistics also indicate that among female academics, 32.2 percent, 23.9 percent, and 44 percent held non-tenure track, tenure-track, and tenured positions, respectively (Catalyst 2010). The wage gap is the largest between female and male full professors, where female professors make on average 90 percent of that of male professors (Catalyst 2010). Institutions of higher education in the United States have implemented various policies to reduce the gender gap in academia. These policies include intensified efforts to recruit female faculty, and once they are hired, to retain them through family-friendly programs and policies. Despite these efforts, both in the United States and abroad the gender gap in academia is still alive and well.

The aforementioned statistics associated with the gender gap are not just numbers; they convey information regarding the differential gender-based socialization process in academia. Long-reigning systems introduce their own socialization processes, which sets the stage for the incoming junior workforce. If the academic socialization process is defined by male academicians, this process will help male junior academicians to socialize and advance in the ranks but lead to the exclusion of female junior academicians. The research (Chandler 1996; Niemann 2002) on male academic socialization shows that male-to-male mentoring relations have a specific structure in that the junior faculty is taken under the wings of a senior faculty member who embodies experience and success. The senior faculty member shares pertinent information with the junior faculty member regarding the culture of the institution and what it takes to advance there. In this kind of a socialization scheme, not having a mentor may even hinder a newcomer's academic advancement. Not only receiving possibly private information about the institution but also being seen under the wings of a senior faculty member would surely make the academic life of a junior faculty member easier. The male-to-male socialization process can be described as a non-egalitarian relationship (or a power relationship), because the senior faculty member's suggestions are often nonnegotiable; they have to be accepted by the junior faculty member. The lack of discussion or reflection on the institution's culture and expectations turns the male-to-male academic socialization into a power relationship whose primary goal is to help a junior faculty advance in his career and not necessarily to help him exchange ideas with a senior faculty member.

Therefore, in the academic world, as in other work places, the senior members communicate the unwritten rules of the work place to the junior member or the mentee. The content of this communication usually includes expected behavioral patterns, rules of the game, ways to identify and engage players, in short, how to become a member of the established group or the power circle. Women can and do become part of the power circle. In fact, the term *tokenism* is used to describe accomplished women or members of a minority group who become a member of the established group. As the token of their representative group, female or minority mentees may feel special or privileged for being part of the power grid. The adverse effect of this special membership may reduce the mentee's willingness to encourage the success of others in her representative group (Chandler 1996; Niemann 2002).

Does this traditional mentor-protégé model or the male-to-male academic socialization process reflect women's expectations from academic mentoring? The answer would be yes, if women merely wanted to assimilate into the academic world with the explicit goal of being connected to a network of senior professors who can make or undo things, at least as perceived in the eyes of the mentee. However, female academics look for authenticity in their assimilation into the world of academics and want to increase their *social capital* through mentoring relations. As opposed to the power-based male-to-male mentoring, female academics value the quality of social interactions, which help increase social cohesion. The underlying element in social capital is not gaining power but building trust-based relationships through which not only one's productivity and well-being are improved but also a positive and cooperative relationship is built with the surrounding environment (World Bank 2014). An application of this concept to mentoring women in academia entails that, as opposed to the aspired vertical cooperation in the traditional male-to-male mentoring, female mentees mostly seek trust-based horizontal associations with their colleagues.

Therefore, what female mentees want from their mentors is more in line with Mentor in Homer's *Odyssey* than any other male-dominated socialization process. Odysseus leaves for war and gives his friend Mentor the duty to keep an eye on his household and, most importantly, on his son Telemachus. Odysseus believes that his son needs guidance in order to develop into the citizen he is expected to become. In the above quote, Mentor comforts Telemachus and speaks to him in a soft and nurturing fashion so that he would not despair. Mentor encourages the mentee, Telemachus, to put his current challenges in perspective and reassures him that he is too important for others around him to be left alone.

This ancient Greek story sets the stage for good mentoring for all ages. In fact, the nature of mentoring proposed in this story has nothing to do with the power-based mentoring-cum-career advancement relationship between the senior and junior academic. On the contrary, *The Odyssey*'s Mentor embodies the trust-based horizontal assimilation of the mentee in the mainstream, and this is exactly what the mentoring literature is telling us to do. As mentors, we use our experiences, our failures as well as our success stories, to communicate to mentees that mentors have not done everything right in their careers. Female mentees are not at all impressed with mentors who show themselves as a walking success story from the beginning of their careers. Even in *The Odyssey*, Goddess Athena sometimes disguised herself as mortal Mentor, which was extremely thoughtful of her. For a goddess, it was very easy to preach to a mortal how things should be done! Instead, Athena wanted to get closer to Telemachus as a mortal who had made and would make mistakes. Mentors share their experiences with honesty and humility with mentees. Even though there may be a difference in academic experience between the mentor and the mentee, the mentor-mentee relationship does not need a power differential. As mentors, we learn from the mentee as well and oftentimes, we see our own experiences under a different light; mentoring involves a mutually beneficial and complementary relationship. We mentors are encouraging, insightful, sharing, helpful, honest, non-judgmental, and collegial (Rogers 1957; Odell 1990; Bey and Holmes 1992; Jeruchim and Shapiro 1992; Beans 1999; Crow and Mathews 1998; Gaskin, Lumpkin, and Tennant 2003).

We contend that female mentees in academia want an egalitarian relationship with their mentors, where they receive insightful feedback, support, and respect for their individuality. Female academicians want and appreciate specific examples and suggestions, because they are much more concerned about how as instructors, they and their material are received in a class environment. They are more open when it comes to talking about their failures and mishaps than their male counterparts (Thoroughgood, Sawyer, and Hunter 2013) because they want to make some sense of them. In short, if we want female academics to continue flourishing in the academic environment, we need to effectively mentor them despite the existing male-dominated models of mentoring in academia. Our next section provides a discussion about how we can restructure the mentoring framework in academia for women.

Can Academia Provide Social Capital-Based Mentoring to Female Academics?

Universities all over the world would like to demonstrate their commitment to recruiting and promoting qualified female academics to comply with legislation. However, a more substantial reason for this commitment is the development of an academically strong and diversified workforce for the ever changing academic landscape. Studies (Gardiner, Tiggemann, Kearns, and Marshall 2007; Wunsch 1993) regarding the effects of pilot programs for mentoring women in academia consider the effects of colleague pairing, mentor training, development workshops, seminars, and networking activities and how these activities affect the pre- and post-participation perception of academic barriers by female academics. These studies suggest that effectively mentored women are more likely to stay at the university, receive more grant income, obtain higher-level of promotions, and have better perceptions of themselves as academics compared with non-mentored female academics. This suggests that not only women benefit from mentoring.

Administrators implementing such initiatives need to be aware of the current network of mentoring relations and critically evaluate them as to what may be missing in these relationships. Common problems for women include the scarcity of potential mentors, the lack of frequent faculty-protégé interaction, and the tension that stems from traditional gender-role expectations. The limited number of senior or even peer women makes it difficult for female mentees to seek out a female mentor. In male-dominated fields, finding a female mentor is further challenged by the lack of access to information networks and tokenism.

University administrations that are planning to provide effective female mentoring programs should focus on:

1. Recognizing and identifying circumstances that are specific to female academics: For example, department- or school-based mentoring programs could document the availability of mentors, work/family time constraints, the unique pressures on women of color, and gender-role expectations.
2. Reflecting on department culture: Departments should solicit feedback on their own culture and what it feels like to be there for various groups of women differing along the ethnic and racial lines.
3. Providing a voice and communicating concerns about the *status* of women: Department-level reflections should lead to actionable items to improve the support of the female faculty.
4. Being proactive: At various administrative levels, programs can be initiated to provide guidelines to mentor female faculty.

The socialization process of junior female academics does not have to adapt to the male patterns of academic socialization. Rather, female academicians can build their career paths drawing from their social roles and life experiences by seeking mentors who understand their social context. This nonhierarchical support network that is not based on disparate status as in the de facto mentoring model represents an alternative to the traditional senior male-based mentorship. A feminist construct for promoting women in academia is certainly not inferior to that introduced by senior males a long time ago. On the contrary, it can contribute to building a truly diversified academic environment.

THE PEER CONSULTING AND MENTORING PROGRAM AT SIUE

The Peer Consulting and Mentoring Program (PCMP) was created at SIUE in 2008 to offer tenure and tenure-track faculty as well as full-time instructors the opportunity for collaborative exploration of their teaching, research, and service. The program as it is today grew out of an existing program already at the university prior to 2008. The program is designed as a confidential, voluntary, supportive, non-evaluative, and collegial service available to faculty who would like to gather information or feedback from an independent, non-judgmental source about various aspects of their academic activities. As a grassroots effort, it also seeks to promote the realization of the Teacher/Scholar philosophy. This philosophy, according to The Teacher Scholar Philosophy of Southern Illinois University Edwardsville "reflects a serious continuing commitment to teaching, scholarship, and service in the belief that scholarship complements and enriches excellence in teaching and service. As such, it values, elevates, and balances the teaching, scholarship, and service functions of the faculty" (SIUE 2008, 4). It is common knowledge that the demands of a tenure track appointment at any university can be overwhelming to a junior faculty member, particularly female and minority faculty. Thus, one of the goals of the PCMP is to assist the faculty succeed in their teaching and scholarship to ultimately attain tenure.

To ensure the success of any mentoring program, mentors should be selected with care. In an academic environment, mentors should be fellow faculty members from different backgrounds who have an innate ability to relate to another faculty member's challenges which can stem from discipline-, gender-, ethnicity-, or race-related issues. PCMP's mentors are academics that have diverse backgrounds and are an extremely caring group of people. Positive attitudes, willingness to share one's own challenges and experiences, and professionalism are the characteristics of our mentors. Additionally, the fact that 72 percent of our mentors are female speaks volume. As indicated in the previous section, women in academia face additional challenges compared to their male counterparts, such as feeling torn between academic work and family responsibilities and various biases originating from society's expectations of women. For example, studies show that students expect that female faculty members should also be nurturing, in addition to being a professional (Athena, Collings, Chrisler, and Quina 1998). These gender biases may be magnified for female faculty of different national, ethnic, or racial backgrounds. Thus, the strong representation of female faculty in our mentoring program is a tribute to our female faculty who has a deep understanding of these biases and wants to put their experiences in good use by servings as a mentor.

Our mentoring program, the PCMP, provides a number of services to the SIUE faculty. GIFT (Group Instructional Feedback Technique) allows a consultant/mentor to ask a faculty member's students questions and share students' answers with the faculty member. Both online and face-to-face courses can be observed by mentors, and the results are shared with the faculty member. Faculty members may also request a mentoring session, where they can confidentially and openly discuss their challenge with a consultant/mentor over a cup of java. We find that in all these diverse interactions between faculty members and mentors, female mentees seem to have a clear understanding as to the nature of the challenge and an ability to verbally express these challenges. Clearly, our mentoring program complements other existing mentoring opportunities at SIUE. While departments and schools provide their own mentoring to junior faculty members, they tend to be focused on communicating the department's or the school's expectations to the newcomer. Such mentoring structures have important information content, and they focus to a lesser degree on the newcomer, her struggles and challenges. We contend that a university-level supportive and confidential mentoring program can meaningfully serve the university community.

Gender and Faculty Mentoring

The Peer Consulting and Mentoring Program at SIUE has a core of eighteen faculty mentors from a variety of academic disciplines. Mentors comprise of thirteen female and five male tenured faculty members. Between August 2008 and April 2014, there have been a total of 189 requests for mentoring in all three areas of our Program's service: 112 requests for Group Instructional Feedback (GIFT), sixty-four requests for class observation, and thirteen requests for one-to-one mentoring. The majority of these requests came from female faculty (62 percent) and only 38 percent from their male counterparts. Requests have been made overwhelmingly by junior faculty in tenure-track positions. We note that the utilization of the types of services suggest a gendered issue. For example, all thirteen of the One-to-One Mentoring requests, sixty-five of the 112 (58 percent) GIFT requests, and thirty-eight of the sixty-four (59 percent) requests for Class Observations came from female faculty.

From the data, it appears that women and faculty of color have special mentoring needs and therefore seek more of such relationships and services. As indicated in the previous section, this result may stem from the fact that women strongly reflect on their teaching and would like to know how they are perceived by their students. Additionally, female academics would like to maintain trust-based relationships through which they receive instrumental and emotional support for a broad range of intellectual endeavors at various points in their careers (Grant, Ward, and Forshner 1993). According to Hall and Sandler (1983) and Gaskin et al. (2003), it is also common for female faculty to have profound and specific needs for mentoring to address a variety of personal and professional concerns, including need for more personal encouragement in career advancement. This is particularly true of women in fields traditionally defined as male-dominated fields, which is also true for other minority faculty.

Similarly, Schwyzer (2008) believes that there are cultural forces that make it more likely for women to ask for help when they need it, and it makes sense that the majority of the mentoring services our Peer Consulting and Mentoring Program provides are utilized by the female faculty. Grant et al. (1993) notes that female faculty may have more limited access than men to the particularly distinguished advisors in their respective departments who can provide special advantages to them as beginners in their career. In sum, our experiences support the literature that suggests women faculty typically will identify programs, such as ours, that have other women faculty or faculty oriented toward women as important sources for mentoring and encouragement.

Experiences and Testimonies of Female Faculty Mentees

It is not surprising to us that the majority of the feedback regarding the usefulness of the Peer Mentoring and Consulting Program have also come from the female faculty members who have been mentored by the program. The comments of a junior female faculty mentee were typical of many others who have received services from the program:

> As a junior faculty, this service is incredibly fruitful. This is my second time doing it, and it has yielded data that is highly informative of my current teaching practices. I get substantially different feedback than I do from the end of the semester evaluations. I highly recommend it for all faculty.

Another mentee noted:

> The mentor provided feedback report in a timely manner. It is always good to "see" a class taught by me through the eyes of others as sometimes I tend to be subjective. I was impressed by the professionalism of the peer mentor, by the promptness and willingness to discuss the observations. This is a wonderful service.

Feedback obtained from faculty also indicates that the mentees use the experience and interactions to improve their careers and chances for tenure, as indicated in this comment:

> The experience was helpful. I used this opportunity to explore some areas of concern based on my mid-tenure reviews. Not only did I get valuable feedback about those areas, but my mentor noticed a few things I had never considered.

A good mentoring program is built on effective mentoring provided by caring, highly motivated, and knowledgeable mentors. This comment by another female faculty mentee captures the essence of this notation:

> My mentor was a tremendous wealth of knowledge. She shared her experience and resources to help me diagnose the problems and develop a plan of action. She was incredibly generous with her time and suggestions. I was truly impressed with her ability to tap in to my concerns so easily. She definitely has provoked my thinking to a new level of awareness that I had not considered even possible.

Another had this to say:

> The feedback and the follow-up meeting I had with my mentor were invaluable. She sat down and walked me through the methods that she has incorporated in her courses. It helped me see actual examples, and allowed me to learn from her expertise, but also tailor it to fit to my own needs in my courses.

Several female mentees have also commented on the utility of the service to their research endeavors and even offered suggestions on how to strengthen the mentor-mentee experiences. For example, one faculty member wrote:

> I received some good ideas about where to look for research ideas, how to find collaborators, and time management strategies. I would suggest getting mentors in each school or discipline so that they have a basic understanding of the general field the mentee needs help with. For example, my research as a qualitative educational researcher is very different from the persons who mentored me. She had good general tips, but it was hard to take that and put it into a context that helped one more meaningful level. Maybe you could have a few mentors and the mentee could pick the person with the closest area of expertise? Possibly have a database or list of people in the different methodologies willing to answer questions, provide feedback and help in other ways specific to qualitative or quantitative methodologies? Overall, the mentor I had was very kind and helpful in general ways.

Finally, this comment captures the overall sentiment and the goals of the program:

> I think it is a great way for new faculty to meet established faculty throughout the university. It is a great source of support and feedback for faculty who decide to take advantage of the program. I think this is a great resource, but just recently found out about it. (This could definitely be my fault, not yours!) I like the informality of it. It was very casual and provided me with some excellent resources and another connection here at the university. Thanks.

ESSENTIAL INGREDIENTS OF MENTORING FEMALE ACADEMICIANS

If the goal is to effectively mentor women in academia, mentoring programs in academia need to understand the circumstances in which women find themselves as junior faculty members. The first fundamental obstacle to the assimilation of female academicians into the university environment is the structure of the environment itself. We believe that institutional mentoring in reality has to some extent strayed from its original content in *The Odyssey*. Over the centuries, the male-dominated academic power structure has reduced mentoring to a climbing-through-socialization activity, where the selected junior faculty members are taken under the wings of the powerful senior professors. Women and persons of color who have experienced the essence of this power structure all their lives are just not comfortable with this structure. If we have learned anything about our female mentees in our program, we know that they do not want to be a member of an exclusive club. They would like to experience, as in *The Odyssey*, what the mentoring literature has prescribed all along as a functional and effective mentoring relationship that is based on positive, respectful, supportive, motivating, and egalitarian interaction.

Our experience with female mentees has shown that women are very concerned about how they are doing their job, how they are perceived as teachers by their students, and so on. Female academicians' heightened self-awareness does not stem from baseless worrying; it stems from their experience with facing different expectations than that of their male counterparts. It is an added stress for female academics that they are expected to be caring and nurturing to their students in addition to be professional, something that is not expected from a male academician.

Successful mentoring of female academicians requires taking an inventory of societal as well as institution-specific pressures on women. Such efforts need to identify specific obstacles to their assimilation into the academic life where assimilation does not mean to become part of the existing system that has caused problems for them in the first place. Assimilation of women and persons of color in academia entails building new structures in which they experience positive feedback and support so that they can be effective teachers and productive scholars.

REFERENCES

Athena, A., L. H. Collings, J. C. Chrisler, and K. Quina. 1998. *Career Strategies for Women in Academe*. Thousand Oaks, CA: Sage Publications.

Beans, B. E. 1999. "Mentoring Program Helps Young Faculty Feel at Home." Retrieved from http://www.apa.org/monitor/mar99/mentor.html.

Bey, T. M., and C. T. Holmes. 1992. *Mentoring: Developing Successful New Teachers*. Reston, VA: Association of Teacher Educators.

Catalyst. 2010. "Statistics about Female Academics." Retrieved from http://www.catalyst.org/knowledge/women-academia.

Chandler, C. 1996. "Mentoring and Women in Academia: Reevaluating the Traditional Model." *National Women's Studies Association Journal* 8(3): 79–100.

Crow, G. M., and L. J. Matthews. 1998. *Finding's One's Way*. Thousand Oaks, CA: Sage Publications.

Gardiner, M., M. Tiggemann, H. Kearns, and K. Marshall. 2007. "Show Me the Money! An Empirical Analysis of Mentoring Outcomes for Women in Academia." *Higher Education Research and Development* 26(4): 425–442.

Gaskin, L. P., A. Lumpkin, and L. K. Tennant. 2003. "Mentoring New Faculty in Higher Education." *Journal of Physical Education, Recreation & Dance* 74(8): 49–53.

Grant, L., K. B. Ward, and C. Forshner. 1993. "Mentoring Experiences of Women and Men in Academic Physics and Astronomy." In C. M. Urry, L. Danly, L. E. Sherbert, and S. Gonzaga (eds.), *Women at Work: A Meeting on the Status of Women in Astronomy*, 81–86. Proceedings of a workshop held at the Space Telescope Science Institute, Baltimore, Maryland, September 8–9, 1992. Baltimore: Space Telescope Science Institute.

Hall, R. A., and B. R. Sandler. 1983. "Academic Mentoring for Women Students and Faculty: A New Look at an Old Way to Get Ahead." *Project on the Status and Education of Women*. Association of American Colleges.

Jeruchim, J., and P. Shapiro. 1992. *Women: Their Mentors and Success*. New York: Fawcett Columbine.

Niemann, Y. F. 2002. "The Psychology of Tokenism: Psychosocial Realities of Faculty of Color." In G. Bernal, J. E. Trimble, A. K. Burlew, and F. T. Leong (eds.), *Handbook of Racial and Ethnic Minority Psychology*, 100–118. Thousand Oaks, CA: Sage Publications.

Odell, S. J. 1990. *Mentoring Teachers*. Washington, DC: National Education Association.

Rogers, C. R. 1957. "The Necessary and Sufficient Conditions of Therapeutic Personality Change." *Journal of Counseling Psychology* 2: 95–103.

Schwyzer, H. 2008. "On Male-Female Mentoring and the Wisdom of Openly Disavowing Sexual Interest." Retrieved from http://www.hugoschwyzer.net/2008/04/02/im-not-a-creep-on-male-female-mentoring-and-the-wisdom-of-openly-disavowing-sexual-interest/.

Smith, M. V. 2005. "Modern Mentoring: Ancient Lessons for Today." *Music Educators Journal* 92(2): 62–67.

Southern Illinois University Edwardsville. 2008. "The Teacher-Scholar Philosophy of SIUE." Retrieved from http://www.siue.edu/graduate/pdf/TEACHER_SCHOLAR_PHILOSOPHY_Apr2011.pdf.

Thoroughgood, C. N., K. B. Sawyer, and S. T. Hunter. 2013. "Real Men Don't Make Mistakes: Investigating the Effects of Leader Gender, Error Type, and the Nature of the Task on Leader Error Perceptions." *Journal of Business & Psychology* 28: 31–48.

World Bank. 2014. "Social Capital." Retrieved from http://web.worldbank.org/WBSITE/EXTERNAL/TOPICS/EXTSOCIALDEVELOPMENT/EXTTSOCIALCAPITAL/0,,contentMDK:20185164~menuPK:418217~pagePK:148956~piPK:216618~theSitePK:401015,00.html.

Wunsch, M. A. 1993. "Mentoring Probationary Women Academics: A Pilot Programme for Career Development. *Studies in Higher Education* 18(3): 349–362.

TEN

Mentoring Practices for Female Faculty

The Role of Professional Networks

Emma Previato

Mentoring is an activity that, especially in education and academia, emerged in the late twentieth century and has not reached the status of traditional disciplines which benefit from funding and research to identify best practices. It may therefore be valuable to compile commented surveys of mentoring activities organized around particular themes, which is one purpose of this chapter. Its primary target are underrepresented women professionals, who may find resources and support by learning of such activities; a broader target audience are those interested in analyzing, constructing, or improving existing institutionalized mentoring programs. Indeed, mentoring can take several forms (for example, personal or group); it involves different aspects according to the area (for example, healthcare, management, education), and calls for a variety of assessment techniques. This chapter's theme is the role of professional organizations and institutionalized programs (that is to say, a recognized, sustainable program within, say, a university or a company).

My experience and focus is the field of education, and research, in the area of science, technology, engineering, and mathematics (STEM). As a mathematician coming of age in the early years when women were underrepresented, namely the 1970s, I received informal mentoring in the form of experiential advice from rare encounters with females who had achieved professional recognition; their words of wisdom were substantive resources that allowed me to persevere. I am inspired by the book

Every Other Thursday (Daniell 2006) which tells the story of a group of professional women, including scientists, university professors, and administrators, who met twice a month for more than twenty-five years, establishing specific practices such as goal setting, networking, and checking on each other's progress. I am inspired to see more intentional examples of mentoring taking place for women and girls interested in the STEM field. For example, concerned about the status of women in war-plagued regions of the world, lawyer Nina J. Lahoud, of the United Nations (UN) Department of Peacekeeping Operations and an Advanced Leadership Initiative senior fellow at Harvard, designed a project aimed to "enhance opportunities for women from conflict-affected countries to obtain legal education and cross-regional mentoring and peer networking support" (*Harvard Magazine* 2014). The response to her call for professional mentors was outstanding, and matchings were swiftly established; to facilitate the process, Lahoud actually took an unpaid leave of absence from her UN job and funded her own travel.

Recently, in the United States, programs for girls have proven effective in building confidence and a sense of community. An online program launched in 2014, "Million Women Mentors," is an engagement campaign and national call to action that mobilizes corporations, government entities, nonprofit, and higher education groups around the imperative of mentoring girls and young women in STEM fields. Million Women Mentors will support the engagement of one million science, technology, engineering, and math (STEM) mentors (male and female) to increase the interest and confidence of girls and young women to persist and succeed in STEM programs and careers. Anyone willing can "take the pledge" and become part of this mentoring community.

Following, I provide an overview of some issues and briefly discuss institutionalized programs for female faculty or (prospective) professionals. I primarily focus on the Association for Women in Mathematics (AWM) and briefly discuss the Association for Women in Science (AWIS) and the Radcliffe Institute Mentoring Program. These programs demonstrate how mentoring can facilitate women's academic pursuits and achievements and I hint to areas where organizations may still fall short with mentoring efforts.

UNDERREPRESENTATION

The personal need for mentorship in my early search for a professional pathway led me to be sensitive to the challenges faced by underrepresented minorities, such as African Americans: I was struck by reports that observed cultural differences between African American and Asian American students facing academic challenges. While the former tend to isolate (Osborne 1997), the latter congregate (An 2007) and work in groups to resolve challenges and draw strength from family networks through the celebration of traditions and support. This resonated deeply with me. I attempted to "institutionalize" a celebration of achievements, and in 2004 created AFRAMATH: African-American Mathematics, an annual symposium at Boston University (BU) that has reached its tenth anniversary this year. The vision of this one-day event was to assemble local communities of teachers and mentors, showcase a distinguished scientist to give a keynote address, debate issues, and provide opportunities for faculty/student panels. While this event and its ramifications were not designed specifically for an audience of faculty or professionals, in a way it was a mentoring resource, both for professionals that work with underrepresented groups and for professional mentors who came to share their experiences with us and among themselves. For example, in 2008 the keynote speaker was Raymond L. Johnson from the University of Maryland at College Park (UMD); he was awarded the 2006 Mentor Award for Lifetime Achievement from the American Association for the Advancement of Science (AAAS). His initiatives and efforts have resulted in UMD being second only to Howard University in the production of African American PhDs. He has personally mentored twenty-three students who have received PhD degrees in mathematics, twenty-two of these students were African American, and among these, eight were female. Professor Johnson's recipe for success was couched into a piece of advice about perseverance to get funded by the administration.

Invitations to AFRAMATH included all ethnic groups, but the speakers were black, for the purpose of providing rarely seen role models. Indeed, a 2004 student panelist said of a black mentor in graduate school, "That was the first time I saw someone on the faculty who looked like me" (personal communication). Another attendee was encouraged by the event to quit his job, to go back to graduate school to earn a master's in mathematics from BU.

In STEM, the National Science Foundation (NSF) defines ethnic groups that are significantly underrepresented at advanced levels of engineering and science as: blacks, Hispanics, Native Americans, Alaskan Natives, and Native Pacific Islanders (NSF 2014). The Field of Dreams Conference is an annual three-day event for underrepresented minority undergraduate students to be matched with mentors who facilitate their applications to graduate school, sponsored by the NSF and by the National Alliance for Doctoral Studies in the Mathematical Sciences (http://mathalliance.org). One of the Alliance's cofounders, Philip Kutzko, was honored by the American Mathematical Society with its 2014 Award for Distinguished Public Service, for his leadership of a national effort to increase the number of doctoral degrees in the mathematical sciences earned by students from underrepresented groups. Additionally, the NSF-funded Alliance for Graduate Education and the Professoriate (AGEP) forms alliances, consisting of institutions dedicated to supporting underrepresented minority students, women, and students with disabilities to complete advanced degrees in the STEM fields. BU is a member of this alliance, so I invited several faculty from other alliance colleges to AFRAMATH with the hope they may become "feeder" partners for our graduate program. We succeeded in bringing in one Medgar Evers College student for her master's degree. BU is also a member of the National Graduate Education for Minorities (GEM) Consortium, which promotes the participation of underrepresented groups in post-graduate science and engineering education and the technical workforce. Another notable program is the Summer Undergraduate Research Fellowship (SURF) Program at BU. It is designed to promote access to graduate education for talented undergraduate students, especially those from minority groups traditionally underrepresented in the sciences. The SURF Program is supported by funds from the National Science Foundation (NSF-REU; NE-AGEP), the Department of Defense (ASSURE), and BU.

I close out this section with a cautionary account about institutionalization (which does not lessen my gratitude to BU, but will be part of the evidence given in the concluding remarks to this chapter) to identify weaknesses and a call for action. After a few years of continuous support, the Boston University Humanities Foundation rejected my further applications on the grounds of the event having insufficient "humanities" content. I suppose, an institution can only allot so much funding with so many competing initiatives. As such, I now run AFRAMATH on a pro bono basis and a shoestring budget, long hours of administrative effort, and last-minute logistic uncertainties. It is constantly edifying to see the generosity and positivity that are bestowed on this event. On the other hand, BU does provide extensive and successful mentorship to students with underprivileged backgrounds, such as the Posse Foundation Scholars and Upward Bound program or the Boston Public High School students. To support these mentoring opportunities, I have made a commitment to allow the leaders of these programs to have a booth to advertise their initiatives at each AFRAMATH symposium.

STRENGTHENING LEADERSHIP

I want to highlight an initiative related to professional mentoring that seems very valuable to me; I have not seen it implemented in gender/minority contexts. Several foundation-sustained initiatives aimed to "close the achievement gap," particularly ones that address the teaching of mathematics, provide training and community building for teachers, with the provision that the selected participants will then go back and become models (mentors, arguably) to their colleagues. Examples are:

- The Knowles Science Teaching Foundation — the signature program awards fellowships to early-career science and mathematics teachers;
- The MAA Project NExT, "New Experiences in Teaching" — provides a year-long fellowship to new and recent PhDs in the mathematical sciences — in particular, it offers participants an ongoing network of peers and mentors. Many Project NExT fellows go on to become leaders within the profession;
- The Simons Foundation's Math for America — prospective and experienced teachers form a community gathers to exchange ideas and define excellence.

Additionally, the American Chemical Society (ACS) runs a Scholars Program, awarding scholarships to underrepresented minority students; moreover, the ACS provides its members with personalized career coaching with guidance on interviewing techniques, career transitions, networking, resume writing, and salary negotiation. These skills are critical for advancing towards leadership positions; it has been noted that females in the workforce still lag behind their male competitors when it comes to skills such as public speaking and negotiations (Tucker 2007; Houflek and Warren 2005). Finally, I mention the Enhancing Diversity in Graduate Education (EDGE) program, sponsored by Morehouse and Pomona Colleges. This program has the goal of strengthening the ability of women students to successfully complete PhD programs in the mathematical sciences and place more women in visible leadership roles in the mathematics community (http://www.edgeforwomen.org/).

The Association for Women in Mathematics (AWM)

The AWM was founded in 1971, as an organization intended to bring together a sparse and lagging community (Valian 1997). Women felt that it was imperative to encourage girls to embrace their mathematical talent, to create financial incentives in the form of prizes and travel support, and to build an image through a speakers' program. Many women felt marginalized; they had experienced discrimination or even explicit advice against their call. This situation has largely improved; however, when I finally obtained funding (through the sponsorship of a scientific company) to create the BU student chapter of the AWM (November 2013), one of the members reported: "a male classmate remarked to me, you can't be a professional mathematician because you are a girl. Nobody would marry you!" She cited this as the reason why she wanted to contribute to the AWM activities. At our first AWM event at BU, our guest speaker chose to give a conversation/interview rather than a formal lecture. We asked her about the goals of the AWM and her own experience, and she highlighted how the organization, though now supported by the NSF and institutional partners, is still run on a volunteer basis. When asked about the impact that the AWM had on her, she mentioned that as an early-career mathematician, the most valuable aspect of the AWM, and one that largely contributed to her persevering in the profession, was that it facilitated finding female colleagues. They would meet at conferences and spend time together, building relationships that would last through-out their lives—one of the closest such connections was not working in her area, but they felt a bond because of being females and loving their subject, within a male-dominated community.

The AWM is of course open to men, who can be members, administra-tors, or professional contributors. However, women are the professional target. An article (Blum 1991) written by one of the earliest AWM presi-dents, chronicled the AWM as one of the most influential organizations for promoting women in mathematics. This organization funds yearly awards for travel and mentorship activities and showcases achievements during annual conferences. Professional support in the form of commen-taries, testimonials, and job tips is provided bi-monthly by the AWM newsletter. The newsletter published an article on professional gender bias which was very enlightening for me (Koblitz 1990); the author noted that a lot has been written on the question of whether or not student ratings tend to discriminate against women, but this topic was not typi-cally published in journals which mathematicians normally read. This author's wife, Ann Hibner Koblitz, went on to found the Kovalevskaia Fund, a small foundation which aims to encourage women in science and technology in developing countries: Kovalevskaia was the first female mathematician to achieve professional recognition (Hibner Koblitz 1983). In another provocative article, Koblitz (2012) offers striking evidence for a list of the obstacles that women typically encounter on the road to a successful career in math, science, and technology.

The AWM Mentoring Program

Recognized in January 2013 for the inaugural AWM service award I depart from the typical style of this book and share snippets of a conver-sation with the recipient (with her express permission):

Q. How did you first identify the need for a Mentoring Network sited within the AWM—was it a novel effort or did you have other profession-al/informal models in mind? If so, which aspects of them did you feel they were most needed/successful?

A. *At a career workshop of the Institute for Math and Applications in 2000, it targeted junior women researchers—there was a common theme that women needed better access to networks and mentors beyond their immediate supervis-ors. Depending on their local environment or department, they may or may not have access to this kind of help and advice, so it was clear they needed access to other networks. They also needed a broader range of advice, not just on their* *specific work but on career navigation and planning, how to be successful at different stages of their careers, how to gain access to opportunities, etc.*

Q. How did you go about instituting the program, did you speak to the AWM president?

A. *Yes, I worked directly with the AWM, both their president and executive, and the web master, who was/is terrific!*

Q. What do you think of the current proliferation of mentoring networks? Most professional organizations or institutions of higher learning have been creating them: do you see duplication as problematic? For example, a Harvard undergraduate may feel herself faced with e-mail proposals to join half a dozen established, institutionalized, professionally oriented mentoring networks, with mentor cadres representing peers, faculty, graduate students, alums, or professionals. Would that be confusing?

A. *If you search best mentoring practices for women in academia, you should come up with quite a number of reports and references. Research on mentoring indicates that a key element to any successful mentoring program is providing a number of options for different types of mentoring—formal, informal, individual, group, online, in-person, peer, senior/junior. The need for different types of mentoring can also change depending on circumstances or career stage. So having a choice is not only good, it is essential to ensure the broad access to mentoring.*

Q. What is special about female networks? And, what is special about women in mathematics? What is special about women faculty, particularly those who belong to underrepresented groups? Please specify if you are addressing the national or the global community.

A. *Research indicates that underrepresented groups typically benefit from established mentoring programs, since they do not necessarily find the same access to informal networks or connections that are found by those from groups in the majority. So female mathematicians are of course an underrepresented group in mathematics, and are not always finding connections locally. Women faculty are not always an underrepresented group, but they do experience the unconscious biases and glass ceilings that are observed in career advancement in organizations in general. Intersectionality—by intersectional, I mean that sometimes it is not gender or gender alone—there are other reasons or combinations of factors such as race/ethnicity, culture, ability, sexuality, gender identity, etc., that can be playing a role or combining with gender to contribute to various biases or disconnects. It is also important for women who are members of other underrepresented groups to have access to different types of mentoring again plays an important role. In addition, there are a variety of aspects that continue to be experienced more often by females, so having female networks can provide advice and understanding on those topics, such as balance of family and career, experience of subtle, unconscious biases, chilly climates, having fewer role models, etc. In the AWM mentor network, mentors are both male and female, and mentees can indicate whether or not they have a preference to have a female mentor.*

Q. How do you feel the AWM mentoring network has most succeeded? Can you quantify its growth? Are there plans to create statistics? Have you yourself ever done or consider doing research on mentoring?

A. *The AWM mentoring network has helped women as they have advanced through their careers and has experienced regular demand over the years. It is flexible in that people can ask for mentoring on different topics—some have been research specific, some career oriented, some on work and family balance, some on how to get into grad school, some on how to get started in a permanent position. So from that point of view it has been able to address a variety of needs for junior women in their mathematical careers. Some mentees have also gone on to be mentors.*

The actual numbers for growth should be accessible from reports available on the AWM website. As for evidence of growth, a few years ago, the AWM Mentor Network committee was established, along with financial contributions from the Math Institutes. This made the network sustainable, both in terms of volunteers to do the work and staff to support the work. At that point I stopped being the chair of the network, a new chair was appointed together with the committee, and I moved into an advisory role. I have not done research in mentoring, but I read about it regularly, as part of my present position as senior advisory to the provost on women faculty at UBC.

Q. My personal experience on networks has been, on occasion, a disenchantment because of mentees who disappeared after signing up and perceived lack of focus and goals. Did you ever experience that, and do you have any antidotes? Some programs routinely ask for evaluations and intervention (which may be overbearing) precisely to prevent such (previously experienced) problems.

A. *We did experience this, and I expect the present network still does somewhat. Since we found this happening early on, we added various guidelines for the mentoring commitment and asked mentees (and mentors) to agree to these before the mentoring contact was set up. This was an additional step in the request process, and we found that this eliminated most of the casual requests for mentors that were lacking the commitment. We also provided suggestions for questions and discussion, to help establish the mentoring relationships. As part of this process, we indicated that the commitment would typically be for about six to twelve months, with some expectation of regular contact. There were of course still a few cases where mentees disappeared, and I would expect that is inevitable in any network of this type. Since we realized that the mentoring need was not always something that was long term, annually we would survey the network to see which matches were still active, and which were no longer active. We would then use this information to see if new mentors needed to be assigned, or to free up mentors for other mentorship opportunities.*

Q. What are your concluding reflections in assessing strengths and weaknesses? Can you identify best practices or something that we can do better?

A. *I found this work very rewarding, as we regularly found that the mentoring connections helped to support success in our students and junior colleagues. The mentors also indicated their enjoyment of the program. Since a key aspect of a successful mentoring program is flexibility, it does require regular maintenance and check-ins, so it not feasible to fully automatize it: running each cycle requires renewed effort and ad hoc solutions. However, I think we found a good mix of volunteerism and staff support, and of course support from the AWM, to make it a sustainable model. As I previously mentioned, many organizations are recognizing the need for good mentoring options, as it is critical to developing diversity and leadership in the next generation* (Personal communication, R. Kuske).

The Association for Women in Science (AWIS)

Another professional association which has a chapter in the Boston area has been key for one of my junior colleagues who joined a mentoring network; she said that one of the most helpful features was having a variety of mentoring structures. She had both a senior mentor, who could center her in her efforts to excel in her career and make her faculty position sustainable, and a mentoring circle, which allowed her to feel validated and safe. The organization is the Association for Women in Science-Massachusetts Chapter (MASS AWIS); their mentoring program is entering its seventh year, while the chapter was formed ten years ago. In view of AWM, I found it interesting to contrast the AWIS structure, highlighting a few descriptions from their website:

> A mentoring circle is a group of individuals that meet together on a regular basis for an agreed upon length of time. The group's primary purpose is to help mentees accomplish two tasks:
> 1. Set important development goals
> 2. Build competence and character to reach those goals
> The group exchanges experiences, challenges, and opportunities for the purpose of enhancing self-confidence, communication skills, leadership practices, and commitment to one's career.
> Each mentoring group consists of 1–2 mentors and 4–5 mentees, carefully matched using information gathered from Mentee and Mentor Applications. Mentors are an experienced group of women working in either academia or industry. The time commitment is 2–6 hours per month over an 8 month period (Sept–April). All Participants attend a mandatory orientation session in early September. (http://mass-awis.org/mentoring-circles/)

AWIS invites professionals to volunteer as mentors; I was honored to receive an invitation to volunteer. I believe an interesting distinguishing feature of this program is that scientists of different disciplines are matched, which could also spark innovative professional projects.

The Radcliffe Mentoring Program (RMP)

I include this program for students because in my opinion it has a significant impact on the mentors, career women who had been students themselves. Through their mentorship, they ask important questions about career directions and fulfillment, which I witnessed when we came together for "Career Panels," our signature yearly event.

To provide perspective on this community, I will relate how the program came about. The Radcliffe College has long been the "Harvard for females" and was fully integrated with Harvard College in 1999. I became a Radcliffe Alumna and was asked to serve on the Radcliffe Mentor Program (RMP) Steering Committee, which oversees matches of approximately 200 alumnae with students each year. The program also organizes community events, runs biannual surveys to fine-tune the program's structure and advises the participants on best practices. The program is now open to male students.

The RMP is run completely on a volunteer basis with student alumnae and staff (who typically work for the Harvard College Women's Center). Through many years of experience on the board as well as volunteer mentorships, I have seen a surprising variety of life-changing mentoring relationships. A board member reported on one anonymous survey response:

> Especially during freshman year, it was great to have an additional advisor, friend, and mentor who was an adult and who cared about me.

Another survey response that made the volunteer mentors smile was:

> I will say that when I was in college, I wanted to be a mathematician, and there was one person who mentored me and got me into a position where I could make that happen, and I will forever be grateful!

It is important to report the mentors' experiences as well, to assess the value of a mentoring program for a professional. An identified the source of failure was:

> My mentee was unclear on what she wanted from the mentorship and unfortunately I think that translated into passivity/perhaps disinterest. . . . I am hoping to discuss again what she would like from our relationship.

To assist with an identified failure, we follow up by asking if there is anything that we can do to support the mentor.

Support, closeness, guidance, and self-reflection are the positive outcomes of the RMP. For members of the Steering Committee, the camaraderie, the team work on ideas, the few minutes spent catching up and sharing setbacks, or announcing and cheering for someone's achievements, have been tangible means of growth.

CONCLUDING THOUGHTS

Women in STEM disciplines experience exceptional challenges. Often viewed as operating outside traditional gender roles, they enter a potentially biased, highly competitive arena; this leads them to constantly question themselves. Formal mentoring programs bestow the aura of legitimacy on groups of women who can share their strategies; as such, professional societies and academia are becoming more responsive. At BU, female STEM students have their own special housing and participate in mentoring workshops (Pfund, House, and Asquith 2013). There have been BU social activities, such as a book club for STEM female faculty, which brought us together over cookies; it was intellectually challenging with undiscriminating support. Programs created to last, such as the AFRAMATH symposium, are necessary for formal mentoring relationship development. As for lessons learned, an area of weakness, shared by many professional societies, is that their nonprofit status makes it is difficult to support programs and people. Reflecting back, I found that funding was typically put together through individual initiatives rather than university sponsored initiatives. One organizational chapter offered a $1,000 scholarship to students to offset the membership fee of women with extenuating circumstances. The organization leader noted funding as the single largest challenge for her program. While there is a positive impact from organizations devoted to creating awareness of issues faced by STEM women, it is also evident that systems for sustainability are lacking.

REFERENCES

An, S. 2007. "Book Review: *Asian Americans in Class: Charting the Achievement Gap among Korean American Youth* by Jamie Lew." *Harvard Educational Review* 77(2).

Blum, L. 1991. "A Brief History of the Association for Women in Mathematics: The Presidents' Perspectives." *Notices of the American Mathematical Society, Special Issue on Women in Mathematics* 38(7).

BUAG. 2014. Retrieved from http://www.bu.edu/today/2014/six-women-who-broke-new-ground/.

Daniell, E. 2006. *Every Other Thursday: Stories and Strategies from Very Successful Women.* Yale University Press.

Harvard Magazine. 2014. "Global Change." Alumni Department, Sept.–Oct., 2014.

Hibner Koblitz, A. 1983. *A Convergence of Lives: Sofia Kovalevskaia: Scientist, Writer, Revolutionary.* CRC Press.

Koblitz, N. 1990. "Are Student Ratings Unfair to Women?" *Association for Women in Mathematics Newsletter* 20(5).

Koblitz, N. 2012. "Are Programs for Women in Science Unfair to Men?" *Kovalevskaia Fund Newsletter.* Available at http://kovfund.org/articles/kov12a.pdf.

NSF. n.d. Retrieved September 14, 2014, from http://www.nsf.gov/pubs/stis1991/nsf91122/nsf91122.txt.

Osborne, J. W. 1997. "Race and Academic Disidentification." *Journal of Educational Psychology* 89(4): 728–735. doi: 10.1037/0022-0663.89.4.728.

Pfund, C., S. House, and P. Asquith. 2013. *Mentor Training for Clinical and Translational Researchers*. W.H. Freeman & Company.

Valian, V. 1997. *Why So Slow? The Advancement of Women*. MIT Press.

Wedeman. 2014 Retrieved from wedemangallery.com/2014/09/15/larger-than-the-sum-of-its-parts.

Conclusion

Lessons Learned

Brenda L. H. Marina

In developing the final chapter of *Mentoring Away the Glass Ceiling in Academia: A Cultured Critique*, I viewed this task as a case study analysis. Following the work of Kochan (2002) and Kochan and Pascarelli (2003), I considered each chapter as a case from which to extrapolate data. Reading and rereading the manuscripts, I conducted a content analysis to situate this discussion about mentoring within the context of the glass ceiling in academia. Rather than draw conclusions about the status of the glass ceiling in academe, I discuss the emergent themes from the intersecting realities of each case. I also framed this analysis around the following question: What are the mentoring experiences of women of diverse backgrounds that influence identity development and internal coping mechanisms in environments often characterized by marginalization? The narratives of these women of diverse backgrounds serve as theoretical contributions, personal advice, and insights, providing practical strategies for mentoring to improve the current context of higher education for women and thus continue to shatter the glass ceiling in academia.

In Section I, "On the Road to Academe," I noted that the authors from these three chapters were intentional to note their use of autoethnography. However, all the chapters communicated a unique narrative journey of continued persistence. By using autoethnography, each author created a rich narrative framework (Muncey 2010; Siddique 2011) to analyze and reflect upon their experiences. In this text, autoethnography has been the way to celebrate rather than demonize the individual story (Chang 2008).

What follows are salient themes that emerged from the women featured in this text who so willingly and eloquently shared the positives and negatives of their mentoring experiences in academia. Consistent with the precepts of intersectionality, these themes reference various culturally and socially constructed categories, such as race, gender, class, and ageism, which interact on multiple and often simultaneous levels, contributing to systematic social inequality, or in other words, a glass ceiling in academia. Glass walls and ceilings have been systematically constructed as a consequence of cultural attitudes, behaviors, and practices (Marina 2011). While progress has been made, barriers to women's advancement in academia continue to exist, including cultural norms, stereotypes, and employment policies and practices.

Furthermore, in considering this cultured critique, with caution, Yosso's theory of cultural capital (2005) scaffolds the discovery of cultural patterns, variations, and similarities for mentoring. My decision to use cultural capital as a framework in this section of the text was based on the subject matter of this book with the illumination of racialized and gendered experiences in academia. Yosso (2005) names six forms of cultural capital that marginalized groups (in this case, women are the marginalized group) bring into the conversation: aspirational, navigational, social, resistant, familial, and linguistic capital. The forms of cultural capital further the notion of intersectionality and illustrate the complexities of issues faced by women of diverse backgrounds. Drawing from Yosso, I briefly describe each of these forms of capital for application to mentoring and academia.

Aspirational capital refers to the ability to sustain high aspirations even when one's circumstances make them seem impossible to achieve, such as living in poverty or in this particular case, remaining diligent in carving out a space for women in historically male-dominated structures. Navigational capital refers to the skills to navigate through social institutions, particularly institutions that systemically disadvantage marginalized persons. Social capital refers to the networks of people to whom women can turn to obtain information, emotional support, and access to key institutional personnel, such as those who may help them through the tenure and promotion process. Resistant capital emphasizes minority individuals' ability to challenge the status quo by resisting negative stereotypes and labels and claiming counter identities of their own. Familial capital refers to the knowledge built up through ties to kin, which includes emotional and moral learning. Lastly, linguistic capital refers to the communication skills accrued by multilingual communities of color. I use three of these six forms of cultural capital as identity markers; both mentors and mentees may consider these areas to identify barriers and address concerns.

In Section I, "On the Road to Academe," the authors describe their graduate school experiences and discuss the role mentoring played in their identity development. Embarking on graduate education, *navigational capital* was the major concern. In "PhorwarD Progress: Moving Ahead through Mentorship in the Academy," Johnson and Snider found role models who embodied confidence and poise because that is what they wanted to see for themselves. They wanted mentors who embodied success so there would be footprints for them to follow. For Tickles and Foxx in "I Am My Sister's Keeper: A Dual Mentoring Perspective of Women of Color in STEM," the authors were not struggling with learning or the learning process. Their need of guidance and direction for coping with the social issues and politics surrounding degree attainment was reiterated. Furthermore, they felt that they lost valuable time finding their own way as they encountered glass ceiling structures and obstacles. In "Navigating the Turbulent Boundaries of a PhD Program: A Supportive Peer-Mentoring Relationship," Ostrom-Blonigen and Larson-Casselton needed emotional support to guide them as older-than-average females struggling with life challenges and where formalized mentoring structures were very limited. Informal mentoring and/or peer mentoring proved to be the mechanism to help lessen the feelings of isolation and face obstacles as they navigated through academe. However, each woman's individual inner strength coupled with the social networks developed over time brought them to a place of self-confidence.

In Section II, "Tapping on the Glass Ceiling in Academe," *social capital* presented itself as the dominant issue for mentoring and moving toward success in academia. Again, *social capital* is developed from those networks of people one can turn to and obtain the key institutional information as well as emotional support. In "Burdens of the Gifted: Moving inside the Margins," McWilliams described academic socialization as neither a consistent nor an institutionalized process and dependent upon the discipline, institution, or individual; socialization occurred mainly on the job, through trial and error, and with little formal training or formal mentoring. Similarly, McCallum, in "A Novice Is a Novice at Any Level: A Narrative of the Experiences of Two Female Academics in Their Beginning Years of Teaching in a Higher Education Institution in Jamaica," noted that formal mentoring as an aspect of workplace socialization is not embedded in the organizational culture of several higher education institutions in her country. Haddock-Millar and Sanyal's chapter on "The Role of a Mentor in Supporting Early Career Academics: The Relationship Is More Important Than the Label," furthers the notion that both informal and formal mentoring relationships are beneficial. The four authors firmly believe that informal mentoring relationships have been the basis for academic socialization. Additionally, the four authors expressed the need for the adoption of formal processes and structures to support the professional well-being of faculty and staff. Departing from the dominant theme of this section, in "The Courage to Give, the Courage to Receive: Mentor-Protégé Relations with Women of Color," Ben's early life reflections hint to the development of *aspirational capital*. Beginning at age four, she grew up working in her immigrant family's restaurant. While she felt disempowered because she had no choice but to stay in her family environment. At the same time she found the good in those early lessons and held fast to the wisdom and work ethic she gained as a protégé.

In the third section, "Steps toward Successful Mentoring," the conversation of *social capital* continues with "Beyond Sisterhood: Using Shared Identities to Build Peer Mentor Networks and Secure Social Capital in the

Academy," authored by Bertrand Jones, Wilder, and Osborne-Lampkin. These authors expressed that mentors were needed to build the social capital necessary for success and survival in academia. Peer mentoring was offered as the avenue for gaining access to critical knowledge, networks, and other professional development opportunities for individuals who have not acquired sufficient amounts of social capital. Similar to four of the authors in section II of this text, Bertrand Jones, Wilder, and Osborne-Lampkin maintain that informal mentoring experiences can be extremely effective tools to build social capital. Following, Blankson, Brown, and Evrensel's "Surviving the Academy: Reflections on Mentoring Female Faculty in Higher Education" conveys information regarding the differential gender-based socialization process in academia. While their chapter adds voice to the social capital issue, their contention that relevant academic structures have been formed by male academics for centuries applies to *aspirational capital* as women have found these structures not necessarily conducive to thriving in academia, yet, they continue to tap on the glass ceilings. "Mentoring Practices for Female Faculty: The Role of Professional Networks," by Previato, also evokes *aspirational capital* with her commitment to provide formalized programs to offer mentorship for women (and girls) working their way into the male-dominated STEM fields.

WHO IS RESPONSIBLE FOR MENTORING AWAY THE GLASS CEILING?

While each chapter in this text describes mentoring experiences, relationships and programs, several chapters also suggest that women are responsible for mentoring away the glass ceiling. For example, Johnson and Snider's chapter "PhorwarD Progress: Moving Ahead through Mentorship in the Academy" noted that the success of black Americans in higher education can be attributed in part to the opportunities they created for themselves with one another. They were intentional in selecting graduate programs with faculty members who shared their research interests and perspectives in higher education. The authors empathically stated, "We each engaged in positive mentorship relationships throughout our collegiate and professional careers to achieve academic, professional, and personal success." Similarly, Tickles and Foxx in "I Am My Sister's Keeper: A Dual Mentoring Perspective of Women of Color in STEM" articulated that women should not be afraid to seek support from individuals. In "Burdens of the Gifted: Moving inside the Margins," McWilliams pointed out that it is women who carry the responsibility to move inside the margins and to help other women to create their identities. With the lack of intentional mentoring within the academy she continuously reflects upon her obligation to be a role model and mentor now that she is closer to "the center." While she had very poignant suggestions for institutions, she indicated that the individual must take ownership for her own career and choices.

Reflection and Confidence for Mentoring Away the Glass Ceiling

I portend that women are in large part responsible for mentoring away the glass ceiling. Several authors in this text support this notion and suggest that critical reflection and building one's confidence can construct and maintain empowering definitions of self. In their own unique manner, each author confirmed that mentorship early on can help build the confidence, which is necessary for navigating the challenging spaces of the academy. In "PhorwarD Progress: Moving Ahead through Mentorship in the Academy," Johnson and Snider felt that scholarly reflection on one's own experiences helped them to understand the experiences, issues, and obstacles they faced along their journey. Blankson, Brown, and Evrensel's "Surviving the Academy: Reflections on Mentoring Female Faculty in Higher Education" suggests that being mindful and reflective on one's own experience in academia is an important ingredient of meaningful mentoring. In "The Role of a Mentor in Supporting Early Career Academics: The Relationship Is More Important Than the Label," Haddock-Millar's mentor helped her to reach her own conclusions, through reflection and critical dialogue. Through this relationship of mutual respect and acceptance, her mentor served as a sponsor, advisor, counselor, and friend, which spurred the development of Haddock-Millar's confidence and self-esteem. In the same chapter, Sanyal, energized by her mentoring experience, took the initiative and regularly reflected on the mentoring process, which caused her to be open to change and new ideas. In "Beyond Sisterhood: Using Shared Identities to Build Peer Mentor Networks and Secure Social Capital in the Academy," Wilder's mentoring alliance greatly improved her sense of efficacy and worth as a scholar in the academy, and Bertrand Jones noted that her mentoring relationship with Osborne-Lampkin was the beginning of rebuilding her confidence in her ability to succeed as a faculty. These individual (self-initiated, self-reflective) and collective experiences suggest that if mentors and mentees both are diligent in identifying aspirational, navigational and social capital issues (a reflective process) from within and without the academy, individual confidences will be bolstered and viable (collective) platforms will be created by women drawing from their own experiences. These collective experiences suggest that support networks are the next steps as a mechanism for operating in male-dominated or male-oriented organizations and workplaces.

Supportive Networks for Mentoring Away the Glass Ceiling

Peer Mentoring

   While each chapter in this text invoked the theme of supportive networks, several authors in particular described peer mentoring for the
cultivation of their aspirational, navigational, and social capital which
allowed them to thrive. Ostrom-Blonigen and Larson-Casselton ex-
claimed that peer mentoring was key for them. Johnson and Snider suggested that there is a need for more emotional support structures, understanding from peers and colleagues, or "sistering." Such relationships
with other caring and nurturing women increase positive self-identity
and self-efficacy (Packer-Williams and Evans 2011). Bertrand Jones, Wilder, and Osborne-Lampkin expressed that their peer network brought
them together as sisters, which facilitated in the development of social
capital. In particular, Osborne-Lampkin described peer mentoring as an
opportunity for mentoring that meets the needs of faculty of color. Because faculty of color receive less social support than their white counterparts (Jackson 2004; Ponjuan, Martin Conley, and Trower 2011), peer relationships provide greater access to mentoring (Thomas, Hu, Gewin, Bingham, and Yanchus 2005). In speaking of the academic environment in
general, but faculty in particular, Blankson, Brown, and Evrensel capture
the essence of peer mentoring in stating that mentors should be fellow
members from different backgrounds who have an innate ability to relate
to another member's challenges which can stem from discipline-, gender-
, ethnicity-, or race-related issues.

Informal and Formal Mentoring

   Every chapter author mentioned informal or formal mentoring networks, relationships, or programs. It is a common theme throughout the
literature that most often, due to missing or inadequate formal mentoring, women in the academy rely on themselves and others for support
and guidance (Fries-Britt and Kelly 2005; Myers 2002). Ostrom-Blonigen
and Larson-Casselton expressed that the informal mentoring relationship
between them was the support necessary for them to complete their PhD
journey. Johnson and Tickles and Foxx noted that the informal interactions with mentors provided an understanding of the role that mentors
should play and for one of the authors, such occurrences helped in the
development of her own identity as a mentor. McWilliams furthers the
importance of informal mentoring as a fundamental part of students'
socialization processes to the academy and the various disciplines. Snider
contends that formalized mentoring programs at the university level
must be created and supported for women by women. McCallum noted
that formal processes need to be adopted for the professional well-being
of new members of the academic staff. Haddock-Millar and Sanyal sug-

gest that institutions need to move from informal mentoring that relies on individual initiatives to more formal mentoring programs to accommodate the diverse needs of early career professionals aspiring to move into leadership roles. Bertrand Jones, Wilder, and Osborne-Lampkin also agree that informal mentoring experiences are extremely beneficial, however, the benefits of formal policies and programs that provide formal, structured mentoring experiences cannot be overlooked.

SUGGESTIONS FOR MENTORING AWAY THE GLASS CEILING IN ACADEMIA

In this final section of emergent themes from the intersecting realities of the chapter authors, I present their insights offered to educate intuitions and organizations about gender-based obstacles that have been consistently observed at many universities, businesses, and governmental organizations. Some of the authors in the book now serve as mentors because of the supportive networks and environments they have experienced. For others, the stark opposite was the case; they now serve as mentors because of the lack of mentorship throughout their academic journey.

For Mentees

It is critical to build a team of mentors; it is wise to have at least one mentor that can relate to the personal (for example, gender-wise, social, cultural, racial, geographical) issues faced by women. The mentoring experience can facilitate emotional and cultural adjustments—adjustments to the emotional and cultural dynamics of institutions, disciplines, or departments. A team of mentors can help to lessen those feelings of isolation, low confidence, cultural alienation, and disillusionment that women often feel in male-dominated spaces (Herzig 2004; Ponjuan, Conley, and Trower 2011). Some authors cited a preference for mentors who "looked like them"; however, the overall advice throughout the texts suggests that women should be open to mentorship from other well-intentioned and qualified individuals (for example, mentors from other ethnic groups and/or gender, or institutions). Being open to unconsidered mentorship is an opportunity to capitalize on being at the right place at the right time for career development, advancement, and potential success. Mentorship, in various forms, is critical for establishing the belief that women deserve to have a place at the table in the academy. As women cultivate self-definition, they will be able to resist the oppressiveness of university environments.

- Glass Ceiling Breaker Words of Wisdom: Seek out a mentor so this statement will not be repeated by another women in academia. . . . *I lost valuable time finding my own way and encountered many detours, roadblocks, and brick walls.*

For Mentors

Through the stories in this text we encourage mentors to continue developing strategies to move forward the agenda of diversity and the mentoring support needed to increase the number of women working in leadership roles in academia. Mentors must be intentional about mentoring by identifying the challenges faced by women. Mentors of women in the academy must consider the aspirational, navigational, and social capital issues and assist other women with gaining access to critical knowledge, networks, and other professional development opportunities. Insights into the dynamics of the institution will help mentees to understand how to engage and build relationships with key people in the academy.

Feelings of isolation, alienation, or being "an only" within their course, department, college, or discipline was a common theme expressed (Stanley 2006) throughout the text. In Section III, the development of alternative forms of a "community" or a sisterhood to diminish feelings of isolation and alienation was described and prescribed by the chapter authors.

- Glass Ceiling Breaker Words of Wisdom: To begin or continue to shift the current academic culture, it is necessary for women of diverse cultures to share their stories for the purposes of expression and empowerment and to facilitate a better understanding of other women's experiences.

For Institutions

The stories in this text were presented as a way to enact change in higher education. There remains, in many instances, deeply rooted institutional, organizational, departmental, individual values, beliefs, and perceptions that perpetuate issues around race and gender that impede the success of women in academia (undergraduate and graduate education, faculty, staff, and administrators). As such, the authors have highlighted needed areas of change and discussed ways in which such changes can be sustained. While mentoring support is needed to increase the number of women working in leadership roles in academia, the goal is to change institutional cultures and not to just add women. It has been noted that effectively mentored women are more likely to stay at the university, receive more grant income, obtain higher-level promotions, and have better perceptions of themselves as academics compared with non-mentored female academics.

There is a lack of development and intentional mentoring within the academy, where academic socialization is neither a consistent nor an institutionalized process. There is a need for some common starting points which will pave the way for women to begin and advance in their careers. However, there must be an understanding and appreciation for the differing paths taken and challenges faced that will exist between and among women. Moving from a "one-size fits all model" for mentoring relationships can potentially improve the quality of mentoring and better meet the needs of women seeking mentors (Peña and Wilder 2011).

Higher education institutions should create structures and processes by which all faculty and staff can find and develop effective mentoring relationships and learning networks, both formal and informal. As previously noted, several chapter authors firmly believe in the benefits of informal mentoring relationships for academic socialization; however, it is incumbent upon higher education institutions to put into place structures and processes to support both informal and formal mentoring relationships and programs. Institutions will benefit by diminishing exclusionary practices.

- Glass Ceiling Breaker Words of Wisdom: Members of university leadership must take decisive and proactive steps to support women and create spaces for both informal and formal mentoring relationships.
- When women make it to the top, they must reach out to other women coming up the ranks behind them.

REFERENCES

Chang, H. 2008. *Autoethnography as Method*. Walnut Creek, CA: Left Coast Press.

Fries-Britt, S., and B. T. Kelly. 2005. "Retaining Each Other: Narratives of Two African American Women in the Academy." *Urban Review* 37(3): 221–242. doi: 10.1007/s11256-005-0006-2.

Fullerton, S., and D. Moore, eds., *Global Business Trends Contemporary Readings 2011 Edition*, 117–122. Ypsilanti: A Publication of the Academy Business Administration (ABA).

Herzig, A. 2004. "Slaughtering this Beautiful Math: Graduate Women Choosing and Leaving Mathematics." *Gender and Education* 16(3): 379.

Jackson, J. 2004. "The Story Is Not in the Numbers: Academic Socialization and Diversifying the Faculty." *NWSA Journal*, 172–185.

Kochan, F. 2002. "Examining the Organizational and Human Dimensions of Mentoring: A Textual Data Analysis." In F. K. Kochan (ed.), *The Organizational and Human Dimensions of Successful Mentoring Programs and Relationships*, 269–286. Greenwich: Information Age Publishing, Inc.

Kochan, F., and J. Pascarelli. 2003. *Global Perspectives on Mentoring: Transforming Contexts, Communities, and Cultures*. Greenwich: Information Age Publishing, Inc.

Marina, B. L. H. 2011 "Breaking Ground and Breaking Barriers in a Globalized World." In S.

Muncey, J. 2010. *Creating Authoethnographies*. London: Sage.

Myers, L. 2002. *A Broken Silence: Voices of African American Women in the Academy.* Westport, CT: Greenwood Publishing Group.

Packer-Williams, C. L., and K. M. Evans. 2011. "Retaining and Reclaiming Ourselves: Reflections on a Peer Mentoring Group Experience for New African American Women Professors." *Perspectives in Peer Programs* 23(1): 9–23.

Peña, M., and J. Wilder. 2011. "Mentoring Transformed: When Students of Color See Diversity in Leadership." *Diversity in Higher Education* 10: 345–363.

Ponjuan, L., V. M. Conley, and C. Trower. 2011. "Career Stage Differences in Pre-Tenure Track Faculty Perceptions of Professional and Personal Relationships with Colleagues." *The Journal of Higher Education* 82(3): 319–346.

Siddique, S. 2011. "Being In-Between: The Relevance of Ethnography and Auto-Ethnography for Psychotherapy Research." *Counseling and Psychotherapy Research* 11(4): 310–316.

Stanley, C. A. 2006. "Summary and Key Recommendations for the Recruitment and Retention of Faculty of Color." In Christine A. Stanley (ed.), *Faculty of Color: Teaching in Predominantly White Colleges and Universities*, 361–373. Bolton, MA: Anker Publishing Company, Inc.

Thomas, K. M., C. Hu, A. G. Gewin, K. Bingham, and N. Yanchus. 2005. "The Roles of Protégé Race, Gender, and Proactive Socialization Attempts on Peer Mentoring." *Advances in Developing Human Resources* 7(4): 540–555.

Yosso, T. J. 2005. "Whose Culture has Capital? A Critical Race Theory Discussion of Community Cultural Wealth." *Race, Ethnicity and Education* 8(1): 69–91.

Index

"academic cloning", 62

AFRAMATH, 177–178, 185
African American, xii, xiii, 4, 7,
    144–145, 164
Asian, 119, 133
Asian American, xv
aspirational capital, 188, 189, 190
Association for Women in
    Mathematics, 179–182
autoethnography, 4, 49–50, 52, 187
AWM. *See* Association for Women in
    Mathematics
"baptism by fire", 67, 70
"bitchy", 115

black, 3, 4, 23; "smart black girl", 7
blind mentoring, 33

Caucasian, xii, 8, 53
communication privacy management
    theory, 45–48, 49, 52, 53
confidence, 7, 9, 14, 27, 35, 36, 86, 116,
    121, 132, 150, 155, 176, 188, 191, 193
CPM. *See* communication privacy
    management theory
culture; cultural, xii, 61, 107, 112, 150,
    165; cultural capital, xiii, xvi, 188;
    culture of mentoring, 73;
    organizational culture, xiv, 81, 108;
    university culture, 84, 96
culture shock, 31, 92, 95, 95–96

dance of identities, 65–66

emotional caretaking, 69, 73

formal mentoring, xiv, 18, 19, 41, 52, 72,
    81, 107, 138, 189, 192; formalized
    academic mentoring, 52–53

gender: gendered institutions, 65;
    genderless institutions, 66
gender-neutral, 62
GIFT. *See* Group Instructional
    Feedback Technique
glass ceiling, vii, xi, 84, 108, 113, 187,
    190
"good girl", 70, 71, 73
"good mother", 66, 70, 73, 74, 76
good-old-boy networks, 65, 113
Group Instructional Feedback
    Technique (GIFT), xvi, 169, 170
guidance, 22, 29, 43, 188

HBCU. *See* historically black colleges
    and universities
Hispanic, 164, 177
historically black colleges and
    universities (HBCU), 23, 25–27, 147

incidental learning, 65
induction, 81, 82, 106
informal mentoring, 41, 44, 51, 138,
    189, 192; informal peer mentoring,
    52
insider-outsider, xiv
intersectionality, xvi, 188
interview: episodic interview, 82, 89;
    exploratory interview, 88; narrative
    interview, 88
isolation, 9, 24, 33, 35, 106, 189, 193, 194

Jamaica, 81, 86, 87, 99, 107

KOM, 120
Korean, xii, 111

Latino, 23
linguistic capital, 188
lived experiences, 61, 63

About the Contributors

Lillie Ben is the first generation to be born in America to her Korean parents who immigrated in the late 1940s; she is the youngest and only daughter among her two older brothers. As a lifelong learner, she has acquired three master's degrees that range from medical school as a physiologist to business school as a fiduciary financial advisor. She is the president and CEO of her financial planning firm, the Essentria Financial Experience, LLC, working with business owners and individual financial-planning clients. As an adjunct professor in the Denver area, Ben combines her medical acumen on neurophysiology with her business acumen on the decision-making process to teach primarily women about personal finance with a different twist that she coined as "neurofinancing." She also volunteers her time to mentor students and professional women and men on leadership skills. Currently, she is completing her PhD in the School of Applied Management & Decision Science at Walden University. Her research focuses on best practices pertaining to gender differences for mentorship programs in businesses and academia.

Tamara Bertrand Jones is assistant professor of higher education in the Department of Educational Leadership and Policy Studies at Florida State University. Bertrand Jones's research builds on interests developed while conducting dissertation research, her own academic and social experiences during graduate school, and her previous professional roles as an evaluator and college administrator. Her current work explores the socialization experiences of black female early-career scholars, doctoral students, and pre-tenure faculty. As a co-founder of Sisters of the Academy Institute, a national organization created to facilitate the success of black women in the academy, her current research naturally aligns with this broader goal.

Isaac A. Blankson earned his PhD from Ohio University in Communication, an MA from the University of Oslo in Norway, and a BA from the University of Ghana. Currently, he is associate professor of public relations and communications and chair of the Department of Speech Communication at Southern Illinois University Edwardsville. He is also the special assistant to the Dean of the College of Arts and Sciences on international and diversity initiatives. Blankson teaches courses in public relations, social media, electronic communication, and intercultural communication. He has published papers on public relations and is the co-author of the book *Negotiating Democracy: Media Transformations in Emerging Democracies* (2008). Blankson has been engaged in SIUE's Peer Consulting and Mentoring Program (PCMP) since 2005 as a member of the Program's Executive Committee and a consultant/mentor and has participated in mentoring conferences and faculty training and orientation.

Venessa Ann Brown holds a PhD from Clark Atlanta University in social work. Currently, she is associate provost for institutional diversity and inclusion and holds a tenured appointment in the Department of Social Work at Southern Illinois University Edwardsville (SIUE). Her current position is chief diversity officer of the university, and she works to ensure diversity and inclusion is central to the mission of the university. She is also the author of the book *Child Welfare Case Studies* and has a book in progress titled *Community-Based Child Welfare with Multicultural Families*. She oversees a number of mentoring programs at SIUE and has been engaged in SIUE's Peer Consulting and Mentoring Program (PCMP) since 2007 as a member of the Program's Executive Committee and has participated in mentoring conferences along with the other Executive Committee members of the PCMP.

Ayşe Evrensel holds a PhD from University of Zurich (Switzerland) in economic and social geography and a PhD in applied economics from Clemson University (SC). Currently, she is associate professor of economics and chair of the Department of Economics and Finance at Southern Illinois University Edwardsville (SIUE). Her teaching focuses on courses such as international finance, international trade, macroeconomics, and financial markets and institutions. She has published papers on corruption, exchange rate regimes, the IMF, and preferential trade agreements and is also the author of the book *International Finance for Dummies*. She has been engaged in SIUE's Peer Consulting and Mentoring Program (PCMP) since 2008 as a member of the program's executive committee as well as a consultant/mentor and has participated in mentoring conferences along with the other executive committee members of the PCMP.

Krystal Foxx holds an EdD from the University of North Carolina at Charlotte. She most recently worked as a graduate research assistant for a NSF-funded project related to improving the retention of underrepresented groups in engineering and serves as a mentor to women doctoral students through her department. Her research agenda includes mentoring, retention and graduation for non-traditional undergraduate students, social justice and equity, and STEM education. Prior to enrolling in a doctoral program, Foxx served as a mentor coordinator for three years where she trained and coached adult volunteers and directed programming related to career and life skills for college-bound/college students.

She has a BS in information science, a masters in public administration (MPA)—nonprofit management, and is currently seeking her EdD in educational leadership—higher education. She also serves on the Sisters of the Academy (SOTA) STEM committee. Her unique perspectives in mentoring are valuable in understanding how mentoring can help women better navigate higher education institutions and prepare for successful careers.

Dr. Julie Haddock-Millar is senior lecturer and teaching fellow in human resource management and development at Middlesex University Business School, UK. She brings a unique multi-layered perspective to the book; prior to joining Middlesex University and making the transition to higher education, she trained as a lawyer and gained her LLB (Hons), LLM in public international law, and BVC from the Inns of Court School of Law. Subsequently, she worked in the private sector in a variety of business, project, and human resource roles, ultimately responsible for the talent management and development of 10,000 employees, across thirty-six stores with Tesco Plc. She completed her doctorate in professional studies with Middlesex University in 2013. She now specializes in the design, implementation, and evaluation of mentoring programs associated with employability and early career transitions utilizing a range of approaches, frameworks, and techniques/tools. She currently leads on two UK-wide multi-stakeholder mentoring programs.

Dr. Cindy Larson-Casselton serves as associate professor of communication studies and theater art at Concordia College, Moorhead, Minnesota. Concordia is a private, coed, four-year liberal arts college. Concordia is a community of more than 2,500 students who come from thirty-four states and thirty-one countries and represent thirty-seven religions and denominations. Concordia employs nearly 200 full-time faculty including NASA and NSF scientists, award-winning composers and writers, and national experts in a wide range of fields.

Jennifer M. Johnson, PhD, is the retention coordinator for the College of Education at Bowie State University. Her scholarship explores the educational experiences of first-generation and lower-income college students. She received her PhD in higher education at the University of Maryland, College Park. Johnson is a first-generation college student and shares the importance of connected with knowledgeable others (both students and faculty) to successfully move through higher education as a student and professional.

Dr. Dian McCallum is a coordinator and lecturer of history education and facilitator of teacher mentor training at the School of Education, Faculty of Humanities and Education, University of the West Indies, Mona

Campus, Jamaica. Her research interests include teaching, learning, and assessment in history; induction and mentoring of beginning teachers; and mentor professional development

Allison McWilliams is the director of mentoring and alumni personal and professional development within the Office of Personal and Career Development at Wake Forest University. As director, McWilliams provides support, guidance, and resources for formal and informal mentoring relationships and programs, and collaborates with faculty and staff to fully prepare students for life during and after college. Prior to joining Wake Forest in June 2010, Dr. McWilliams was a public service faculty member at the University of Georgia, where she created, administered, and served as a facilitator for leadership development, organizational development, and mentoring programs and initiatives both for higher education and public sector audiences.

La'Tara Osborne-Lampkin is an associate in research at Florida State University. She holds a PhD in educational leadership and policy, with coursework focusing on educational policy, the politics of education, and methods for policy research and evaluation. Her primary research focuses on accountability policies and reform efforts designed to improve the academic outcomes of students. She also broadly explores various aspects of policy making and decision making, including the implementation of policies surrounding the recruitment and retention of minority faculty and graduate students.

Dr. Jean Ostrom-Blonigen serves as the interim assistant vice president for Information Technology Services (ITS) at North Dakota State University (NDSU), Fargo, North Dakota. NDSU is a student-focused, land-grant, research university—an economic engine that educates students, conducts primary research, creates new knowledge, and advances technology. The university provides affordable access to an excellent education at a top-ranked research institution that combines teaching and research in a rich learning environment, educating future leaders who will create solutions to national and global challenges that will shape a better world.

Emma Previato is professor of mathematics at Boston University and a fellow of the American Mathematical Society. She earned a PhD in mathematics from Harvard University, has published over seventy research articles, and (co-)edited three books. She has given over 200 domestic and international presentations and organized several research workshops and conferences. She was the recipient of the MAA/Northeastern Section 2003 Award for Distinguished College or University Teaching of Mathematics. She teaches and mentors mathematics students and founded the

BU Student Chapters of the Mathematical Association of America (MAA) and of the association for Women in Mathematics. Since 2004, she has organized an annual outreach symposium, AFRAMATH. She serves as mentor in several programs at Boston University and in the community, including: Menino Scholars, graduates of the Boston Public School system, STEM, special-residence students. She has provided service to the Responsible Conduct of Research Program, the Boston University and Pre-Dental Advisory Board, the Women in Science and Engineering network, the Radcliffe Mentor Program Advisory Committee, and the Resource Scientist for National Science Foundation Graduate Research Fellowship Program (NSF-GRFP).

Chandana Sanyal is senior lecturer and chartered fellow (CIPD) in human resource management and development at Middlesex University Business School, UK. She brings a unique insight into the international and cultural dimensions of mentoring to this book. Sanyal is a practitioner academic with over seventeen years experience as a manager and senior learning and development practioner and now in an academic role specializing in individual and organizational learning and development. She is particularly interested in coaching and mentoring as a learning intervention both for individual and teams within organizations. Her area of research for her doctorate in professional practice is on mentoring and employability which will build on this area of expertise and explore models of mentoring to support employability of students in higher education.

Jeanette Snider, MA, is academic advisor for the Robert H. Smith School of Business at the University of Maryland, College Park (UMCP). She earned her master's degree in higher education at UMCP and began the PhD program there in the fall of 2014. Prior to becoming a full-time advisor, she served as a graduate assistant in the Smith School's Office of Undergraduate Studies. Her scholarship explores multicultural student development and mentoring relationships for students of color in higher education. Snider draws upon her experiences with mentorship, beginning as an undergraduate student, on her experiences in higher education.

Dr. Virginia Cook Tickles currently serves as an aerospace engineer in the Office of Strategic Analysis and Communications' Engineering Cost Office at Marshall Space Flight Center. Tickles began at NASA performing engineering analysis in propulsion systems, engine systems, and space transportation systems before transitioning into the Engineering Cost Office. In 2008, she entered the NASA Administrator's Fellowship program and served as a visiting professor at Tennessee State University and Jackson State University integrating cost analysis concepts into the engineering curriculum and mentoring engineering students. She has a BS in mechanical engineering (Tuskegee University), MS in systems engineering management (Florida Institute of Technology), and PhD in urban higher education (Jackson State University). She is currently the chair of the Sisters of the Academy (SOTA) STEM Initiative and has mentored students extensively in academia and industry. Her greatest achievement is her role as the mother of six young adult women.

JeffriAnne Wilder is associate professor of sociology in the Department of Sociology, Anthropology, and Social Work at the University of North Florida. She holds a PhD in sociology from the University of Florida. In addition to her studies in sociology, she also completed a concentration in women's studies and gender research. As a race scholar specializing in issues of cultural diversity, her primary areas of research include race and ethnic relations—specifically the contemporary experience of black Americans; the intersections of race, class, and gender; and the experiences of black women in higher education.

About the Editor

Brenda L. H. Marina, PhD, is associate professor, teaching graduate courses in educational leadership and higher education administration. Dr. Marina is on the board of directors for the International Mentoring Association (IMA). She is also a peer reviewer for the *International Journal of Mentoring and Coaching in Education* and has served as a moderator for the Research and Mentoring strand for the European Mentoring and Coaching Council (EMCC) E-Conference. Dr. Marina is the author and co-author of several publications related to the areas of leadership though mentoring, women in leadership, multicultural competence in higher education, and global education issues. She currently serves as a faculty advisor for the Student Abolitionist Movement (S.A.M.), an organization that promotes awareness about human trafficking in the United States and across the globe. Additionally, she serves on a Women & Gender Studies advisory board and also is the editor for the *Georgia Journal of College Student Affairs*, a journal sponsored by the Georgia College Personnel Association (GCPA). Dr. Marina holds professional affiliations at the state, national, and international levels and serves as a speaker for state, national and international conferences and other venues on issues related to her research.

"I believe my experiences in graduate school ignited the spark to a fulfilling professional career of guiding students in decisions that impact them for a life-time. I also credit my mentors for modeling the true meaning of higher education professionalism. Such experiences and mentorship have impacted and shaped my ideas for mentoring women in general and women of color in specific and for preparing twenty-first-century higher education and student affairs profession-als."

CPSIA information can be obtained at www.ICGtesting.com
Printed in the USA
BVOW03*1321020615

402535BV00003B/3/P